From *Motorcycle Consumer News*

Proficient Motorcycling

SECOND EDITION

The Ultimate Guide to Riding Well

By David L. Hough

BOWTIE
P R E S S®

A Division of BowTie, Inc.

Karla Austin, *Director of Operations & Product Development*

Nick Clemente, *Special Consultant*

Barbara Kimmel, *Editor in Chief*

Amy Stirnkorb, *Designer*

Indexed by Melody England

Library of Congress Cataloging-in-Publication Data

Hough, David L., 1937–
  Proficient motorcycling : the ultimate guide to riding well / by David L. Hough.
— 2nd ed.
      p. cm.
  At head of title: From Motorcycle consumer news.
  Includes bibliographical references and index.
  ISBN 978-1-933958-35-4
  1. Motorcycling—Safety measures. 2. Motorcycling accidents—Prevention. 3.
Motorcycling—Study and teaching. I. Motorcycle consumer news. II. Title.

  TL440.5.H67 2008
  629.28'475—dc22
                            2007035379

BowTie Press®
A Division of BowTie, Inc.
23172 Plaza Pointe Drive, Ste. 110
Laguna Hills, CA 92653

Printed and bound in Singapore
11 10 09   2 3 4 5 6 7 8 9 10

Dedication

While the content of this book is really collective wisdom gleaned from fellow motorcyclists and the school of hard knocks, two individuals were instrumental in allowing this book to come to life.

First, it was Bob Carpenter, the editor of *Road Rider*, who salvaged my first article back in 1972. Bob encouraged me to keep submitting, showed me by example how to write, and then suggested I tackle the "Proficient Motorcycling" series that eventually served as the basis for this book. Thanks, Bob. It's been quite a trip so far.

Second, my wife Diana has been tolerating my travels, travails, and tantrums since we got married. She accompanied me on many long motorcycle journeys on a variety of motorcycles that weren't very comfortable; endured more than a few cold, wet, windy days; put up with my motorcycling fanaticism for the past forty years; and kept me moving on this project even when I would rather have gone riding. We got married in a little country church on Bainbridge Island in 1958, and we're still together. Pretty amazing, huh?

Contents

Preface 7
Introduction 9

Chapter 1: Risk!
Canyon Bites 13
The Taboo 14
How Far Are You Hanging It Out? 16
Fixing the Odds 28
I Didn't See You 40

Chapter 2: Motorcycle Dynamics
What Keeps It Balanced? 45
What Makes It Turn? 53
The Lowdown on the Slowdown 67
Taking the Panic out of Panic Stops 77

Chapter 3: Cornering Tactics
Cornering Habits 87
Cornering Lines 97
Right Pace, Right Place. 102
Homework 110

Chapter 4: Urban Traffic Survival
City Traffic 113
Snap-Jawed Intersections 118
Suburb Survival 124
Superslab Tactics 130
Aggressive Drivers 138
Evasive Action 144

Chapter 5: Booby Traps

Surface Hazards 151
Curbs Ahead 160
Running Out of Pavement. 168
Deer, Oh Dear! 175
Ferocious Fidos. 183

Chapter 6: Special Situations

When It Rains. 191
Rain Riding Tactics 197
When You're Hot, You're HOT 202
Running Cool 207
Dang Wind 210
Freezing Your Gas on the Pass 219
Night Owls 226
White-Line Fever 233

Chapter 7: Sharing the Ride

Batches of Bikers 241
The Second Rider 252
Let's Get Loaded 260
Sidecars and Trikes. 266

The End of the Trip 277

Resources 279
Glossary 282
Index. 284

Preface

I've always been interested in how things work. I remember taking apart my new cap pistol when I was six years old, then hiding it when I couldn't get all the springs back inside. After a few more years of dabbling in things mechanical, I could overhaul the planetary geared hub on my bicycle and respoke wheels. I worked on outboard motors and built a few boats. In college, I took some mechanical engineering courses and learned about machining, casting, and welding before I switched over to industrial design. I started maintaining the family automobiles out of necessity, and when we needed a new house for a growing family, I learned concrete work, carpentry, plumbing, and electrical.

When I started riding motorcycles back in the 1960s, it was natural for me to wonder about the curious behavior of two-wheelers. I realized that riding a motorcycle involved not only the mechanics but also the dynamics of how to control them. My commuting to work by motorcycle eventually extended to thirty years, during which time I absorbed more than a few lessons about motorcycle dynamics as well as the joys and challenges of long-distance touring, group riding, foreign travel, three-wheeled motorcycles, off-pavement riding, motorcyclist rights, rider training, and yes, writing about it all. In the mid 1970s, I started putting down my thoughts on paper, contributing occasionally to *Road Rider*, a small Southern California touring magazine with a fiercely loyal family of subscribers. I began to offer safety tips at the local motorcycle club meetings, and I taught several "road survival" courses. When the Motorcycle Safety Foundation came into being, I became an MSF-certified instructor.

The "Proficient Motorcycling" column sprang to life in the May, 1984 issue of *Road Rider*, after editor Bob Carpenter asked me to write a six-part skills series, which he intended to publish every other month for one year. I didn't want to call this a safety column because I didn't think people rode motorcycles to be safe. I figured readers might rise to the challenge of getting more proficient. So I named it Proficient Motorcycling. Bob immediately decided to make it a monthly column, which I contributed to for several more years. Little did we realize at the time that "Proficient Motorcycling" would outlive *Road Rider*, capture a few awards from the motorcycle safety folks, stretch out another fifteen years, and start a trend toward the inclusion of riding-skills articles in other enthusiast publications.

By 1991, *Road Rider* magazine had been purchased by Fancy Publications and was reborn as *Motorcycle Consumer News (MCN)*, a black-and white, no-advertisements, no-nonsense, quick-turnaround, product-oriented monthly. The "Proficient Motorcycling" column jumped the gap from *Road Rider* to *MCN* almost without skipping a beat

MCN editor Fred Rau recognized the value of skills articles and encouraged me to keep the column going. Today, it's still a popular feature of the magazine. Back in 2000, when I put this book together from years of past "Proficient Motorcycling" columns, I was approaching age 65, and I recognized the column might well outlive me. So I helped train my replacement, Ken Condon. Ken now writes the "Proficient Motorcycling" column for *MCN*.

When BowTie Press decided to publish the first edition of the book *Proficient Motorcycling,* no one really understood the potential, and it was made very economically. Everyone was surprised and relieved when the first run quickly sold out. Since then, more than 120,000 copies of *Proficient Motorcycling* have found their way into the hands and minds of motorcycle enthusiasts. More than a few readers have told me proudly that they lent their first copy to other riders, couldn't get it back, and had to buy a second copy for themselves.

Considering the enthusiastic reception to the first edition, it's time for an update, so here's the second edition—a little bigger, sharper, and better organized. I hope you find it useful.

Note: contents based on the "Proficient Motorcycling" series as published in *Motorcycle Consumer News* and *Road Rider* magazine, 1981–1999.

Introduction

BEGIN AT
THE BEGINNING

I've been trying for years to break the taboo about discussing the risks of motorcycling. Motorcyclists know instinctively that the risks of riding are higher than those associated with other vehicles, but there seems to be a general consensus that ignoring the risks will make them go away. Certainly, motorcycle salespeople tend to sidestep the safety issue for fear of squelching a sale. Mainstream motorcycle magazines have focused on the bike as a machine, a lifestyle, or an addictive pursuit, but seldom have there been articles on how to control the bike or how to get through traffic unscathed. And if a motorcyclist is still trying to convince the family that riding a two-wheeler is an acceptable mode of transportation, maybe it would be smart to not bring the risks out into the open. In my opinion, it is possible to reduce the risks of motorcycling to an acceptable level through skill and knowledge, and we really need to get that concept out in the open.

I'm pleased to see that today other authors are starting to talk about riding skills. There are a number of excellent books available, mostly by authors with a background in motorcycle racing. The ex-racers tend to focus on fast cornering and deal only superficially with the business of negotiating the hazards of riding on public roads. My focus is the opposite. I deal primarily with riding tactics appropriate to public roads, with much less emphasis on rapid cornering. That's why this book includes lots of photos of situations on public roads and fewer photos emphasizing the motorcycle as the center of attention.

Let's face the risk questions openly and honestly. Yes, motorcycles are potentially dangerous, but whoever is holding the handlebar grips at the moment can significantly change the odds. If you want to avoid pain and lost dollars, you need to understand what the risks are and take positive steps to control any situation to your advantage. The proficient motorcyclist knows what trouble looks like and has the

The big payoff is that becoming a proficient motorcyclist can be immensely satisfying.

skills to negotiate whatever happens along. The big payoff is that becoming a really proficient motorcyclist can be immensely satisfying.

I've tried to keep discussions of motorcycle dynamics simple, but some people may still have difficulty understanding the concepts. Sometimes the dynamics won't become clear until you take the book out to the garage and do some experimentation with your motorcycle or until you take your machine for a spin and feel what it's telling you. You can study this book in any sequence you choose, but the contents are arranged so that one subject leads to the next. It will probably make more sense to you if you start at the beginning and read through to the end.

I'll try to give you all the no-nonsense information I can, but this is only a book, not a training course. When experimenting on your motorcycle or practicing a skill, please wear your best crash padding. I believe that appropriate protective gear includes abrasion- and impact-resistant full jacket and riding pants, tall leather riding boots, full-fingered gloves, a genuine DOT-approved helmet, and shatterproof eye protection.

Throughout *Proficient Motorcycling*, you'll encounter some characters whom you may suspect you've seen somewhere. Here's Biker Bob, riding along minding his own business, when suddenly—*crash, wham, bam*—Bob's bike slams over on its side in a shower of sparks and shattered plastic. Wait a minute! Who is this guy Biker Bob, anyway? Be aware that most of the characters in this book are fictitious, although many of the situations are based on real crashes and incidents. Think of the tales of woe as myths, which may not be completely factual but are all potential learning experiences. You may even recognize a bit of yourself in these fictional folks. In some cases, I know I've played the part of Bob myself. And, please, do us both a favor and don't get hung up on the names or the sexes.

Consider this book only the beginning of a journey toward becoming a proficient motorcyclist. Take advantage of skills seminars at motorcycle events. Read different books on motorcycling skills. Take a training course, or attend a track school. Mostly, keep yourself attuned to what's happening as you motor off toward the horizon. There are many other lessons waiting to be learned.

CHAPTER 1

Risk!

CANYON BITES

I t's a sunny Sunday morning in the Colorado mountains. Perfect weather. Light traffic. The pavement is clean and dry. Motoring eastbound through the scenic Boulder canyon, Norman and Christine are enjoying the ride and the view. Both riders are wearing protective gear, including high-quality full-coverage helmets. Norman is paying attention to the curves, planning good cornering lines, and keeping his Suzuki well in control.

Westbound, four motorcyclists on fast sportbikes are dicing with each other, enjoying their race-bred machines, the excellent road conditions, and the rush of friendly competition at the spirited pace, albeit with little regard for speed limits or double yellow lines. At the moment, Mark is slightly more willing than the others to jack up the risks, and his Honda is pulling ahead of the pack.

Just east of Hurricane Hill, Norman slows the Suzuki for the sharp blind turn through the rocks and leans the bike over into a nice curving arc that should kiss the centerline at his apex. At the same instant, Mark carves into the same turn westbound on his Honda. Mark realizes too late that the curve through the rocks is tighter than he had assumed. He tries to lean the Honda more, but he can't prevent the bike from drifting wide across the double yellow lines, right into the path of the approaching Suzuki.

Frantically, Norman shoves the grips toward the right to swerve the Suzuki away from a 120-mph head-on collision. Mark frantically tries to get the Honda turned, but the tires lose traction, and the bike lowsides in a shower of sparks and plastic. The sliding Honda clips the Suzuki just hard enough to send it cartwheeling into the rocks. Mark tumbles to a stop, bleeding profusely but alive. A second later, Mark's buddies carve around the corner and spin through the mess of wadded-up bikes and bodies. Norman dies instantly, his helmeted head ripped from his body. Norman's wife, Christine, dies an hour later at the hospital. Mark and his buddies all survive.

This is a true story, and I'm not relating it just to gross you out. Similar crashes occur over and over again on various twisty highways across America that are popular with weekend motorcyclists. The term *canyon racing* comes from California, where the twisty roads leading up the canyons are the playgrounds of aggressive motorcyclists. The East Coast has its canyon roads, too, including the famously twisty road through Deals Gap between North Carolina and Tennessee, known by motorcyclists as The Dragon.

The Taboo

You won't hear much about motorcycle fatalities from your local motorcycle dealerships or in mainstream motorcycle magazines. Discussing fatalities has long been a motorcycling taboo. If a rider survives the crash, the experience might provide some bragging rights. But talking about the fatalities tends to take all the fun out of the sport for riders, and for those in the industry it has a chilling effect on sales. In general, motorcyclists and motorcycle dealerships don't understand how to manage the risks of riding, so it's more comfortable to avoid the topic. Since the motorcycle industry pays big bucks to the Motorcycle Safety Foundation (MSF) to solve the problem, the industry attitude is just stay out of their way and let them do whatever it is they do.

Yes, I understand the discomfort of bringing the risks out in the open and talking about them. After all, part of the thrill of motorcycling is challenging the odds. We ride motorcycles partly because they are more dangerous than other vehicles. Perhaps not talking about the risks will hold them at bay. Maybe talking about risks is inviting the odds to strike. Or maybe we just don't know enough about managing the risks to know how far we're hanging it out. For instance, all road racers understand the need for crash padding because they intend to ride at 99 percent of their limits, and they know how easy it is to punch through the envelope. But the street rider may also be riding at 99 percent of the risk envelope when entering a busy intersection. If that's the case, then why don't all street riders wear quality crash padding?

I believe that if we're to manage the risks of riding, we need to take it personally. We need to understand what's happening and figure out what to do to keep our risks in check. So let's ignore the taboo and talk seriously about what's happening.

Risk Acceptance

You'll encounter lots of other motorcyclists charging ahead aggressively on public roads, seriously captured by a road-race mentality, always measuring their worth in terms of who passed and who got passed. Odds are 10 to 1 the road is clear today, with no sleepy drivers wandering across the centerline and no fresh boulders lying on the road halfway around a blind turn. Of course, on every sunny Sunday on twisty roads across America, a few of those daring riders with a higher risk acceptance lose the gamble. Blind corners are one reason some riders almost always arrive at the biker hangout first. Personally, I'm not willing to gamble my life that the blind curve ahead isn't blocked by a fallen tree, logging truck, or wandering horse. But, I've also ridden with those who don't share my conservative attitude about gambling my life, and I've let them speed ahead.

The point is, each of us has a different level of awareness about potentially hazardous situations and a different risk acceptance. There are a growing number of motorcyclists who measure their self-worth in terms of their own skill and their personal enjoyment of the ride, not someone else's. As you grow older, it gets easier to accept that riding on public roads must have a very different focus from riding on a racetrack. I'm out to have a good time, which includes not only arriving home with body and motorcycle parts unscathed but also enjoying the scenery and taking some satisfaction from having the motorcycle well under control.

If you believe the covers of today's motorcycling magazines, the purpose of motorcycling is to ride as fast as you can and lean over in the curves until your chicken strips and knee sliders get respectably scuffed. Road racers are held up as our heroes, and race-replica sportbikes are what you really should want. Of course, today's sports machines really *are* good. If you could roll a box-stock Honda CBR100RR, a Kawasaki ZX-14, or a Yamaha YZF R1 off the showroom floor and into a time machine and transport it back just ten years, you'd have a faster, better handling motorcycle than the big-buck factory race bikes of the day.

And that's really a dilemma for today's motorcyclists. There's this image of me on a high-zoot sportbike, passing every other motorcyclist on the road, half Mike Hailwood and half Joey Dunlop. OK, if I were younger, it might be Valentino Rossi and Kenny Roberts Jr. But I don't ride the track. The dreamy perfect racer image gets pushed aside by the nightmare of a gravel truck making a left turn out of a hidden driveway, a horse that has escaped from a pasture, a splash of spilled diesel oil, or a rusty pickup truck weaving across the line as the driver flings an empty Jack Daniels bottle into my path.

Sure, I'd like to think of myself as a good rider, but I'd like to stick around for a while longer. I can't escape the knowledge that public roads are full of hazards that could quickly and permanently end my motorcycling. There are lots of riders who are willing to push the envelope on public roads, but they seem to have very short riding careers. For me, jacking up the risks of a ticket or a crash is unacceptable. I've also discovered over the years that what's important is to enjoy the ride, and only a modest part of that enjoyment relates to speed. There's tremendous enjoyment in riding a motorcycle at the right speed for the situation, rather than at the maximum speed; getting the motorcycle "in the groove," and knowing you have more performance in the bank should you need it or choose to use it.

The Fatality Numbers

In 2005, more than 4,500 motorcyclists died in motorcycle crashes nationwide. What's even scarier, motorcycle crashes were typically more fatal than car crashes. According to the National Highway Traffic Safety Administration (NHTSA), an astounding 80 percent of motorcycle crashes resulted in injury or death, compared with 20 percent of car crashes. The Insurance Information Institute calculates that the fatality rate for motorcyclists in 2004 was 4.8 times the rate for passenger car occupants per registered vehicle. In 2005, motorcycles accounted for only 2.4 percent of registered vehicles but accounted for 10.5 percent of total traffic fatalities.

The moral should be clear: If you want to survive those entertaining canyon roads—or city streets—you need to not only control your own machine but also control the situation, which includes other drivers and yes, other motorcyclists.

The Long Road Ahead

Let's set out on that long road toward managing the risks of riding, starting with a little deeper look into the statistics and your own riding tactics. Then, let's move on through the topics that seem to be related directly to motorcycle crashes, including motorcycle steering and braking dynamics, cornering tactics, and surviving urban traffic. I'll continue the journey with some advice about road hazards I call booby traps, special situations such as riding at night, and sharing the ride with others. You'll notice that this book focuses on riding public roads, so you'll see lots of photos of corners, surface hazards, and traffic, rather than glamour shots of motorcycles leaned over into racetrack corners.

How Far Are You Hanging It Out?

I don't know how you learned to ride a motorcycle, but I taught myself. Back in the mid-sixties, my old buddy Ricochet Red had started commuting to work on a Honda 90 and quickly graduated to a big Honda 160. I tried Red's 160 and immediately saw the potential for beating automobile traffic on and off the Seattle ferry. Within a week, I found a clean used Suzuki 150 twin for $300.

Of course there weren't many training courses around in the sixties. Red coached me through a half hour of practice on his Honda behind the grade school one Saturday afternoon. Monday morning, I climbed on the Suzuki and zipped off into rush-hour traffic. It rained that very first day, and I remember squish-squishing around the office as I mulled over the implications of motorcycles and weather. That was the start of my motorcycling education.

Of course, there were people around the office who clucked their tongues at my foolishness. Everyone knew motorcycles were dangerous, and riding a motorcycle to work in heavy traffic had to be high-risk foolishness. There were snide remarks and stupid jokes. One co-worker even approached me, gripped my shoulder with fatherly sincerity, and offered the opinion, "I sure wouldn't want *my* son to ride one of *those* things." A few days later, when I arrived at the ophthalmologist carrying my helmet, the doctor gave me a twenty-minute lecture on the hazards of riding motorcycles and a five-minute eye exam.

I wouldn't admit it to anyone at the time, but that barrage of antimotorcycle flak caused me to have some serious doubts about motorcycling. I had a wife, two young children, and a mortgage. And I sure didn't want to spend the rest of my life in a wheelchair. I recall one day toward the end of the second week when I nearly gave it up. After work, I'd strapped my lunchbox to the back of the bike, put on my helmet, and started the engine, but I was a little reluctant to get rolling. Factory traffic is notoriously aggressive at shift change. I sat on the bike for a long time in the corner of the parking lot, watching cars wedge into the stream and trying to control my rising panic. Eventually, I forced myself to get on the bike and ride home. And I'm still riding. Over the next forty-plus years, I gradually learned some important lessons about motorcycling. The first lesson was that my co-workers and my ophthalmologist didn't know diddly about motorcycling or motorcycle safety.

Looking back, I have to agree that the basic concern of my colleagues was probably realistic. A lot of people have gotten messed up in motorcycle crashes, and new riders are particularly vulnerable. But what neither my associates nor I understood at the time is that the risks of motorcycling vary significantly from individual to individual. One rider may have a serious crash soon after taking up motorcycling. Another rider may survive years and years without having a single incident.

Is it just a matter of chance that one rider suffers a crash while another rider avoids crashing? Is swinging a leg over a motorcycle just a two-wheeled form of

Is motorcycling a two-wheeled version of Russian Roulette, or can we really manage the risks?

Russian roulette? I don't think so. During the years I've been riding, writing, and teaching, quite a pile of statistics have been collected. We don't have nearly as much specific data available as we'd like, but we have a much better idea of the risks now than anyone had back in the sixties.

Let's take a short, fast ride through risk territory. We'll give you a little quiz at the end to help you see how you're doing.

Uh-Oh . . . Statistics

I am frequently asked for "the truth" about motorcycle crashes, as if someone were trying to hide the evidence. The basic problem with statistics is figuring out how to collect and sort the data. It might seem that it would be a simple task to collect motorcycle fatality statistics from all the states, but the real-world situation is extremely complex. To get the big picture, all the states send in their own results to the feds. But different states have different rules for reporting crashes and fatalities. For instance, California reports motorcycle crashes that occur only on public streets and highways, including mopeds and motorized bicycles. By comparison, Missouri reports motorcycle crashes on public streets and highways plus nonpublic property, including off-highway motorcycles, mopeds, motorized bicycles, and three- or four-wheeled ATVs. Each state has different rules, so we have to temper the national results with a bit of common sense. *(Source: MSF Motorcycle Crash Statistics, 2001.)*

We do have statistics about motorcyclist fatalities that I believe are reliable. Back in the 1970s, there was a surge in motorcycle fatalities. Then, from 1980 until 1997, the motorcycle fatality totals gradually dropped, just as all other forms of transportation were getting safer. But around 1997, the trend reversed. Motorcycle sales began to increase, and the fatality numbers started climbing again. It may be helpful to look at the fatality rate as well as the total number of fatalities per year. The rate takes into account the relative number of motorcycles on the road. The most desirable way to calculate the fatality rate would be comparing fatalities with miles traveled, but I'm suspicious of any "miles traveled" number because that has to be a guess. The other way to calculate the rate is by comparing fatalities with motorcycle registrations. I believe registrations are more reliable, so that's the rate I use for calculating.

In my opinion, if you ride primarily in city traffic, your specific risks are defined fairly well by the Motorcycle Accident Factors Study conducted by the Traffic Safety Center of the University of Southern California, in the late 1970s. The study has become known as simply the Hurt Report, after lead investigator Dr. Hugh "Harry" Hurt. The USC team investigated 1,100 motorcycle accidents that occurred in the greater Los Angeles area over a two-year period and analyzed 900 of those accidents for the report. I had an opportunity to interview Harry several years ago, and I asked

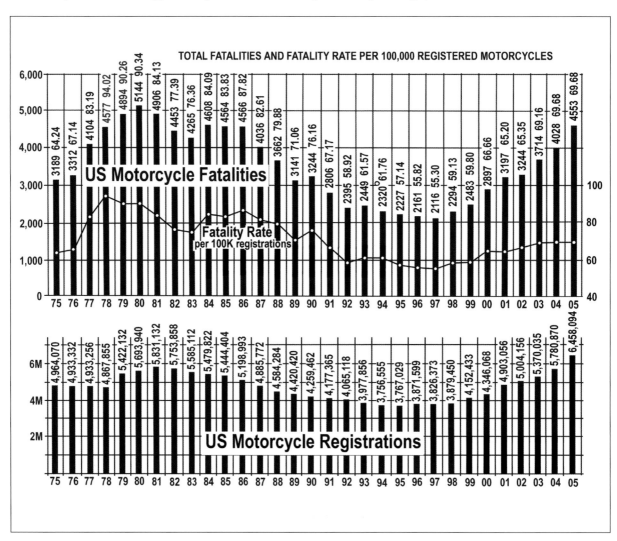

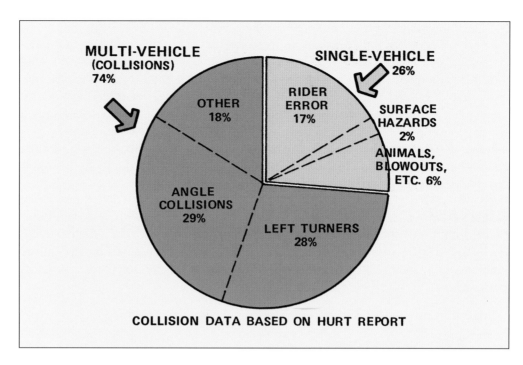

COLLISION DATA BASED ON HURT REPORT

specifically if he felt the report was still valid for this generation's motorcyclists. Harry suggested that motorcyclists were having the same sort of crashes as in the 1970s but at higher speeds, and on more expensive bikes. So it's still worthwhile to look to the Hurt Report for clues about today's motorcycle crashes.

Let's also note that the definitions have changed. Back in the days of the Hurt Report, unfortunate events were called accidents—as if no one could predict what was happening or do anything about it. But today unfortunate events are called crashes. We're getting away from the concept of a motorcyclist being an accident victim because in most situations the people involved can observe what's happening and take evasive action.

The majority of motorcycle crashes in the 1970s were collisions with other vehicles, mostly automobiles. Seventy-four percent were multivehicle—that is, at least one vehicle colliding with another. Twenty-six percent of motorcycle crashes were single vehicle, as when a bike slides out on gravel in a corner without involving another vehicle.

The important point of this big picture is that back in the 1970s almost 75 percent of motorcycle crashes were multivehicle collisions, and roughly half of those collisions were precipitated by auto drivers. About 25 percent of all city motorcycle crashes were collisions with left-turning cars. The two most common errors motorcyclists made were believing the other driver saw them and not taking any evasive action. For example, 32 percent of the riders who collided with other vehicles rode into a collision without taking any evasive action.

Today, that picture has changed slightly. According to a 2004 report of the National Center for Statistics and Analysis (NCSA), 46 percent of fatal motorcycle crashes were single vehicle, and more fatalities occurred on rural roads than on urban streets. In single-vehicle fatal crashes, the motorcyclist collided with a fixed object in approximately 60 percent of the cases.

Only about one-fourth of all motorcycle crashes in the Hurt Report were precipitated by rider error: for example, the motorcyclist went wide in a turn and sideswiped a car or overcooked the rear brake trying to stop and slid out. That's a clue that riders didn't really understand how to control their motorcycles. Apparently, that trend continues. NCSA reported in 1999 that 30 percent of riders involved in fatal crashes didn't take evasive action. Only 13 percent were attempting to brake, and 9 percent were attempting to steer out of trouble. If there is a lesson here, it is that motorcyclists would benefit from proficient control skills. For years we've been able to point the finger at other motorists as being the problem, but today it's obvious that motorcyclists are responsible for at least half of fatal crashes.

Licensing

In the meantime, let's consider the experience and licensing status of riders involved in crashes. In the following chart from the Hurt Report, 1.0 indicates the average of those studied. Numbers higher than 1.0 indicate a greater than average crash involvement.

Motorcycle License Status	Involvement
Motorcycle	0.7
None (or revoked)	2.4
Auto only	2.0
Commercial/chauffeur	0.5
Learner's permit	1.2

These statistics hint that riders with no license, a revoked license, or only an auto license were about twice as likely to be involved in a motorcycle crash as those with a permit and three times as likely as was a properly licensed motorcyclist. The NHTSA Traffic Safety Facts for 2004 reports that 24 percent of operators involved in fatal crashes nationwide did not have a valid license. Now, it should be obvious that just getting a piece of cardboard doesn't change a rider's skill. My suspicion is that it's a matter of attitude. The rider who doesn't get properly licensed is exhibiting an attitude that motorcycling isn't a seriously risky activity. I can see how that attitude would carry over to aggressive riding and ignoring traffic laws. It should be no surprise that 27.4 percent of motorcyclists involved in fatal crashes in 2004 had prior speeding convictions, and 15.2 percent had recorded license suspensions or revocations.

Licensing compliance was actually worse during the 1990s than in the 1970s. NCSA reported that 46 percent of riders in fatal crashes in 1990 were improperly licensed—that is, they were not licensed or their licenses were suspended, revoked, expired, or cancelled. By 1999, license compliance of motorcyclists involved in fatal crashes had climbed back up to 68 percent; better than in 1999, but worse than in the 1970s. Let's hope that getting a higher percentage of riders properly licensed will have an effect on reducing the fatality rate.

Riding Experience

Let's consider risk in relation to riding experience. Does your risk go down as you gain experience? In the following chart from the Hurt Report, 1.0 would be average. Above 1.0 means a higher than average risk; below 1.0 means a lower than average risk.

Experience Riding in Traffic	Risk	
0–6 months	1.40	
7–12 months	0.96	
13–24 months	0.93	
25–36 months	1.52	
37–48 months	0.98	
48+ months	0.83	

These numbers show that a rider with less than six months' experience was almost twice as likely to have an accident as the rider with more than four years. We would expect that. The shocker is that the rider with two to three years of experience was even more likely to crash than the new kid. The lesson here is that riders tend to get cocky when they think they have learned it all—about two years into the learning curve. This is a subject that hasn't been addressed recently by NHTSA or the other statistics-gathering organizations. I'd certainly like to know how motorcycling experience relates to risk in today's riding environment, especially with so many riders getting into motorcycling later in life.

Training

What about training? Did Ricochet Red do me a favor by giving me a few riding tips in the schoolyard? A number below 1.0 would be less risk; a number above 1.0 would be higher risk.

Training	Risk	
Professional training	0.46	
School/club course	0.50	
Self-taught	0.90	
Taught by friends/family	1.56	

I guess Red did me a favor by limiting his advice to just half an hour. Apparently, riders taught by friends or family were about one-third more likely to crash than those who taught themselves. But the smart ones who took a rider training class were half as likely to crash as we do-it-yourself types. Note that the Hurt Report took place at just about the same time as the Motorcycle Safety Foundation came into existence. Obviously, a higher percentage of riders have received professional training since 1980, and training coincides with that gradual reduction in fatalities between 1980 and 1997. Unfortunately, motorcycle rider training philosophy changed around 2000, reducing most courses to "minimum national standards" and coordinating training with what the Motorcycle Safety Foundation calls "improved motorcyclist licensing programs." Is it just a coincidence that fatalities have been increasing since training was reduced to the minimum standard? I honestly believe that rider training helps a new rider get a head start on riding skills, but I'd prefer to see more comprehensive courses available, to give new or returning riders more knowledge about such things as riding in traffic, cornering control, and negotiating surface hazards.

Alcohol

It isn't a popular subject to discuss at motorcycle rallies or biker bars, but apparently too many motorcyclists have a serious problem with alcohol. There seems to be a direct link between alcohol and fatal motorcycle crashes. In the Hurt report, 41 percent of riders who didn't survive the crash had some alcohol or drug involvement. That trend continues today.

We're not talking about an innocently sober rider getting whacked by a drunk driver; we're talking about a motorcyclist riding while under the influence and crashing the bike into something. Since blood-alcohol concentration (BAC) is something that can be measured after a fatal crash, we have more and better statistics that point out the seriousness of riding under the influence. The Insurance Information Institute reports the following for drivers and riders by blood alcohol concentration and vehicle type, for years 2000 through 2004:

Year	Passenger Car		Light Truck		Large Truck		Motorcycle	
BAC level	0.01+	0.08+	0.01+	0.08+	0.01+	0.08+	0.01+	0.08+
2000	28%	24%	26%	22%	3%	1%	40%	32%
2001	27%	23%	27%	23%	2%	1%	37%	29%
2002	27%	22%	27%	23%	3%	2%	39%	31%
2003	26%	22%	25%	22%	2%	1%	36%	29%
2004	26%	22%	25%	21%	2%	1%	34%	27%

Those numbers are embarrassing proof that motorcyclists abuse alcohol more than other road users do. In round numbers, roughly half of all motorcycle fatalities involve a rider under the influence of alcohol or drugs. Somewhere around 10 percent of motorcyclists involved in crashes had been drinking, but drinking riders represent over 40 percent of all motorcycle fatalities. According to NHTSA Traffic Safety Facts for 2004, in fatal crashes, a higher percentage of motorcycle operators had BAC levels of 0.08 g/dL or higher than did any other type of driver.

One big reason why a motorcycle crash turns out to be fatal is speed. The greater the speed, the more traumatic the injuries when the crash happens. Apparently, riders who have alcohol in the brain are much more likely to ride faster than they would while sober. What's the message in all this? Well, the bottom line is that if you allow yourself to ride a motorcycle after drinking, even after just a few beers, you're really hanging it out.

Rider Age

Another statistic that came to the attention of the number-crunchers is rider age. Around 1999, NHTSA statisticians observed an increase in motorcycle fatalities in the forty-and-over age group. The number of fatalities in the younger age groups actually declined. That news got widely reported, and today's folklore includes the myth that the big problem with motorcycling is older riders. However, when NHTSA subsequently factored in the number of riders in the various age groups, it turned out that the twenty- to twenty-nine-year-old age group is overrepresented in fatal crashes. There are fewer younger riders in the total mix, but the younger riders continued to be more involved in more than their share of fatal accidents, at least up through 1999.

	Table 4: Motorcyclist Fatalities by Year and Age Group												
Year	Motorcyclist Age Group												Total
	< 20		20-29		30-39		40-49		> 49		Unknown		
	No.	%	No.	%	No.	%	No.	%	No.	%	No.	%	
1990	198	13	679	46	387	26	138	9	67	5	0	0	1,469
1991	168	13	565	44	358	28	133	10	60	5	1	0	1,285
1992	138	12	466	42	316	28	131	12	63	6	0	0	1,114
1993	99	9	435	41	307	29	153	14	74	7	1	0	1,069
1994	100	10	420	42	249	25	160	16	80	8	1	0	1,010
1995	73	8	404	42	264	28	142	15	77	8	0	0	960
1996	77	8	333	36	270	29	177	19	80	9	0	0	937
1997	50	5	317	34	267	28	180	19	123	13	0	0	937
1998	77	7	321	31	297	29	225	22	122	12	0	0	1,042
1999	61	5	340	30	292	26	271	24	176	15	0	0	1,140
2000	189	7	818	28	707	24	677	23	501	17	5	0	2,897
2001	209	7	919	29	797	25	722	23	532	17	2	0	3,181
Source: National Center for Statistics and Analysis, NHTSA, FARS													

Big Bikes Versus Small Bikes

Doesn't it make sense that bigger, more powerful motorcycles would be involved more often in serious crashes? The Hurt Report didn't show that to be true.

Back in the 1970s, apparently larger machines were less likely to be involved in accidents than were smaller motorcycles, especially if you factored in the estimated numbers of machines on the road. Part of the reason may be that in those days, riders moved up to larger motorcycles as they gained experience.

Engine Displacement Versus Accidents

Displacement	Percent of Accidents	Estimated Machines in Use
0–100cc	9 percent	8 percent
101–250cc	13 percent	9 percent
251–500cc	37 percent	26 percent
501–750cc	25 percent	34 percent
751+ cc	16 percent	23 percent

Government and insurance groups continue to be suspicious of the relationship between engine displacement and fatal crashes. The NCSA number-crunchers have observed that larger bikes are showing up more and more in fatal crashes:

Motorcyclist Fatalities by Year and Engine Displacement (cc)

Year	Up to 500 No.	Up to 500 %	501-1,000 No.	501-1,000 %	1,001-1,500 No.	1,001-1,500 %	> 1,500 No.	> 1,500 %	Unknown No.	Unknown %	Total
1990	247	17	725	49	329	22	0	0	168	11	1,469
1991	194	15	667	52	316	25	0	0	108	8	1,285
1992	173	16	507	46	312	28	0	0	122	11	1,114
1993	143	13	514	48	308	29	0	0	104	10	1,069
1994	132	13	468	46	289	29	0	0	121	12	1,010
1995	122	13	462	48	285	30	0	0	91	9	960
1996	86	9	451	48	307	33	2	0	91	10	937
1997	72	8	446	48	331	35	6	1	82	9	937
1998	83	8	484	46	364	35	8	1	103	10	1,042
1999	73	6	455	40	372	33	12	1	228	20	1,140
2000	203	7	1,261	44	1,092	38	46	2	295	10	2,897
2001	227	7	1,395	37	1,177	37	48	2	334	10	3,181

Source: National Center for Statistics and Analysis, NHTSA, FARS

According to the NCSA numbers, motorcycles 500cc and under have dropped from 17 percent of fatalities in 1990 to 6 percent in 1999. In that same time frame, machines of 1,001 to 1,500cc had increased from 22 percent of fatalities in 1990 to 33 percent in 1999. In other words, larger motorcycles seemed to be involved in the fatality increases. The researchers at first thought they had discovered the smoking gun that would explain the increases in fatalities. But it turns out that it's just a matter of the demographics. When you factor in the sizes of motorcycles being purchased today, it becomes more obvious that the trend toward bigger displacement bikes being involved in fatal crashes is simply a mirror of motorcyclists' buying preferences.

What's more, engine displacement isn't a good measure of motorcycle performance. There are more than a few 600cc sportbikes around with quarter-mile speeds of over 120 mph. At the same time, we have some heavyweight cruisers in the 1,500cc class with top speeds of less than 100 mph.

It might make sense to limit novice riders to less powerful machines. In some countries, novice riders are limited to smaller motorcycles, typically 250cc, during their probationary learning phase. Then, after a year or two, if the new rider can show proficiency, he or she can apply for a license to operate a larger bike. That concept would be hard to implement in the United States, where an individual has been free to purchase whatever machine strikes his or her fancy, with no proof of skill level. For tiered licensing to work in the United States, states would need to stiffen up the licensing process, and that would be a very tough sell in the land of the free and the home of the brave.

The Road Rider Survey

Let's note that the Hurt Report was conducted in the Los Angeles area, so a large percentage of the crashes were in urban (city) riding. Doing a study in California made sense, since around one-third of motorcyclists in the United States live there. But lots of us live in the country or do much of our serious riding on roads far from the city. Years ago, as a contributor to *Road Rider* magazine, I wondered how the numbers would compare between California and elsewhere around the country. I got the brilliant idea to do a survey of the types of crashes and incidents *Road Rider* subscribers had actually experienced. Of course, the *Road Rider* survey wasn't nearly as sophisticated as the Hurt Report, but the responses were spread over the entire United States, and it involved about the same number of cases. Among crashes reported to the authorities, readers indicated approximately twice as many single-vehicle crashes, most notably due to surface hazards and wild animals. Where the Hurt Report showed 26 percent of all crashes were single vehicle, the *Road Rider*

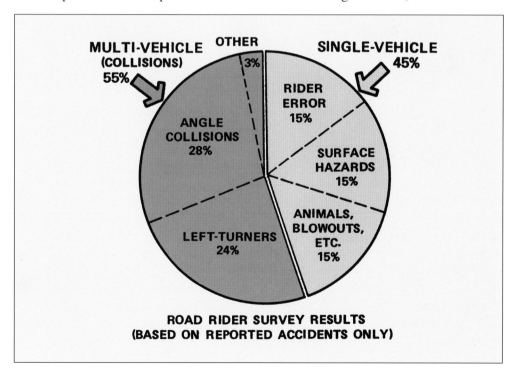

ROAD RIDER SURVEY RESULTS
(BASED ON REPORTED ACCIDENTS ONLY)

survey indicated 45 percent were single vehicle. That would make sense, since many of those crashes were out in the country, away from a major city.

It's interesting that the latest NHTSA numbers show that single-vehicle crashes are hovering around 45 percent of fatal crashes, with multiple-vehicle crashes at around 55 percent—exactly what the *Road Rider* survey indicated.

The *Road Rider* accident survey brought something else to my attention. We asked for both reported and unreported incidents. Apparently, a lot of motorcycle crashes don't get reported. Let's say you slide out on loose gravel and smash your bike into the ditch. If no one calls the police and you are still mobile enough to ride, would you call the authorities and demand to fill out an accident report? Personally, I wouldn't want to initiate any reports that might come to the attention of my insurance company. I suspect that lots of crashed bikes get hauled home in a trailer as clandestinely as possible. When we included both reported and unreported accidents from the *Road Rider* survey, the numbers came out quite differently from the Hurt Report. Single-vehicle accidents accounted for 86 percent of the total.

Note that the *Road Rider* survey showed a much higher percentage of single-vehicle crashes caused by surface hazards, animal strikes, and cornering errors than the Hurt Report indicated. That would make sense because outside of cities we would expect a higher percentage of those types of crashes. While the *Road Rider* survey wasn't one of those huge, government-funded, university research projects, I think it hints that motorcyclists nationwide face a somewhat different mix of hazards than the Hurt Report showed. Let's also note that these days the NHTSA focuses more on fatal crashes, although a rider can be seriously injured in a crash that isn't fatal. That's why in *Proficient Motorcycling* I get a lot deeper into hazards such as edge traps and wild animals than the typical rider training courses include.

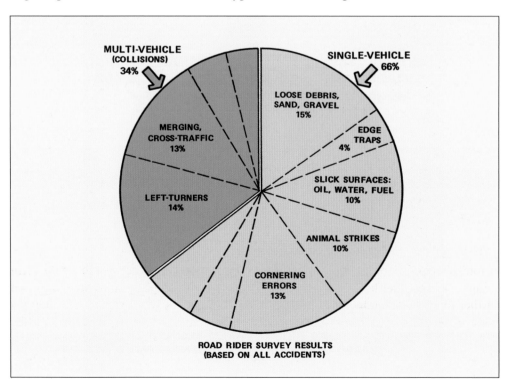

Quiz Time

Now that we've rambled through a few of the statistics, put on your thickest skin and tally up your personal score. The numbers are weighted in an approximate relationship to the statistics.

QUIZ	ADD POINTS	SUBTRACT POINTS
1. Motorcycle license	10	
2. Commercial driving license	5	
3. Learner's permit, no license	2	
4. License revoked		10
5. No motorcycle license		10
6. Less than 6 mos. experience		2
7. 25 to 36 mos. experience	5	
8. More than 48 mos. experience	8	
9. Taught by friends/family		2
10. Learned by self		2
11. Passed novice training course	10	
12. Passed additional course	8	
13. No training within last 5 yrs.		5
14. Sometimes ride after drinking		20
15. Never ride after drinking	20	
16. Often ride in city traffic		5
17. Mostly ride 250 to 600cc		2
18. Mostly ride 750cc or larger	2	
19. Can name 20 common surface hazards	5	
20. Know technique to cross edge traps	5	
21. Practiced quick stops this year	5	
22. Not practiced quick stops this year		5
23. Frequently use countersteering	5	
24. What's countersteering?		5
25. Age between 20–29		5
26. Age 49 or older	5	
27. Always wear armored riding gear	5	
28. Usually wear only denims		5
29. Always wear full coverage helmet	5	
30. Seldom wear approved helmet		5

Hey, It's Subjective

A total score of 85 or higher is a pretty good indication you're doing a lot of the right things. On the other hand, if your score is less than 40, maybe you're hanging it out further than you intended. Sure, sure, I know this is awfully subjective. The point is to be honest with yourself about your motorcycling risk exposure. If you don't like the questions I stacked up, go back through the statistics and write your own quiz. Wherever you are on the risk scale, I'll be offering some suggestions about managing the risks.

Fixing the Odds

All right, we've looked at an accident, reviewed some motorcycle accident statistics, and taken a little quiz to help you get some perspective on your relative risk. I realize that such exercises may be way off track. After all, statistics are based on averages, and there are very few Joe Average motorcyclists. What's more, we might also be a little suspicious of accident studies that look at only how and why people crashed. It's sort of like the patient who went to the doctor complaining of a sore tongue:

> **Patient:** "Doctor, my tongue really hurts."
> **Doctor:** "Does your tongue hurt all the time?"
> **Patient:** "No, but it really hurts when I bite down hard on it."
> **Doctor:** "Well, don't do that!"

The statistics based on crashes and fatalities give us hints about what not to do, but they don't tell us what successful riders *do* to avoid crashing. The traditional approach to getting a helmet full of knowledge is just to keep riding and riding. Experience, the veterans might suggest, is the best teacher. In other words, just ride far enough and long enough, and life will eventually present you with all the lessons to be learned. That's probably true, but the trouble is some of the motorcycling errors can ambush you before you learn enough to avoid them. It's a lot safer and less risky to learn what you can from other people's mistakes and experiences. That's why I pay attention to the grizzled old motorcycling veterans when they occasionally drop hints about lessons learned.

I happened to be along one day when the *MCN* editor was picking up a test motorcycle for a photo shoot. Mostly, he was engrossed in details of the new machine, the fleeting time, the need to find a photogenic location, and the urgency of beating the evening rush hour. The dealer, obviously a veteran rider, was on a different mental plane. He knew I wrote skill articles, and he offered some advice about one small but important detail: adjusting mirrors: "Most people adjust their mirrors so that the view converges behind the motorcycle. I figured out that it is more important to see more of what's coming up in adjacent lanes. So I adjust my mirrors more toward the sides." As we rode away with the test machine, I observed that I also adjusted my mirrors far enough outward that I could pick up only a corner of the saddlebags at the inside edges. *Big deal!* you may be thinking. *Who cares how the mirrors are adjusted? Let's get to the really important stuff!*

Well, maybe a helmet full of such small details adds up to the important stuff. Sure, our physical riding skills have a lot to do with keeping the bike under control. But what goes on between the ears is even more important because that's where we decide what to tell our muscles. Novices start out with the physical skills of mastering the clutch, throttle, brakes, and balance. Veterans understand that motorcycling is really more of a mental process of scrutinizing the situation, evaluating the hazards, and deciding what to do with the motorcycle.

The Noob

Now and then you'll exit a restaurant to find someone circling your machine, a little wide-eyed and irrational, perhaps drooling at the mouth. When you hear the typical questions about fuel mileage, engine displacement, and prices, you know you're talking to someone infected with the motorcycle bug. Do the newbie a favor by pointing him or her toward the nearest rider training course. If the novice decides to become a motorcyclist, that initial training provides a good foundation for gaining experience.

I wish I could be more enthusiastic about today's standard rider training courses, but I believe that the quality of training has slumped in many states, with the emphasis having been shifted away from giving the new rider the tools to deal with riding in the real world, more to getting a new rider licensed and ready to buy a new bike as quickly and efficiently as possible. Training sites with veteran instructors seem to do a good job with the latest simplified curriculum. I've also heard from instructors who are embarrassed at turning out students who passed the simplified test but obviously weren't ready for the road. The good news is that some state programs are taking more responsibility for their training courses, and some are even developing their own training to meet the needs of local riders.

Rider training courses can give you a big dose of information all at once. The trouble with knowledge is that it's a lot like French bread—it doesn't stay fresh very long. You can gain a lot of fresh information from motorcycle magazines and books. A year's worth of monthly reading adds up to a healthy dose of information to help stack the motorcycling risk deck in your favor. A lot of motorcyclists miss out simply because they don't take the time to read what's available. A number of veteran motorcyclists have told me they clip and save helpful articles in a notebook to study again on cold winter nights. You'd think the veterans would have learned it all by now, but that's not the way it works. The veterans are still around because they continue to refresh their knowledge.

I used to teach the MSF Experienced Rider Course (ERC), and I was an enthusiastic supporter for a long time, encouraging everyone to take the ERC and take it again every couple of years as a refresher. But the "new and improved" version of the ERC eliminated most of the crash avoidance strategies and control dynamics instruction, and I'm disappointed with the results. If you're a relatively new rider, take the ERC. In my opinion, the latest ERC will give you an opportunity to practice your control skills. But if you're an experienced rider, it won't give you much of what you need.

Fortunately, there are some alternative street riding courses available, including Lee Parks' Total Control Advanced Riding Clinic, Atlanta Motorcycle Schools Street Smarts course, Bob Reichenberg's Streetmasters Motorcycle Workshops, and the on-road Stayin' Safe Motorcycle Training developed by the late Larry Grodsky. There are also a number of track schools that focus on controlled cornering and braking at real-world speeds, including Keith Code's California Superbike School and Reg Pridmore's CLASS Motorcycle Schools.

Most important, there are several books about riding skills available, including the MSF's *Motorcycling Excellence Second Edition*, Lee Park's *Total Control*, and Nick Ienatsch's *Sport Riding Techniques*. So perhaps the best "training" for an experienced rider is just to study the books and practice the skills on your own. I'll provide references for the books and riding schools later on.

Sight Distance

I often use the phrase "adjust your speed to *sight distance*." Let's be specific about what that means. At a given speed, it takes a certain minimum distance to stop a specific motorcycle. If you expect to avoid that porcupine or those motorcycles splattered on the pavement just around that next blind turn, your speed must be limited to your stopping distance. For example, let's say your machine is capable of coming to a stop from 60 mph in 190 feet. If you can't see any farther ahead than 190 feet, your speed shouldn't be any faster than 60 mph. If your sight distance is limited to 150 feet, you shouldn't be riding any faster than say, 50 mph.

Of course, trying to judge distance in feet or car lengths is unreliable. The pavement goes by in a blur, too quickly to make easy mental measurements of distance. The trick is to make time measurements. While you're riding along, pick out some fixed object ahead such as a signpost, and count the seconds it takes you to get there. Count out loud, "one thousand and one, one thousand and two," and so on. By taking a time measurement of your sight distance and comparing it with your speed, you can make more intelligent decisions about how far you are hanging it out.

I'll offer some guidelines:

Speed	Minimum Sight Distance	
30 to 50 mph	4 sec	↑
50 to 60 mph	5 sec	↑
60 to 70 mph	6 sec	
70 to 80 mph	7 sec	↑

Give these numbers a try, and see if you agree with my suggested minimums. If your reflexes are really quick and you can make consistent hard stops without dropping the bike or highsiding, shave off a second. If these minimums make you a little nervous, add a second. The point is to have a method of gauging honestly how your speed stacks up to your and your bike's stopping performance. If you find that you are consistently entering blind situations at speeds too fast to stop within your minimum sight distances, the message should be obvious: get on the binders and slow down quickly whenever sight distance closes up.

When you are approaching a blind situation such as the crest of a steep hill, is it reasonable to assume that there isn't a problem ahead, even though you can't see the road ahead? For instance, let's say there is a driver on the other side of the hill backing up to make a turn into a driveway. Should you brake just because your sight distance is temporarily limited? Personally, I have seen enough hazards just over a hill or around a corner to be very suspicious. I don't think it is reasonable to assume the road is clear when you can't see the road ahead within your stopping distance.

To Obey or Not to Obey

As traffic grows more congested and aggressive, more motorists are bending the laws. You may find yourself in the dilemma of having to decide whether to increase the risks of a crash or increase the risks of a traffic ticket. For instance, consider those no passing zones marked by double yellow lines. Years ago, road crews were more realistic about the hazards and more frugal with the yellow paint. We could pretty well depend on the double yellow lines warning us of real hazards, such as hidden dips where another vehicle might be hidden from view or side roads where

If you were motoring along at 55 or 60 mph, would you brake for this situation? I don't think it's reasonable to assume the road is clear on the other side of this hill, even if traffic on the road has been light. When sight distance closes up, I believe in immediately reducing speed and preparing for evasive action.

other vehicles could suddenly pull out. But some road crews have gradually extended the double yellow lines farther and farther, until some highways are double-yellowed from one end to the other. If you're riding a quick motorcycle, it's frustrating to hang back behind a creeping motor home or overloaded gravel truck when you can see the other lane is clear and you know you have plenty of zip to get around. More and more of us are giving in to the temptation to just ignore the yellow lines and get on with the ride.

You might be tempted to ignore the no passing lines and get around this slow-moving truck, but before you leap out and accelerate, scrutinize the situation ahead. Are you absolutely certain the truck isn't about to make a left turn into that side road ahead?

Legally speaking, it's no more illegal to pass over a double yellow than to exceed the posted speed limit, but the laws of physics are self-enforcing. Being on the wrong side of the road at warp passing speeds is certainly an invitation to a head-on collision if a car suddenly appears from around the corner or a local resident pulls out of a hidden driveway.

You'll have to decide for yourself when and where you are willing to risk passing over the double yellow. My advice is to never, ever be out in the wrong lane while crossing a bridge, approaching the crest of a hill, rounding a blind curve, or riding through an intersection. But what about a long uphill sweeper where you can see the road eight or ten seconds ahead? And when you come up behind a vehicle waiting to turn left from a busy two-laner, is it smart to come to a sitting-duck stop, or should you swerve over onto the shoulder, pass on the right, and keep moving?

Regardless of the law, before you decide to zip around any slow-moving or stopped vehicle, take a good look at the situation, and try to figure out what's happening and what's about to happen. Is there a side road or driveway into which the other vehicle could turn? Is there a tree-shaded intersection ahead from which another vehicle could suddenly materialize? Is the other vehicle going slowly because the driver is about to make a left turn? It's unwise to pass in any areas where there are roads or driveways along the highway, even if it isn't a no-passing zone. And before you pass a stopped vehicle on the right, take a good look behind you to ensure that someone else isn't in the process of zooming around you.

Wandering Drivers

While around half of all fatal motorcycle crashes are the result of the rider losing control, the other half are collisions. So a big part of managing the situation is to be aware of what the drivers around you are doing. The other day, a mini-van driver who had been tailgating me for several miles finally zoomed on by straddling the centerline. Even though I was maintaining 60 in a 55, I think the close pass was a message, perhaps "you've been holding me up long enough," or "motorcycles don't belong on the highway," or maybe just "move it or lose it, biker boy, I got places to be." While such aggressive actions tend to anger me, they don't scare me quite as much as drivers who wander over the centerline or halfway onto the shoulder or who change speed for no apparent reason. I can only assume that wandering drivers don't have their brains fully engaged in DRIVE, or their brains are fogged with chemicals, or they are distracted by a conversation on their cell phones. Whatever the

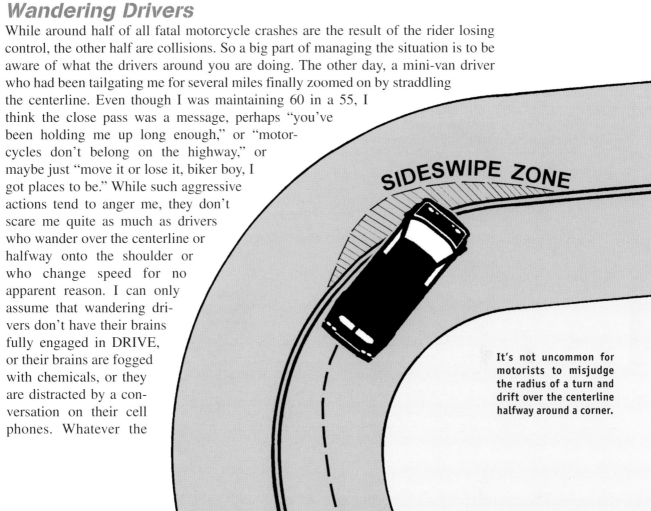

It's not uncommon for motorists to misjudge the radius of a turn and drift over the centerline halfway around a corner.

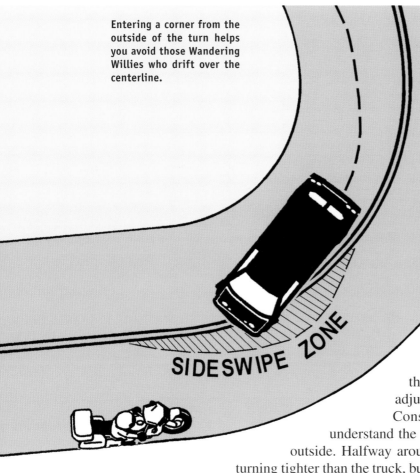

Entering a corner from the outside of the turn helps you avoid those Wandering Willies who drift over the centerline.

SIDESWIPE ZONE

reason, it's a scary situation for vehicles hurtling toward each other at closing speeds of 130 mph, separated only by a pair of four-inch yellow lines painted on the pavement.

Whether it's an act of aggression or a disengaged brain on their part, drivers who wander over the centerline can pick you off if you don't take action to stay out of the way. If there's a collision between a motorcycle and a heavier vehicle, you know who's going to get hurt. On curving roads, there are specific locations where motorists tend to wander out of their lane, whatever the vehicle. You can adjust your line to avoid these areas.

Consider Wandering Willie, who doesn't understand the importance of entering corners from the outside. Halfway around, Willie suddenly realizes the road is turning tighter than the truck, but by then it's too late to prevent an excursion into the opposing lane.

Imagine yourself approaching from the opposite direction, and note that Wandering Willie drifts into your lane about two-thirds of the way around. Drivers also tend to cut corners near the apex of their lane, not realizing the rear wheels track inside of their front wheels.

Emergency Reactions Follow Habits

One of the most important lessons I've learned is that emergency actions follow habits. Riding through the high desert of eastern Oregon one night, my headlight beam suddenly picked up the reflection of two eyes alongside the road. I rolled off the throttle and squeezed the brake lever gently. This is deer country, and the reliable tactic for avoiding a deer strike is to stop short of a collision. Those shining eyes were too low to the ground to be a deer, but whether a deer, raccoon, or skunk, I didn't want to hit it.

When the reflecting eyes suddenly darted toward the pavement, my hand squeezed the brake lever progressively harder, the machine transferred its weight onto the front tire, and my hand squeezed just hard enough to brake the front wheel to the maximum just short of a skid. Twenty feet from impact, the headlight beam illuminated a very large porcupine bobbling out toward the centerline, then changing its mind, making a U-turn, and scrambling back toward the verge. As Porky

ambled off the pavement, my fingers eased off the brake, the suspension stabilized, and my hand rolled back on the throttle.

On a twisty road, it's not uncommon for a driver with a wide vehicle to borrow the other side of the road in curves.

What amazes me still is that I don't recall any decision to brake hard. My right hand just produced a classic quick stop, as if it had been controlled by some animal-sensing device programmed to make a stop in the shortest distance without crashing. Of course, we all carry such a device. It's located on the bike somewhere between your ears. In an emergency, the brain follows whatever programs have been learned through practice. If you always favor the front brake for normal stops, and you have experienced enough power stops to know what an impending skid feels like, your brain has a quick-stop program available for emergencies.

The moral of that story is that if you expect to have the right skills for an emergency, you must constantly practice the right skills every time you ride. If you expect to be able to handle the loose gravel or the wandering motorist you discover as you round a blind turn, you must practice control skills such as countersteering, smooth throttle-to-brake transitions, and aggressive braking while leaned over.

To put this another way, there really aren't any emergency maneuvers you can pull out of your bag of tricks when something goes wrong. You can practice special maneuvers, but the only ones that count are the control skills you practice every day as you ride along. And if we assume there are physical habits to be practiced, then there must also be proficient mental skills that we must practice so that they become habits as well.

The View

The farther you are toward the outside as you enter a turn, the more you can see of what's coming, whether that's Wandering Willie, a wild bull elk, or a patch of loose gravel. It's important to maximize your view, regardless of your preferred traveling speed. The more you can see of the curve ahead, the easier it will be to set up your cornering line.

One common factor in motorcycle crashes on twisty roads is that the riders couldn't see the entire situation ahead. Out in the country, those right-hand turns present some special problems. The view is more limited than in a left-hander of the same curvature. The smart tactic is to enter a right turn from closer to the road centerline. That provides the best view around the corner, which increases sight distance and puts the bike on a better line to exit without sneaking over the centerline.

Avoiding the bite is not just a matter of motoring slowly down the center of your lane and waiting nervously to take evasive action. The best bite remedy is to practice good habits. If you think about all the points I've mentioned, you'll see a pattern emerge. You need to be in control of the situation as well as in control of your bike. Next time you're out on the back roads, evaluate your speed habits with a quick sight-distance time check. Practice good habits every time you ride. Position yourself to see and be seen. And don't be timid about using those big brakes to scrub off speed RIGHT NOW when sight distance suddenly closes up or about swerving away from the centerline when you see an oncoming driver cutting the corner.

If you expect to be able to stop short of the truck that's stopped in the road just around the blind turn, you must practice control skills such as braking while leaned over in a curve.

Entering a right turn from the right

Entering a right turn from closer to the centerline gives you a better view of what's ahead.

Body Armor

Even with the best of licensing, training, and skills practice, some crashes are simply unavoidable. For example, a moose suddenly emerges from the shadows and knocks you off the bike, or an oncoming coal truck swerves over the centerline in a blind corner, forcing you off the road. When you get your chance to crash one of these days, you'll be hitting the landscape in whatever gear you decided to put on before the ride.

If today is going to be your day to crash, what *do you* want between your body and the pavement?

But even if you don't get to crash, your riding gear has a lot to do with your ability to control the bike. I'll leave it up to your imagination how I know this, but a couple of wasps dropping into your boot takes a lot of attention away from the task of keeping the motorcycle pointed between the lines. A sunburned neck can make it too painful to turn your head to find that car hidden in your blind spot. A bouncing stone cracking into your shin can distract you from the slippery manhole cover ahead.

So riding gear is more than just uncomfortable body armor worn reluctantly day after day just in case today happens to be your turn to crash. Good riding gear protects against wind, sun, heat, cold, rain, and flying debris. A shatterproof face shield not only protects your eyes from grit but also keeps your face from getting wind chapped. Leather gloves not only protect your palms from road rash during a spill but also keep your knuckles from getting burned by wind and sun and help your fingers avoid blisters. Tall leather boots provide ankle support as well as protection from a hot exhaust pipe or from nasty biting insects.

But if today does happen to be your turn to crash, it would be handy if your gear also provides impact and abrasion protection. Competition-weight leather will slide for something like 80 to 100 feet on rough concrete before it grinds through to your underwear. Cotton denim will rip to shreds in about five feet. Fabric riding suits with armored patches can be almost as abrasion resistant as leather and a lot easier to clean after a few days of high-humidity travel. Of course, we can adjust our gear to the riding conditions. The more hazardous the situation, the greater the need for good stuff. When I'm making a nighttime transit through deer country on my two-wheeled rocket, I'm inclined to wear my heavyweight leathers. When I'm driving my dual sport sidecar rig up on the logging roads, I prefer a two-piece fabric riding suit.

Good riding gear protects against the weather and flying debris. Leather is the king in terms of abrasion resistance, but fabric suits with internal armor can provide excellent impact and abrasion protection, as well as water resistance.

Abrasion-resistant gear is a number-one priority to keep your skin away from the pavement, but impact pads in the knees, elbows, and shoulders will cushion the blows and reduce broken bones. Leg and arm injuries can be painful, but chest and head injuries are more likely to be critical or fatal. That's why some riders wear a spine protector or upper body armor under their jackets.

The Helmet

The ultimate purpose of a helmet is to prevent brain injuries during an accident. You can crack your leg or your skull and survive, but scrambled brains will bring you to a permanent halt. One really important reason for protecting

You don't really need a real helmet if you are clever enough and skillful enough to avoid crashes. What you wear is your business. But more than a few riders do crash, even when they didn't expect to. It's a bad joke to believe that a thin "party" lid with no impact liner will give you any protection when you go down.

If you find that a full-coverage helmet is claustrophobic or difficult to wear with eyeglasses, consider one of the flip-front styles.

your brain is that the brain doesn't heal itself the way other body tissue does. If you bang your head hard enough to black out for a few seconds, you've injured your brain. And a concussion can turn into epilepsy a year or two down the road. So if you intend to get back in the saddle after the big crash, consider the importance of keeping brain injuries to a minimum. Even a $50 helmet that's DOT approved can provide excellent protection because it's the crushable foam inside that protects the brain, not the outer shell.

There are lots of statistics on helmet use, and there have been way too many heated discussions about mandatory helmet laws—pro and con. I believe that what you wear while riding is your own business, but let's be honest about the situation. A fake "party" lid with no internal crushable liner can't provide any meaningful protection from sharp blows to the head. A DOT-approved helmet will provide reasonable brain protection in the typical street motorcycle crash. A full-coverage helmet can also provide jaw and face protection. According to a German study, the majority of helmet strikes in accidents are to the left and right chin areas. That's something to think about if you have been wearing a shorty or three-quarter helmet.

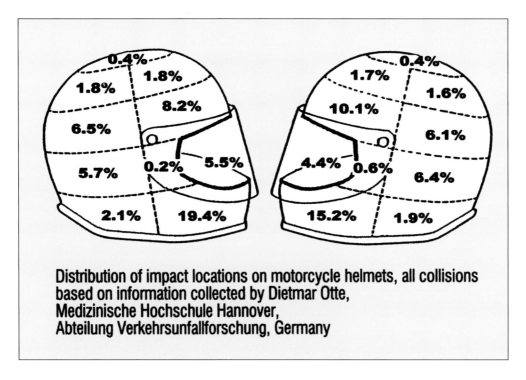

Distribution of impact locations on motorcycle helmets, all collisions based on information collected by Dietmar Otte, Medizinische Hochschule Hannover, Abteilung Verkehrsunfallforschung, Germany

I think I understand the risks pretty well. I have one helmet with a cracked shell right at forehead level, a result of a large stone roosted from a vehicle ahead. I've also been hit by various potentially injurious or messy objects, including June bugs, bees, small stones, straw, hail, and seagull poop. Personally, I never go motorcycling without a helmet. My favorite style is full coverage with a flip front.

I Didn't See You

If you allow another motorist to knock you down, you'll probably hear the same lame excuse: I didn't see you. Sometimes an errant driver has looked down at the poor motorcyclist lying miserably crunched under a bent motorcycle and let slip, "Gosh, I didn't see you. You were coming so fast, and you were wearing black leather, and besides, you didn't have your headlight turned on." Certainly there are occasions when the other driver really couldn't see the motorcyclist, but many veteran motorcyclists have long had a sneaking suspicion that the excuse is mostly a cop-out. When a driver attempts a sudden left turn in front of a motorcyclist and knocks the bike down, do we expect them to say, "I saw you but I was in a hurry and I figured you'd get out of my way?"

This oft-repeated I-didn't-see-you excuse has led some safety experts to believe that the problem is simply that motorcycles are inconspicuous in traffic. The solution, theoretically, is to be more conspicuous. The suggestions are to wear brightly colored riding gear, add a modulator that flashes the headlight, and maybe screw on a Yosemite Sam Back Off mud flap.

Most of the high-mileage riding friends I know roll their eyes at the conspicuity stuff. "Friends don't let friends wear pink vests," they would sneer. Perhaps the veterans have a more realistic understanding of the I-didn't-see-you myth. Does the conspicuity stuff really work, or is it more of a magic talisman than a dependable safety device? (Magic talismans are supposed to ward off evil with no effort on the part of the wearer.) Conspicuity devices are based on the assumption that the other guy will get out of your way if he can only see you. The veterans know that avoiding collisions depends on being prepared to get out of the way of the other guy, whether he sees you or not.

Like it or not, there are some situations in which you have no escape path should another driver wander into your lane. It's helpful to be conspicuous for the benefit of other drivers.

Inattentional Blindness

Psychology research has uncovered an interesting phenomenon that relates to the I-didn't-see-you excuse. It seems that humans are subjected to so much incoming information that one part of the brain serves as sort of a subconscious mental "spam filter." The filter passes on to the conscious part of the brain only information that corresponds to what the person is concerned about, or what the psychologists call attending to. If a driver is thinking about (attending to) buying a new car, the spam filter will pass along anything related to cars, including automobile dealerships and billboards with car ads. The flip side is that if the driver is not concerned about

Although this rider is highly skilled, he wears a conspicuity vest over his leathers to help capture the attention of other drivers. A retro-reflective conspicuity vest is especially useful for night riding, when the stripes light up brilliantly in the headlights of other vehicles.

In addition to the headlights, this motorcycle has amber clearance lights in the front of the mirror housings and extra driving lights in the fairing lowers. The array of lights really helps an oncoming driver comprehend the presence of the bike, and the width of the clearance lights provide a driver with clues to more accurately predict its approach speed.

something (say, motorcycles), the spam filter may delete the image. So it really can be true that a driver looks right at you and sees you, but your image gets filtered out and never gets to the conscious part of the driver's brain. That would explain how a driver might not comprehend a motorcyclist wearing a high-visibility jacket and the bike flashing its head-light—or, for that matter, a freight train with a flashing headlight and the air horns blaring.

Since we can't control every situation, we often depend upon other motorists to not run us over, like it or not. Motorcycles are narrower and more diffi-cult to see in traffic. Other motorists don't always comprehend how rapidly a motor-cycle is approaching because a single seven-inch diameter headlight doesn't really give motorists a clue about your approach speed. So there is a case for motorcyclists to be a little more conspicu-ous for the benefit of those drivers on the road who are really trying to avoid collisions.

Most important, if you are still in the process of learning the tactics of traffic survival, you really are more dependent on other drivers to stay out of your way, and you should help them out by being as conspicuous as you can. Whatever your experience level, you'll have to arrive at a level of conspicuousness that meets your needs and fits your limits of sensibility.

If you think it might help increase your conspicuity, here are some suggestions:

- Consider lighter-color riding gear such as a tan, silver, or bright blue. Add brightly colored vanity stripes to your darker-colored leathers, or wear a bright reflective vest over your jacket.
- Choose a helmet in a lighter, brighter color or a helmet design with bright stripes.
- When shopping for a new machine or repainting your faded bike, give priori-ty to a bright paint scheme.
- Use amber running lights on the front, as widely spaced as practical.
- For nighttime rides, add reflective tape to the back end of your saddlebags, tour trunk, and helmet. Add multiple red taillights, preferably spaced wide apart.

CHAPTER 2

Motorcycle Dynamics

WHAT KEEPS IT BALANCED?

You can get down the road pretty well on your two-wheeler without having to know a lot of details. Once your bike is in motion, it's relatively easy to keep it balanced in a more or less straight line. If the bike wanders a bit in the wrong direction, just lean it back toward your intended line. If you want to turn, all you have to do is lean the bike in the direction you want to go. Simple, huh? Well, maybe not so simple. There are a lot of riders around who demonstrate over and over that they are only half in control of their motorcycles.

Drifting Dan really wants his big tourer to make a nice crisp turn from a stop onto that narrow road, but as he nervously eases out the clutch, the bike seems to take command and swings wide over the centerline. Wandering Wanda wants her cruiser to just motor down the middle of the lane, but it sometimes creeps over toward the edge of the pavement, then back toward the centerline. Beemer Bob does fine at speed, but when he rolls into the parking lot for the breakfast meeting, his new sport tourer seems intent on wobbling over toward parked cars, and it's a constant sweaty struggle to keep it between the lines.

One major reason Dan, Wanda, and Bob have difficulty getting their motorcycles to cooperate is that they don't really understand how motorcycles balance and steer. Drifting Dan panics when his heavyweight touring bike swings wide, but when he attempts to muscle it back toward his lane, it just seems to go wider. Dan doesn't realize he is actually steering the bars in the wrong direction. Wandering Wanda is paranoid about running wide, and she's absolutely terrified of corners, but she is afraid to try that countersteering she's heard about. Beemer Bob breaks out in a sweat when his shiny machine points itself toward car fenders, but he has yet to learn that it is primarily pushing on the grips that controls direction, not pressing his knees against the tank or pushing down on the foot pegs.

Dan, Wanda, and Bob have a common problem in their struggle to control their motorcycles. They all understand that you have to lean the bike to change direction. They just aren't sure what really makes it happen. What they need to know is, to

Controlling your motorcycle in turns is more than just avoiding embarrassment. Crossing the centerline is an invitation to a collision.

lean right, push on the right grip; to lean left, push on the left grip. If your machine tries to snuggle up to a parked car on your right, pushing on the left grip will lean it away from a fender-bender. It's called countersteering because you momentarily steer the front wheel opposite (counter) to the way you want the motorcycle to lean.

It also helps to look where you want to go. If you don't want to hit a pothole, focus on the road to one side or the other. If you don't want to cross that centerline, look ahead down your lane; don't gawk at the line. Even novice riders who haven't mastered countersteering often gain considerable control by just getting their eyes up and looking where they want the bike to go.

Those are the two big secrets for the average situation: countersteer and look where you want to go. Now, go out and play.

Before you thumb the starter, though, let's note that there are lots of hazardous situations out there that demand more skill than the average situation. For example, let's say Beemer Bob zooms out of a tunnel in the mountains, smack into a 50-knot crosswind gusting from his right. The gust slams into the bike, pushing it toward the centerline. What should he do?

Bob needs to push hard on the upwind grip to lean the bike over and maintain enough muscle on the grip to hold the bike leaned over into the wind, but in a straight line. To counter that gust from the right, he needs to push aggressively on the right grip to lean the bike upwind. With the bike leaned over but not turning, steering isn't going to feel normal, so Bob needs to apply pressure on the grips to make the motorcycle go where he wants it to go, and not just think "lean."

Such situations remind us that balancing isn't just a simple matter of nudging on the low grip. To prepare for a wide variety of situations, it might be helpful to look a little deeper into the dynamics of how two-wheelers balance and steer. If you get confused with any of this, I suggest you go out to the garage and try the experiments on your motorcycle.

And, as we get started on balancing dynamics, you should be aware that not everyone agrees about how it works any more than everyone agrees about love or war. From time to time, even the experts get into arm-waving arguments about small details, pens hastily scribbling diagrams on lunchroom napkins. What I'm going to offer here is the opinion of one aging moto-journalist/instructor, based on forty years of arm-waving discussions and napkin scribblings. And note that for what follows in this chapter, *motorcycle* means a two-wheeler, not a rigid sidecar rig or trike.

Two-Wheeler Stability

Occasionally, you'll see a rider let go of the grips and lean back in the saddle at freeway speed. You may marvel at the naiveté of a rider willing to ignore such hazards as a groove in the pavement that might instantly yank the front end into a tankslapper, but hands-off riding is a great demonstration of the unique stability of a motorcycle. The front-end geometry automatically stabilizes the bike in a straight line, self-correcting for minor changes in lean angle.

The simplistic suggestion is that this self-centering action is just a result of the castering effect of the front tire trailing behind the steering pivot axis, similar to the front wheels of a shopping cart at the grocery store. But two-wheelers are quite a bit more complex than shopping carts because they lean into turns. The self-balancing action of a motorcycle front end is a result of the combined effects of a number of details, including rake, trail, steering head rise and fall, mass shift, contact patch location, and tire profiles.

Rake/Trail

When test riders refer to heavy steering, they are talking about a machine that is so stable in a straight-ahead situation that it requires a lot of muscle to get it leaned over and held into a turn. What they mean by a flickable machine is one that is relatively unstable, that can be easily leaned over or straightened up with very little effort on the grips. This is a delicate balance, and sometimes the engineers have to walk a tightrope between low-effort (flickable) cornering and bad manners, such as the front wheel suddenly steering itself toward the curve (tucking), uncontrollable oscillations (speed wobbles), or falling into turns at slower speeds.

The behavior of a bike is related to its steering geometry. If you stand off to one side of your motorcycle and observe the angle of the front forks, you'll notice that the top of the fork tubes are angled (raked) back. And if you look closer, you'll see that the fork tubes aren't exactly in line with the steering head on the frame. While you are standing off to one side of the bike, imagine a laser beam passing through the steering head until it strikes the ground. The laser beam represents the pivot center, or steering axis of the whole front end. When we talk about rake angle, we're talking about how far the steering head is angled back from vertical. Today's cruisers typically have around 30 degrees of rake, while flickable sportbikes have rake of 24 degrees or less. In general, greater rake produces greater straight-ahead stability at speed, and steeper rake produces low-effort steering. But rake is only part of the equation.

The steering axis intersects the ground somewhere ahead of the contact patch where the front tire is sitting on the surface. The distance between the contact patch and the steering axis is called trail (the contact patch trails behind the steering axis).

A motorcycle like this one with greater rake and trail typically has very stable straight-ahead steering but requires more effort to roll into or out of turns.

A motorcycle like this with steep rake and short trail has very easy steering, making it very flickable from side to side.

Typically, street bikes have trail somewhere in the three- to six-inch range. In general, longer trail results in a machine that resists leaning into corners, and shorter trail results in quicker, easier steering, or perhaps even a machine that wants to fall into corners. Since rake and trail are interdependent, the figures in bike reviews are usually given as rake/trail.

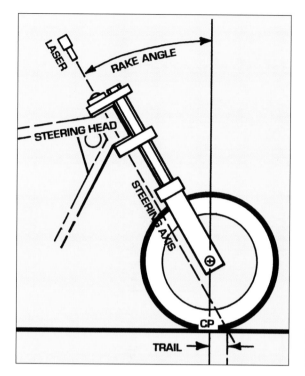

Trail is the distance from which the front wheel contact patch follows behind the steering axis.

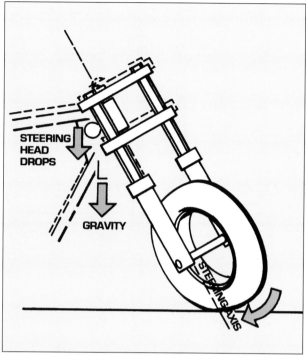

Because of rake, the steering head actually rises and falls when the front end is steered.

Steering Head Rise and Fall

One of the interesting results of rake/trail is that the steering head falls slightly as the front end is pivoted from center to either side, and it rises as the front wheel is turned back toward center. The greater the rake, the more the rise or fall. You can see this for yourself. Straddle your bike, get it balanced vertically, and observe the elevation of the top of the steering head as you turn the handlebars from straight ahead to either side and back to center.

Now, remember, gravity is pulling down on the bike, which is supporting perhaps half its weight on the steering head. So gravity actually helps turn the front end away from center and resists the front end returning to center. That's not a problem, since steering head rise/fall can be balanced against other steering forces.

Mass Shift

While you are straddling your bike, you might also notice that when you turn the handlebars, the steering head also moves sideways (laterally). If you turn the bars to the left, the steering head (and the whole front of the bike) shifts laterally to the left of the contact patch. That means that when the front wheel is turned away from center, the weight on the front end is shifted toward one side. For instance, with the front wheel pointed toward the right, you'll feel gravity pulling the bike over toward the right. In other words, steering from side to side can actually help balance the bike even if the wheels are not rolling. Of course, as the motorcycle begins to roll ahead, it reacts differently than it does when standing still. With the bike rolling down the street, everything moves around in a complex dance.

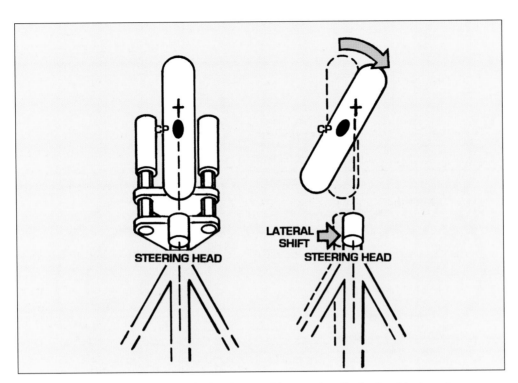

Because of trail, the steering head moves sideways when the front end is steered.

Contact Patch Location

If you were to ride your machine through a puddle of white paint, you'd see a painted stripe all the way around the tread, maybe one or two inches wide. But even though we could see that this contact stripe is a big ring around the tire tread, it's a lot easier to discuss front-end geometry if we agree to think of it as the small contact patch (CP) where the tire touches the road at any particular moment. Be aware that the location of the CP can shift forward and back as well as sideways.

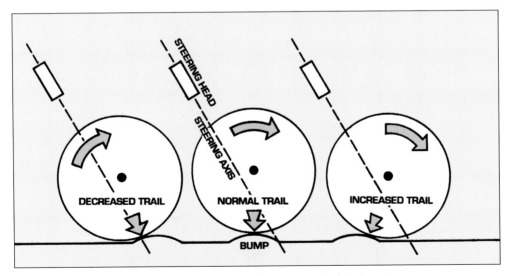

Trail can decrease or increase as the front wheel rolls over a bump.

Consider what happens when the wheel rolls over a bump. As the tire first contacts the bump, the CP instantaneously shifts forward and then follows the bump backward until the tire rolls onto level ground again. If the bump is steep enough (a curb, for instance), the CP can momentarily jump ahead of the steering axis. That's why a steep bump or dip yanks the handlebars around (and why riding no hands over bumps and grooves isn't a clever idea).

Now, lean the bike over on the sidestand, with the front wheel pointed straight ahead. Get down on your hands and knees, and look back toward the front tire. Observe that the CP is no longer in line with the bike centerline. When you lean the bike over into a curve, the CP shifts laterally toward the direction of lean. That causes tire drag to steer the front wheel more toward the curve.

Tire Cross Section (Profile)

With a narrow, round-profile tire, the CP doesn't move far to the side. But with a wide, low-profile tire, the CP shifts farther sideways than with a round-profile tire, for the same lean angle. And the farther out the CP, the greater its off-center drag. The CPs of both front and rear tires shift laterally as the bike leans over, so the sizes and profiles of front and rear tires are interrelated. That's one reason changing tires to different profiles, or changing just one tire to a different size or profile, can change how the bike handles, for better or worse. It's very fashionable these days for cruisers to wear extremely wide rear tires, but handling usually suffers when function takes a backseat to style.

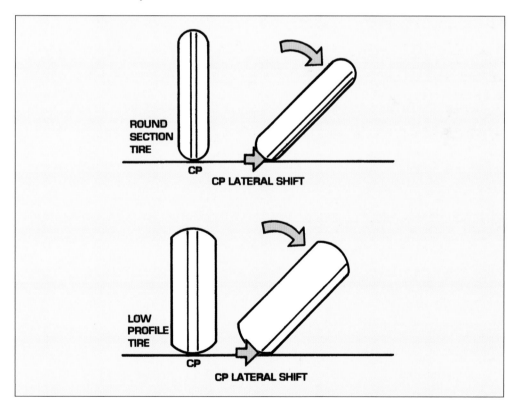

When a wheel is leaned into a curve, the contact patch on the tire shifts toward the edge of the tread. CP shift is greater with a wide, low-profile tire than with a narrower tire.

Self-Balancing

With carefully selected rake, trail, and tire profiles, a machine can have good self-balancing dynamics, whether moving upright and straight ahead or leaned over into a curve and turning, and whether at fast or slow speeds. The point I don't want you to miss is that the front-end geometry is designed to balance itself. If the bike leans over to the right, the CP shifts farther right, steering the front wheel more toward the right. As the wheel tracks away from center, that rolls the bike back toward vertical. When the machine returns to vertical, the gravity, steering head position, and CP all balance again.

When the motorcycle begins to fall over, the location of the front tire contact ring moves slightly, increasing drag on that side of the tire and countersteering the front wheel back under the center of mass.

As the front wheel steers itself back under the mass, the bike is rolled upright and balanced again but on a slightly different path.

If you watch a motorcycle cruising down the superslab (freeway), you'd swear it follows an absolutely perfect straight line. But if you could measure accurately, you'd discover that it rolls ever so slightly from one side to the other as it balances itself, sort of like a clock pendulum. This self-balancing act is more obvious at slower speeds because the front tire requires greater steering input at slower speeds than at higher speeds to get the same effect.

If you were to ride your bike slowly through a puddle of white paint and then go back and look at the tire tracks, you would observe that the front tire sometimes tracks to the left and sometimes to the right. In other words, the front tire rolls along in a snakelike track as the bike continuously rebalances itself.

Gyroscopic and Inertial Stability

Two big contributors to straight-ahead stability are the inertial effect of the motorcycle/rider mass and the gyroscopic forces generated by the spinning wheels. Perhaps the best way to think of inertia is that objects "want" to keep on doing whatever they are doing. Kick a brick sitting on the ground, and you'll discover that it

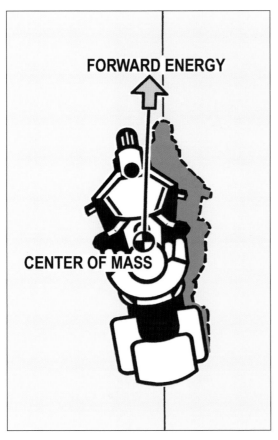

Even if the front wheel tracks off on a tangent, forward energy attempts to pull the mass of bike and rider back into a straight line again.

doesn't want to move. Throw the brick, and it's obvious it wants to keep moving, at the same speed and in the same direction. The popular unscientific term for property of matter is *momentum*. The correct name for this is *inertia*, but if we start to add vectors and forces, we'd need to start calling it *kinetic energy*. To avoid a war over definitions, I'll just call it *forward energy*.

A motorcycle, once up to speed, wants to keep rolling along, straight ahead, at the same speed. Forward energy contributes to straight-ahead stability by pulling the motorcycle's mass back toward center and by providing a resistance against which the tires can react. For example, if the motorcycle starts to drift away from center, forward energy attempts to pull it back into a straight line again.

The wheels of a motorcycle also contribute to stability but in a different way. Spinning wheels generate gyroscopic energy that resists changes in position. A spinning gyroscope wants to stay spinning at the same angle. The gyroscopic effect of the wheels helps keep the motorcycle from making any sudden changes in direction.

There are four main forces acting on a motorcycle to cause it to roll (lean) toward the curve, and engineers have attempted to quantify them. It appears that tire traction is the dominant force that initiates the roll. The tire traction is balanced against gravity pulling the bike over, while rider steering input is balanced against gyroscopic stability. If it were not for the gyroscopic stability of the wheels, the rider would tend to overcorrect, and it would be very difficult to keep the bike balanced. This explains why a heavier front wheel steers more slowly than a lighter wheel does. A lighter front wheel assembly allows more flickable steering, which is an advantage on a race bike.

What Makes It Turn?

In the previous section, I discussed a number of factors that cause a motorcycle to balance itself and what the rider can do to help. Now, let's consider what we do to make a motorcycle turn. I'll try to keep turning as understandable as possible and still give you the information you need to achieve better control of your motorcycle.

Turning Equals Unbalancing

As already noted, a well-engineered motorcycle wants to go straight. The front-end geometry automatically steers the bike toward straight ahead and vertical, and forward energy and gyroscopic forces help stabilize it. To get a two-wheeler to turn, we need to get it leaned over. So turning is really a process of unbalancing the bike to get it leaned over, then rebalancing again in a curving path.

Turning is really unbalancing the bike to get it leaned over, then rebalanced in a curving path.

Bikes Versus Cars

One of the big differences between how two-wheeled motorcycles and automobiles turn is that a motorcycle must first be leaned over before it starts to turn. An automobile starts to turn as soon as you yank on the steering wheel. The same is true for a trike or sidecar outfit, or for any other multitrack vehicle. But two-wheelers are different. Even with a flickable sportbike, it may take a half second to get the bike leaned over before it actually starts to change direction. And with a heavyweight tourer, that initial lean may require more than one second.

A lot of arm-waving and heated discussion has taken place around the campfires and Internet forums about how we really cause motorcycles to turn. The discussions always get around to countersteering, but there doesn't seem to be much common understanding of what we really mean by countersteering and exactly what the forces are that make it work. Let's see if I can clear up some of the mystery.

The Leaning/Cornering Process

Leaning can be initiated by a number of different factors, including rider's body English, steering the handlebars, and even road camber or a crosswind. The most powerful input is steering the handlebars, so we'll focus on that first.

Experienced riders usually refer to a rider's steering input as countersteering because the handlebars are steered opposite, or counter, to the intended lean. Push on the right grip to lean right; push on the left grip to lean left. That's where some of the confusion starts because leaning and cornering is really a process of several steps, whereas countersteering is only the first very brief step in the process. The leaning/cornering process all happens within a couple of seconds, so let's slow down the action and go through it step by step. We'll illustrate this from the front and exaggerate the graphic a bit so you can understand what the front end is doing.

The rider initiates the lean by a brief press on the grip to steer the front wheel away from the intended direction of turn. From the saddle, it may appear that the front wheel continues in a straight line while the top of the bike leans over, but what really happens is that the front wheel steers off on a slight tangent, which causes the contact patch to track away from the turn. The bike's mass resists lateral movement, so the tire tracking out forces the top of the bike to lean in toward the turn. For example, let's say the rider wants to make a right turn. Pushing on the right grip steers the front wheel off more toward the left, which forces the bike to lean toward the right. The actual countersteering takes only about a half second for an aggressive lean, or one second for a leisurely lean. Let's use the term *roll* in place of lean, to borrow an aviation term that's a little more descriptive.

If you have been practicing countersteering for a while, it may seem as if you just press on the grip and maintain the same pressure. But it should be obvious that if the front wheel continues to track off on a tangent, the bike will continue to roll over until it slams into the ground. So as soon as the bike rolls toward the turn, you must ease up on that initial countersteering push to allow the front wheel to steer itself back toward center. If the bike rolls over too far, you actually add some pressure on the grip to stop the roll and stabilize the lean angle. The gyroscopic stability of the wheels helps smooth out the steering input.

Approaching a right turn, the rider momentarily countersteers the front wheel away from the turn. The front wheel tracking left forces the bike to roll right.

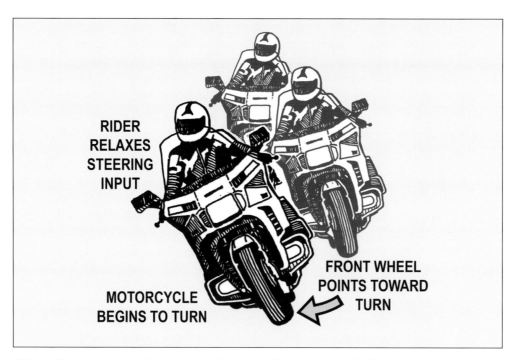

RIDER
RELAXES
STEERING
INPUT

FRONT WHEEL
POINTS TOWARD
TURN

MOTORCYCLE
BEGINS TO TURN

With the bike leaned toward the curve, the rider steers the front wheel slightly toward the curve, and the motorcycle begins to turn.

Now that the bike is leaned over and the front wheel is pointed toward the curve, the bike starts to turn. Tire traction is actually pushing against the road surface to overcome inertia and force the front end into a curving path. The front wheel is pointed slightly toward the curve, and the rider applies just enough steering input to keep the bike leaning and turning.

Of course, the bike's forward energy tries to force it back into a straight line. We usually refer to that effect as centrifugal force. If you were to tie a connecting rod on the end of a string and swing it around your head, the outward pull on the orbiting rod would represent centrifugal force, and the string would represent the front tire. With the bike leaned over, gravity is pulling strongly on the curve side to pull the bike over; at the same time, centrifugal force is trying to roll the bike upright. Gravity and centrifugal force balance against each other. Or, more correctly, the rider balances gravity against centrifugal force by small steering corrections.

One of the interesting characteristics of gyroscopes is *gyroscopic precession*. What that fancy term means is that if you hold a spinning motorcycle wheel vertically by the axles and steer it toward the left, the wheel wants to lean over toward the right. Since this seems to correspond to what happens when a motorcycle is leaned into a turn, many people are fooled into believing that gyroscopic precession is the dominant force that causes a motorcycle to roll into turns. It's a nice, simple theory but a little too simple to explain why a motorcycle behaves the way it does.

Since a motorcycle tire is in rolling contact with the road surface, tire traction enters the equation, and traction can produce much stronger forces than precession at normal road speeds. Secondarily, the steering angles are so slight during initiation of the lean that very little gyroscopic roll torque is generated. What's more, as the motorcycle is leaned over, the front wheel is first turned away from the direction of

It is primarily tire traction that forces the bike to turn away from center.

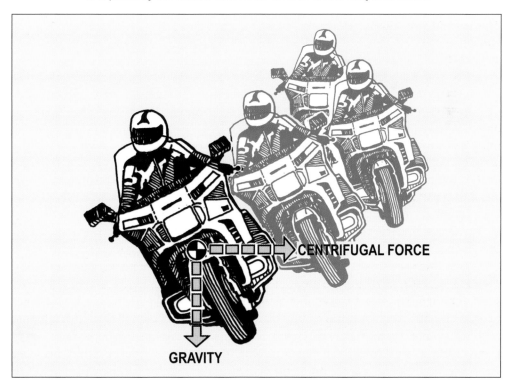

Now leaned into the curve and turning, the bike is stabilized by gravity balanced against centrifugal force.

lean and then turned back toward the lean. The net effect is that gyroscopic precession almost cancels itself out in terms of affecting roll. But the gyroscopic stability of the wheels is a necessary part of steering. If the wheels had little or no mass, it would be extremely difficult to balance the bike because of the instability.

Feedback

Part of the confusion over motorcycle balancing and steering is that different machines handle differently and give different feedback to the rider. It's not easy to differentiate between what the bike is doing and what the rider is doing. Ideally, if the rider maintains a slight press on the low grip, the bike will continue around a turn at the same lean angle. If the rider eases pressure on the grip, the motorcycle should roll itself upright and settle into a straight-ahead path. This would be called neutral steering, although it really isn't neutral at all. And not all motorcycles have neutral steering.

Consider a motorcycle with a tendency to fall into turns. With such a machine, you can initiate a right turn by pressing on the right grip; but once the bike starts to lean, it just wants to keep on rolling over farther and farther. So you need to counteract the motorcycle's self-induced roll by maintaining a pull on the low grip to keep the bike from leaning over any farther than you need for the turn. It might seem that you are steering the front wheel toward the curve and that your steering input is what is causing the motorcycle to turn. What you are actually doing is limiting the bike's own characteristic of falling into turns.

So if you encounter a rider who is convinced he or she consistently steers the front wheel toward the turn, it's most likely a matter of a bike that falls into corners. Generally, motorcycles that fall into turns are earlier designs with narrow front tire profiles and short steering trail.

Center of Gravity

When you hear someone attributing a motorcycle's good or bad manners to the elevation of its center of gravity (CoG), remember that it's mostly steering geometry that makes a machine feel sluggish to steer or top heavy in turns. Certainly, a cruiser that's built low to the ground will have a lower CoG. But some CoG cruisers with a low CoG have heavy steering. And there are tall dual sportbikes with the engine mass up in the stratosphere but flickable manners. My point is that the actual height of the CoG is only a concern when you are balancing at a stop or pushing the bike out of the garage. In motion, front-end geometry has a lot more to do with how the bike balances. And if your favorite machine has some strange cornering feedback, be aware that you can do some fine-tuning by setting up the suspension and, if necessary, changing tire diameters and profiles.

Body English

Remember Drifting Dan, who can't seem to control balance of his big road burner by throwing his weight around on the bike? It worked fine with Dan's little 250 that he rode years ago, but it doesn't work with his heavier touring bike. Sure, body English can cause a bike to change direction. But the result you get from throwing your weight around depends to a great extent on the relationship of your weight to the weight of the bike. The heavier the bike, the more its inertial and gyroscopic stability. For instance, slam your knee into the tank on a contemporary 250 lightweight, and the bike will head off in a new direction. Slam your knee against the tank of an 1800cc tourer, and the bike may wobble once or twice and then straighten right back up on its original path. With the heavier machine, Dan needs to focus more on countersteering and less on body English.

The next time you are out riding, think about what you're doing to control balance and direction. Are you sitting rock-solid in the saddle and just resting your boots on the pegs? Are you shifting your butt? Are you shifting weight from one foot peg to the other? In a turn, do you place more weight on the inside peg or the outside peg? Are you pushing on the grips or pulling on the grips? Are you pushing on the low grip or pulling? I'm not offering any correct answers here, just pointing out that part of becoming a proficient motorcyclist is figuring out what it takes to balance your machine and what it's trying to tell you.

Direct Steering Versus Countersteering

A road racer pointed out to me an interesting phenomenon about steering input. While leaned over at speed on the racetrack, this rider observed that about half the time he was pushing on the low grip, steering the front wheel slightly away from the turn, and half the time he was pulling on the low grip, steering the front wheel toward the turn, all the while attempting to hold the bike on his desired racing line. He knew whether he was turning the front wheel toward the turn or away from the turn because he was hanging off the bike and could see the front wheel. He described pulling on the low grip as direct steering and pushing on the low grip as countersteering. The racer was struggling with the concepts of direct steering and countersteering. Somehow he had come to believe that motorcycle steering had to be either direct steering or countersteering, but not both. His observation was that he was alternating between the two.

To help clear this up, let's define *direct steering* as pointing the front wheel toward the intended direction of travel, in other words, steering the front wheel toward the left in a left turn. Was the racer direct steering? Yes, much of the time. But was he also countersteering? Yes, but only some of the time. We should understand *countersteering* to mean momentarily steering the contact patch opposite to the direction we want the bike to roll. Let's be clear that countersteering isn't a matter of whether the bars are turned left of center or right of center, or whether that takes a push or a pull, whether the bike is upright or leaned over, or whether speed is fast or slow. Whatever the position of the bike or front wheel, you momentarily steer the front wheel opposite the way you want the bike to roll.

Countersteering is momentarily steering the contact patch opposite the direction you want the motorcycle to roll. Direct steering is pointing the front wheel toward the intended direction of travel.

For example, if the motorcycle is leaned over in a tight left turn and then a crosswind pushes it over a little too far, momentarily pulling on the left grip will keep it from rolling over farther. Is that still countersteering, even though the front wheel is pointed to the left of center in a left turn? Sure. Countersteering is a momentary, dynamic input, not the direction the front wheel happens to be pointed toward at the moment. Or let's say you are leaned over into a left turn and it's time to lift the bike up and exit the corner. Momentarily steering the front wheel slightly more toward the curve (by pressing the grips more toward the right) forces the bike to roll more upright. The momentary press on the grip to roll the bike vertical is countersteering. You can't determine countersteering from a still photograph because it's a dynamic motion.

In this situation, the rider is momentarily steering the front wheel more toward the left to roll the bike more upright, but the wheel is still pointed toward the curve.

Push Steering

If you're still a little confused about this countersteering business, I suggest a little experiment. The simplest way to describe countersteering is to push on the right grip to turn right or push on the left grip to turn left. Take your bike out for a spin; get up to 35 mph or so on a straight, vacant road; and consciously push lightly on the left grip. The bike will lean over slightly left and move over toward the left side of the lane. Now, push on the right grip. The bike will lean slightly right and steer back toward the right side of the lane.

This isn't something new because it's how everyone steers motorcycles, whether they realize it or not. Lots of riders concentrate on body English such as knee or foot pressure, unaware that the important input is through the hands. Accurate cornering is much easier once you realize that the primary input is through the grips. But once you've experimented with push steering, it's time to move on. Different machines and different situations provide different feedback to the grips when leaned over in a corner. So we need to understand countersteering as more than simply pushing on the low grip.

Out-Tracking

When you countersteer, it may seem as if pressure on the grip pushes the bike over without actually pivoting the front wheel. Does the front end actually pivot away from center as the bike leans over into a curve? Yes. The movement is slight, but if the front end isn't free to pivot in the steering head, the motorcycle can't be balanced or turned.

If you could watch a slow-motion video of a motorcycle running through a puddle of paint and then making a turn, you would see that the front tire momentarily

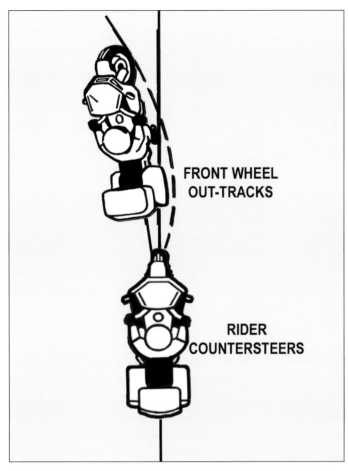

FRONT WHEEL
OUT-TRACKS

RIDER
COUNTERSTEERS

When the rider countersteers, the front wheel momentarily out-tracks opposite the intended direction of the turn, then returns to center as the motorcycle leans over.

tracks toward the outside during the initial countersteer, then eases back toward the direction of turn. In slow-speed turns, the front tire generally tracks outside the rear tire.

If you'd like a good example of out-tracking, record some motorcycle road race footage, and play it back in slow motion. In those shots where the camera is looking back down the straight toward a corner, you can see the lean angle of the bikes head-on. If you mentally plot the path of the motorcycle's center of mass, you'll see that the bottom of the front tire out-tracks, even arcing over onto the rumble strips as the rider uses every last inch of pavement to get the bike leaned.

Coning

While your bike is leaned over in a curve, you might wonder why the bike continues to turn even though the front end seems to be pointed straight ahead. Part of the reason is that the front wheel really is pointed slightly toward the curve. The other part of the reason is called coning. To understand the concept of coning, let's consider the shape of the front tire where it meets the road surface.

The motorcycle pictured above is in a straight line, approaching the turn-in point.

As the rider countersteers, the front wheel actually tracks away from the intended direction of turn.

With the motorcycle leaned, the front wheel recenters and then steers toward the turn.

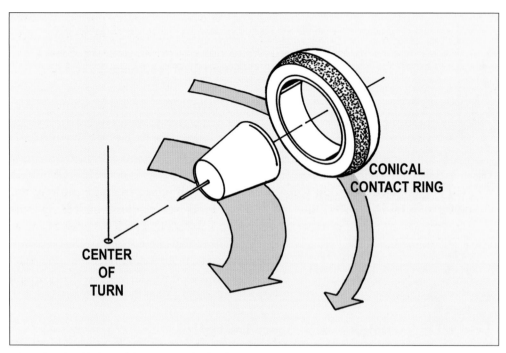

When the wheel is leaned into a turn, the flexible tire forms a contact ring that is conical in shape, similar to the shape of a foam coffee cup on its side.

Although we can see that the top of an inflated tire forms a rounded shape, we have to imagine that the tire momentarily gets flattened where it contacts the ground at the CP. And we also know that the tire CP isn't really a single point but rather a continuous ring around the tread. It's important to recognize that with the bike leaned over into a turn, this contact ring forms a conical shape, similar to a foam coffee cup on its side.

If you nudge the cup forward, it wants to roll in a circle because the circumference at the closed end is smaller than the circumference at the open end. If you stick a toothpick through the center of the cup bottom, the toothpick will point approximately at the center of the circle. A motorcycle tire responds similarly when the bike is leaned over, with the inside of the tire contact surface covering less distance than the outside. So when leaned, a motorcycle wheel wants to roll in a circle, with the axle pointed more or less at the center of the turn. In a very tight turn, the axle may actually point at a center that's below the surface of the ground.

Fast Flicks

The more muscle you put into countersteering, the harder the front tire will push to roll the bike into a lean, and the quicker it will roll (up to the limit of traction, of course). The longer you hold pressure on the grip, the farther over the bike will roll. Those are key points to remember when riding a twisty road where you need to flick the bike left-right-left in a series of turns. Remember, it may take a half second to get the bike rolled upright from a tight turn and another half second to get it leaned over the other way before it changes direction.

Is it possible to muscle the handlebars hard enough to snap the tires loose? Yes. You may have seen this in a road race, where a bike suddenly jumps into a heart-stopping wiggle in the middle of an S-curve, or the front tire loses its grip and the bike crashes off on a tangent. In an aggressive S-turn, the rider needs to counteract the roll when the bike is leaned to the desired angle, and that demands some traction.

A motorcycle rolls around its center of mass (CoM) without a lot of resistance but resists being pushed up, down, or sideways. That's why a bike speeding over a lumpy bridge on the Isle of Man can get airborne. The bike's mass wants to keep going straight ahead, even as the ground drops away beneath the tires.

Even if you aren't flying over a steep bridge, the bike's inertia will momentarily resist gaining or losing altitude. When a bike is leaned over into a turn, the CoM must lose altitude. The bike's inertia momentarily resists the pull of gravity, so the tires will have reduced traction when rolling toward the turn. But when rolling the bike up out of a turn, the CoM must be lifted up again, momentarily increasing traction. As the bike is rolled upright, you may notice that suspension compresses, at least for a moment.

The practical application of this is that the front tire is more likely to lose traction when the rider is countersteering hard into a turn, and the tire gains traction as the bike is rolled back to vertical. It also explains why it takes more muscle to roll a bike up out of a lean than to roll it into a lean.

As the motorcycle is rolled into a lean, the mass has to drop slightly to maintain contact with the road. That can cause a temporary reduction in traction. When the bike is rolled up out of a lean, the bike's mass has to be lifted vertically, which demands more muscle but results in a temporary increase in traction.

U-Turns

If you're paranoid about slow speed U-turns, you're not alone. Heavyweight machines can be a handful at slow speeds and in tight quarters. The novice technique is to drag the foot skids, turn the bars to the stop, and feather the clutch to creep around. The novice may also discover that the bike has a larger turning diameter than the space available (often discovered just as the front tire threatens to drop off the pavement onto a loose gravel shoulder).

Scott Wilson demonstrates a tight turn. Note that he is slipping the clutch to keep the engine pulling. He has shifted his weight to the outside of the saddle and is looking where he wants to go, not down at the pavement in front of the bike.

The trick for tight U-turns is being aware that as the bike is leaned over farther, it will make a tighter turn. So rather than drag your boots on the ground with the bike vertical, what's needed is to lean the bike over to a steeper angle.

The technique is to place most of your weight on the outside, lean the bike wa-a-a-y over, and keep the engine pulling. It's OK to slip the clutch if needed to keep the engine from stalling, but squeezing the clutch in a tight turn is usually followed by the sound of a bike hitting the ground. Don't try to coast around a tight turn; you need to keep the engine pulling to balance centrifugal force against gravity. In tight turns, it helps to swivel your head around like a barn owl and look where you want to go. Staring at the ground three feet ahead of the bike may result in finding yourself on the ground right where you were looking.

If the bike seems to go wider than you want it to, you need to lean it over farther. Shift your weight to the outside edge of the saddle or stand more on the outside foot peg. Grab those grips and push the bike over. To avoid any confusion over whether you are pulling or pushing on the low grip, imagine pushing both grips toward the turn to lean the bike over more and pushing both grips away from the turn to keep it from falling over or to straighten up. By now it should be obvious that we are using direct steering most of the time and brief countersteering adjustments to help control lean angle.

Ergonomics

If you've been ho-hum about the subject of ergonomics (how the rider fits on the motorcycle), consider that how you sit on the bike and reach toward the grips has a lot do with steering control. You'll have better control of the bike when you can reach the grips in a natural position, with your arms slightly bent and your feet braced under your body weight, not forward. So if you find your motorcycle difficult to control, take a close look at the ergonomics. It's not just an *I* thing.

If you ride a cruiser-style machine with the foot pegs or boards mounted far forward, you'll find it somewhat more difficult to steer accurately because you can't use your legs to brace against your steering input. Since the feet-forward seating position means you will normally be pulling on both grips to counteract wind pressure, you'll need to modify your countersteering technique. Rather than press on the grip on the turn side, pull on the opposite grip. That is, approaching a left turn, pull on the right grip.

The feet-forward seating position also makes it difficult to support your weight on your feet. For tight turns, you can simply slide your butt toward the edge of the saddle. For instance, when making a tight U-turn to the left, you can slide over to the right edge of the saddle.

Cruisers with forward-mounted footboards require slightly different steering techniques.

I've got a warm-up exercise for you to practice tight turns. It's just a long figure 8 about eighteen feet wide and forty feet long. Enter at one corner, make a tight turn at the other end, reverse direction, make another tight turn, and continue out the far end.

If tight turns make you nervous, this is just what you need to practice. Shift your weight to the outside, push both grips in the direction you want to go, and keep the engine pulling. Slip the clutch as needed, but don't pull the clutch and try to coast. Most motorcycles can turn a figure 8 within the eighteen-foot by forty-foot area. If you can't turn within the eighteen-foot width, move the cones out to twenty or twenty-five feet at first, then pull the cones in as you gain skill and confidence. If your bike has independent front/rear brakes, try easing on a little rear brake to give the engine something to pull against.

ABOUT 18 FEET

EXIT

WEIGHT ON RIGHT FOOTPEG

KEEP ENGINE PULLING

WEIGHT ON LEFT FOOTPEG

ABOUT 40 FEET

ENTER

The figure-8 box is an exercise to help you practice tight U-turns. Enter at one corner, make a U-turn at the other end, make another U-turn at the near end, and exit at the far corner. Keep the engine pulling, even if you have to slip the clutch.

If you don't have time to lay out the figure-8 exercise, try making a figure 8 before you park the bike at the end of a ride, or practice a few figure 8s as you arrive in the company parking lot each morning. Anyone can ride straight because the bike is doing most of the balancing. It's in the tight turns where we find out who can ride and who is just going along for the ride.

The Lowdown on the Slowdown

Remember back to those statistics about motorcycle crashes, where I mentioned that many motorcyclists aren't as proficient at braking as they need to be? Let's consider what's involved in braking, and then I'll outline some practice exercises you can use to increase your braking skills.

Once in a while, you need to brake aggressively to avoid a hazardous situation.

Laying It Down

Back in the old days, lots of people got killed in motorcar and motorcycle accidents exacerbated by weak brakes. Lawrence (of Arabia) didn't die falling off a camel; he died crashing his Brough Superior into a stone wall as an alternative to plowing into some children who popped into view on the narrow English road. In the United States, the standard quick-stop technique for yesteryear's motor officers was to throw the black and white on its side and hope it would grind to a stop on the axle nuts and crash bars. Many police academies still teach the technique of laying it down, even though officers may be riding machines with sticky rubber and ABS brakes, which can stop a lot quicker on the rubber than on chrome. Frankly, I've always assumed that laying it down *is* a crash.

Have you ever heard a fellow rider describe a panic stop during which the tires were sliding? For example, here's Zoomie Zed explaining a near collision: "I'm cruising along minding my own business when this chickie babe in a Cherokee zooms out of an alley. I jam on the brake real quick. I'm braking so hard the rear tire is smokin' right to a stop. My engine stalls just as my front wheel ends up about two inches from her front door. You shoulda seen the stupid look on her face!"

Good news, bad news, Zed. The good news is that you didn't score another accident in your file and didn't drop the bike. The bad news is that you didn't stop as quickly as you could have. First, the front brake is the one that stops the bike. And jamming on the rear brake too quickly caused the tire to skid, which increased your stopping distance and could have resulted in a highside flip. Even if you had squeezed the front brake lever, you would have wasted a lot of stopping distance reaching for the lever. A clever rider would know that cars pulling out of alleys account for about one out of every six motorcycle fatalities, so you should have been prepared to make a quick stop when you saw the car nosing out. One more thing, Zed: it helps to squeeze the clutch during a quick stop, so you can concentrate on the brakes and keep the engine from locking up the rear wheel.

Up on those twisty mountain roads, lots of experienced riders think it's clever to ride a steady pace that doesn't require any braking. The idea is that smooth is good and that speed changes are the opposite of smooth. Riding a steady pace is enjoyable, but the problem is that those back roads contain hazards such as farm tractors, wild deer, loose gravel, and mud-lubricated corners. You don't usually get much advance warning of such hazards, so you may have to brake hard at the last moment to avoid a disaster, and you may have to do that aggressive braking while rounding a corner.

What's more, that twisty mountain road eventually comes to town. As you come off the hill and find yourself slogging through urban traffic, your biggest challenge might be avoiding a left-turning motorist or a car dodging the wrong way across a parking lot. So whether you ride conservatively or closer to the edge of the envelope, hard braking should be a part of your habit patterns. Rather than think of smooth as never using the brakes, I prefer to think of smooth as being able to brake right up to the limits of traction without upsetting the bike or getting excited, whether rounding a corner or negotiating traffic.

Inertia

Let's consider how to make quick, painless, maximum-effort slowdowns. First, there are forces we're trying to overcome with the brakes. Inertia is the physical property of objects wanting to keep moving in a straight line at the same speed. A speeding motorcycle wants to keep speeding along pointed straight ahead, even if we roll off the gas. What's important about inertia is that it increases significantly with speed. Gravity is a constant—it's the same regardless of speed. But the higher the speed, the greater the forward energy. To slow down a motorcycle or bring it to a stop, we've got to overpower its forward energy.

Of course the bike will slow down if you just roll off the throttle. Wind resistance, rolling friction, and engine compression braking all help overcome forward energy. But if you need to slow down quickly, you've got to use the brakes, and braking successfully requires both knowledge and skill.

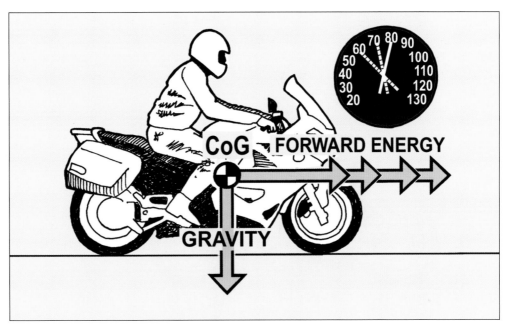

Gravity is a constant that doesn't change with increased speed, but forward energy increases dramatically with speed.

Braking Forces

You may have observed that rear-wheel braking can make lots of smoke and noise but doesn't slow the machine nearly as quickly as the front brake does. Braking the wheel to a stop doesn't necessarily stop the bike. That's because the maximum braking force you can apply to a wheel depends upon traction, and traction is a function of the weight on the tire as well as the stickiness of the tire and roughness of the road.

Theoretically, if one-half of the total weight of the motorcycle, including rider and load, is carried on the rear tire, the maximum braking force you can get out of the rear tire is one-half the weight of the machine. So if the total weight is 800 pounds with a weight bias of 50/50, the maximum rear-wheel braking force would be 400 pounds However, since even rear-brake application transfers weight forward, rear-wheel brake force would decrease, encouraging the rear tire to skid.

Front-Wheel Braking

During braking, the load on the wheels isn't a constant. When you apply the brakes, the weight seems to transfer forward onto the front tire, increasing front tire traction. Consider that whether it is engine compression or brake friction trying to overcome forward energy, the braking force is applied way down at the tire contact patches, while the center of mass is much higher on the machine. The mass wants to keep moving straight ahead, and the result is that when the brakes are applied, the motorcycle pitches forward. This feels as if the weight had suddenly been transferred forward onto the front wheel. Since the available braking force is determined by the load on the tire, as the machine pitches forward, more traction becomes available on the front. So more front-brake force can then be applied. Assuming tractable pavement and sticky rubber, it is relatively easy to brake hard enough on a light bike to do a front wheel stoppie, with 100 percent of braking force on the front and the rear wheel in the air.

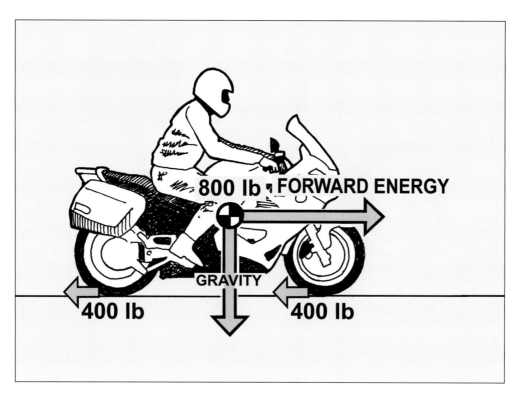

Braking force is proportional to weight on the tire.

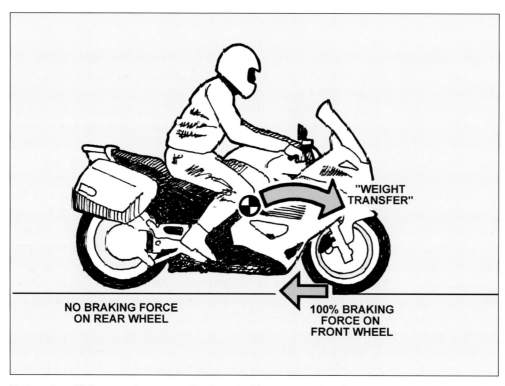

If there is sufficient traction, aggressive front braking can transfer all the weight onto the front tire, resulting in 100 percent braking on the front and no braking on the rear.

Some riders are cautious about braking hard on the front for fear the motorcycle will flip over the front wheel. That wasn't much of a problem in the good old days of harder rubber, but with today's sticky tires on short-wheelbase bikes, it's now the limiting factor. However, most of us could brake a lot harder on the front than we do, even in the rain. Our greatest concern with hard front braking should be smooth, progressive squeezing of the lever to keep the tire from sliding during the time it takes for the bike to pitch forward. It takes about one second for that weight transfer to occur.

Highsiding

While many riders are paranoid about sliding the front tire, the greatest danger from overbraking is not on the front but on the rear. The danger is flipping yourself into a painful highside crash if the bike slides sideways during a quick stop. If the rider overbrakes on the rear and the rear end starts sliding out to one side, the unfortunate survival reaction is often to let up on the pedal to reduce the skid. But when the tire regains traction and spins up, it snaps the rear end back toward center so violently it can flip the bike over the high side.

Highside flips are simple to avoid. Just stay in the habit of using more front brake than rear brake all the time. Lightweight sportbikes are particularly susceptible to rear-wheel skids because the weight bias is often more on the front wheel, yet the rear brake is typically a powerful hydraulic disc. When the rear brake is applied on a light sportbike with just a solo rider, it is very easy to skid the tire.

If you realize that your lightweight machine tends to slide the rear tire even with just a light dab on the pedal, ignore the rear brake and use just the front brake. A sliding tire has much less traction than a tire that's still rolling over the road surface.

Directional Control

To keep the bike pointed straight ahead with the rubber side down, we need to squander a bit of tire traction to keep the rear end straight and some of that front-tire traction to keep the machine balanced. We maintain directional control by modulating, or adjusting, brake-lever pressure to keep either tire from sliding at any point in the stop. That's the technique to strive for, whether your machine has an integrated, linked, or antilock brake system. Manufacturers are offering antilock brake systems on some machines to help prevent a slideout if the rider grabs the front brake too quickly or aggressively. But the best antiskid system is still mounted between a rider's ears.

A sliding tire has much less traction than does a tire that's still rolling over the road. Maximum traction occurs at around 15 percent slip. During a quick stop, it is important to adjust pressure on the levers to apply maximum braking just short of a skid. During that first second while the motorcycle is pitching forward, squeeze progressively harder until the weight transfer allows maximum front-wheel braking.

Practice that now. Make a pretend brake lever with the thumb and index finger of your left hand. Now, squeeze the "lever" while counting out loud, "one thousand and one." If you are full on the brake before you're through counting, that's too fast.

As the weight transfers forward, the rear tire will lose traction, so less braking can be applied to the rear wheel. As the front lever is squeezed progressively harder, you must let up on the rear brake. Toward the end of the stop, as forward energy dissipates, it is necessary to ease up on the brakes slightly. And if you must cross a slippery spot such as a plastic arrow or an oil slick, it's important to ease off the brakes

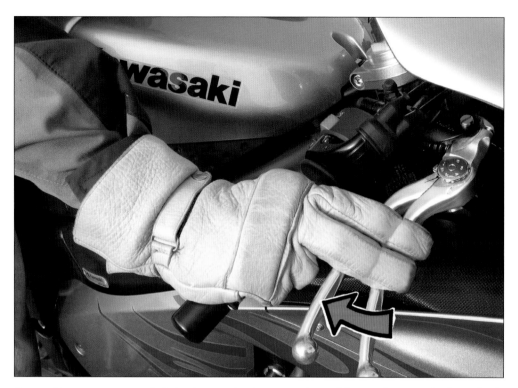

You need to squeeze progressively harder over about one second as weight transfers onto the front wheel.

momentarily as the tires cross the slippery surface. In the rain or when carrying a passenger, more rear brake can be applied because there will be comparatively more weight on the rear wheel.

Real-World Quick Stops

Theoretically, maximum braking force on a tire is limited to the force of gravity pulling down on the wheel. An 800-pound bike should be able to generate 800 pounds of front-wheel braking force given smooth pavement with a perfect coefficient of friction of 100 percent (1.0). A motorcycle with good brakes should be able to make a maximum-effort stop from 60 mph in something like 120 feet.

But if you check the stopping distances in the bike reviews such as those in *Motorcycle Consumer News*, you'll find 60 mph to 0 braking distances as short as 108 feet. Do motorcycles defy the laws of physics? No, it's just that in real life, the pavement isn't perfectly smooth. Obviously, an extremely smooth surface such as a shiny steel plate will never have traction greater than 1.0. But the little stones in the surface of typical concrete or asphalt pavement act somewhat like the teeth in a cog belt drive, boosting available traction somewhat above that theoretical 1.0 coefficient of friction.

Reading the braking tests, you might believe that if the bike you are riding has been tested in a 60 mph to 0 stop in 120 feet, you can stop your bike that quickly in a real-world situation. But it's not very likely you would be able to duplicate a test rider's quick stops. First, a test rider knows he is going to make an aggressive stop and knows exactly where and when. When you are riding in the real world, you don't know when you are going to have to pull off a quick stop. When you suddenly realize you need to stop quickly, it takes a fraction of a second to actually get on the brakes. The test reports don't include reaction time, only the actual stopping distances. An extremely quick reaction would be 0.5 sec. A very skilled rider might be able to react within 0.7 sec. An aging rider or an inexperienced rider might have a reaction time of 1.0 sec or even longer.

Second, a test rider gets to repeat the stop over and over until the shortest distance is achieved, and that's what gets published. After several runs, the professional rider may get a deceleration rate of 1g, or 32 ft/sec per second. When you need to make your first quick stop your best, you'd be doing well to pull off a deceleration rate of 30 ft/sec per second, even with sticky tires on clean, dry pavement. The bottom line is that a really aggressive stop for a proficient street rider would be in the neighborhood of 195 feet from 60 mph to 0, assuming a quick reaction time of 0.75 sec. And from higher speeds, stopping distances really stretch out. Remember, the bike doesn't slow at all during the time it takes to react, and reaction distance increases with speed. The lesson is to cover the brake lever and ease on a little brake when approaching hazardous situations.

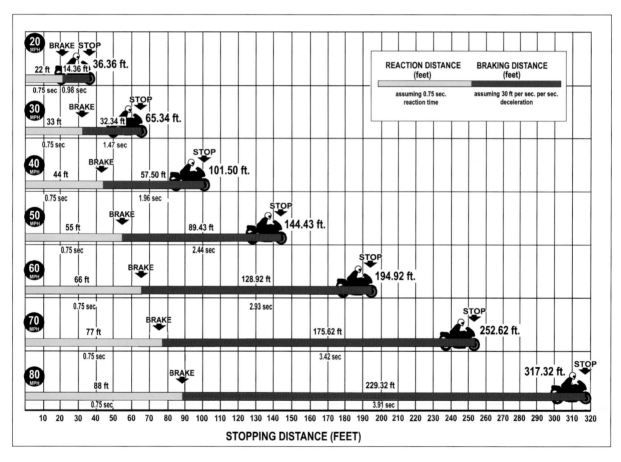

Brake Systems

One reason a quick stop is so useful is because of the amount of power the brakes can muster. Some motorcycles have integrated brake systems that tie together the front and rear brakes to make it easier for the rider to do the right thing. Fully integrated systems have the front and rear brakes tied together so that applying either the rear pedal or the front lever applies both front and rear brakes together. A partially integrated system means the front lever activates both front and rear brakes but the rear pedal activates only the rear brake.

Linked brake systems use multiple hydraulic lines with proportioning and delay valves to activate different pistons in the front and rear calipers. The Honda linked brake system (LBS) uses triple piston calipers on two front disks and one rear disk. Each of the three pistons on each caliper is independent, so activating only one piston produces about one-third of the potential braking force on each caliper.

Squeezing the front brake lever activates the outer two pistons of both front calipers plus the middle piston of the rear caliper. Stepping on the rear brake pedal activates the two outer pistons on the single rear caliper plus the middle pistons on both front calipers. The result is that squeezing the front lever applies about 33 percent of rear braking; stepping on the rear pedal contributes to approximately 33 percent of front-wheel braking.

Antilock brake systems (ABS) help you avoid a spill if you brake too hard. ABS works by releasing the brake pressure in pulses when the wheel speed sensor detects that wheel rotation has suddenly slowed. The ABS controller momentarily releases brake pressure to allow the wheel to spin up and regain traction, then reapplies the brake. ABS can save you from a spill if you overbrake on a slick surface, but ABS doesn't differentiate between straight line stops and braking while leaned over. The shortest stop requires that you brake to a maximum just short of a full skid, which means you should be braking as hard as possible without activating the ABS. You should consider ABS a safety net, not an automatic brake system, and even ABS riders should learn to apply the brakes just short of a skid. That's doubly important for braking in curves, since ABS won't sense a lateral slideout or loss of traction caused by engine braking on the rear wheel.

The Ideal Quick Stop
Let's put all of the details together now and describe an ideal quick stop:

- You've been enjoying a twisty back road and arrive back in the city. The locals are hurrying around to the various stores and seem to be more focused on getting their shopping done than on watching for motorcycles.
- Entering the busy downtown area, you check to be sure you aren't being tailgated, cover the front brake lever, and watch for pedestrians or bicyclists who might dart across the street or other vehicles that might swerve across your path.

Suddenly, you need to make a quick stop to avoid a left-turner.

- Approaching a busy intersection, you observe a motor home in the opposite lane that could turn left. You shift down a gear, squeeze lightly on the front brake to reduce speed and prepare for a possible quick stop, and scrutinize the front end of the van for clues the driver is beginning to turn. You see the front tires pointed in your direction.

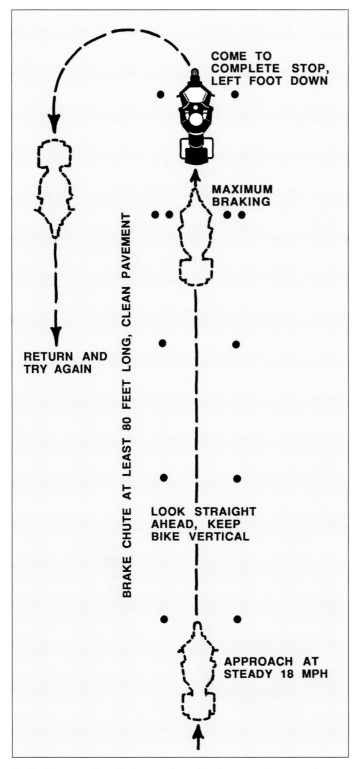

COME TO COMPLETE STOP, LEFT FOOT DOWN

MAXIMUM BRAKING

RETURN AND TRY AGAIN

BRAKE CHUTE AT LEAST 80 FEET LONG, CLEAN PAVEMENT

LOOK STRAIGHT AHEAD, KEEP BIKE VERTICAL

APPROACH AT STEADY 18 MPH

For braking practice, find some clean, level pavement you can borrow for a while. Start your braking runs at 18 mph, and gradually increase approach speeds on subsequent passes as you gain confidence and familiarity with the characteristics of the bike you are riding.

- The hood of the truck rises slightly as the driver accelerates into a left turn across your path, trying to squeeze through the gap in traffic.
- You squeeze the clutch and apply both brakes simultaneously, pressing lightly on the rear brake pedal but squeezing progressively harder on the front lever as weight transfers onto the front wheel.
- The left-turner suddenly wakes up to the potential collision and jams on the brakes, stopping halfway across your lane.
- Concentrating on a quick stop, you maintain maximum braking on the front just short of a skid, and shift to first gear just before you bring the motorcycle to a stop with your right foot still on the rear brake and your left foot on the ground. You glance briefly in the mirror to be sure you're not about to be rear-ended, signal the driver to go ahead, then ease out the clutch and continue on your way. You've taken charge to turn a potential nasty accident into a minor inconvenience.

Quick-Stop Practice

Quick stops require skill and experience with the machine you are riding. That's especially important if you are riding a different bike from your usual mount. The only way to build braking skills is to practice the right techniques until they become habits.

I'm not talking just quick slowdowns from 80 to 60 here; I'm talking quick stops from road speed to zero, with no smoking tires, no falldowns, and no highsides. If you intend to ride fast on public roads, you should be as good at hard braking and quick stops as you are at cornering lines and rolling on the gas. Riders of ABS-equipped machines are not excused from the drill.

Find some long, smooth, tractable piece of pavement somewhere that you can borrow for an hour or so. An abandoned section of road will do if it's reasonably clean and dry. Perhaps you have a nearby parking lot that is vacant early in the morning. It helps to set up some cones or markers to define a braking chute, but all you really need is a long strip of clean, level pavement.

- Get the machine stabilized at about 18 to 20 mph in second gear. Trust me here, don't try your first run any faster. Maintain speed right up to the braking point. Keep your head up and maintain your awareness of where you intend to be stopped. Avoid glancing down at the instruments or levers.
- When your front tire passes the braking point, squeeze the clutch, roll off the throttle, and simultaneously apply both brakes, progressively squeezing harder on the front as you count out "one thousand and one." Stop as quickly as you can without skidding either tire.
- Toward the end of the stop, shift into first gear. Come to a complete stop with your right foot on the rear brake pedal and your left foot supporting the machine. The habit of shifting to first prepares you for a quick getaway to avoid a rear-end collision.
- Return to the end of the chute and try it again. See if you can better your previous distance without skidding. As you gain confidence in your front tire traction, bump your approach speed up another 2 mph on each subsequent practice pass.

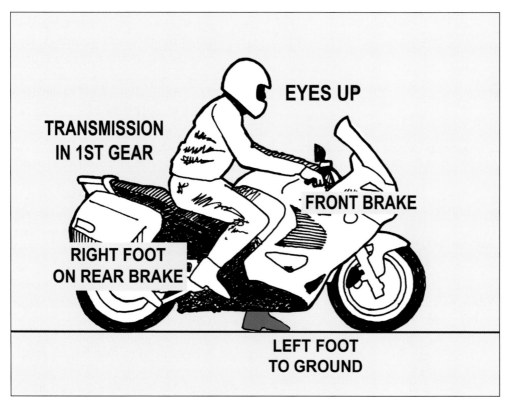

At the end of the stop, you should have the clutch squeezed, the transmission in first gear, your right foot on the rear brake pedal, and your left foot to the ground. It's a good habit to check your mirrors after stopping.

Skids

An impending front tire skid allows the front wheel to wiggle from side to side. Steering will feel less responsive. If the front tire does start to skid, immediately release the lever to regain traction, then squeeze a little more gently. Be aware that as you increase approach speed, the rear tire will be more likely to skid due to the increasing inertial forces. If you accidentally skid the rear tire, my best advice is to stand on it and slide to a complete stop to avoid the possibility of a highside flip. Then make a point of using less rear brake next time. If you can't seem to avoid skidding the rear tire, rest your right foot on the passenger peg, and try stopping with the front brake only. A machine with a longer wheelbase will have less of a tendency to lift the rear wheel. When practicing aggressive braking, it's very helpful to have another rider watching your technique. If you have a buddy to practice with, one rider can signal the other when to stop, to add some spontaneity to the drill.

One other little item: before you try any skill practice on your bike, do us both a favor and climb into your best crash costume. If you do it all right, I'm happy, too. But if you don't get it right, I'm not going to be there to point out bad habits or help you pick up the pieces.

Taking the Panic out of Panic Stops

Roger doesn't know it, but he's about to encounter a mule deer just around the corner.

Roger Rider is out for a spin in the country. It's a beautiful day, the weather is comfortably warm, and the bike is running sweetly. The road twists and turns predictably, dipping down into tree-shaded hollows and climbing back up to snake between the farms and meadows. It's too nice a day to hurry, but Roger isn't loafing, either, because it just feels right to roll on the gas exiting the corners and accelerate through the flickering shadows and sunlight.

But Roger's fun is about to end for the day. Approaching a downhill curve, he is startled by a brown object rising up from the roadside ditch and pivoting in his direction. Roger instantly recognizes the two big ears of a mule deer and hopes it will just freeze there as he rides on by. Without thinking about it, his right hand rolls off the gas and his left hand nudges the bike over to a course farther away from the deer.

But the deer doesn't just freeze. As Roger gets within the last thirty feet, the deer suddenly springs to action, bounding onto the road and clattering away in graceful leaps. The deer tries to zigzag away from the motorcycle, and Roger tries to swerve around the deer, but they both guess wrong. Too late, Roger makes a panic grab for the front brake lever. The front wheel slides out, deer and motorcycle careen off each other, and both sprawl onto the pavement. Fortunately, neither rider nor deer is seriously injured, and both manage to stagger back onto their feet after a few seconds.

The deer limps off into the trees. Roger limps over to look at his bike, now a mess of broken plastic and bent metal.

Whether it's a left-turning van at an intersection, a stalled hay truck in a blind corner, or a deer alongside the road, aggressive braking is often the best tactic for avoiding a collision. Some riders call a maximum-effort quick stop a panic stop because the situation calls for immediate action. Of course, *panic* means sudden, unreasoning terror, and certainly Roger reacted in panic when the deer jumped in front of him. But what Roger really needed was deliberate, reasoned, and correct evasive action. Let's see what we can do to take the *panic* out of panic stops.

Is a Quick Stop the Best Maneuver?

Now, you may or may not agree that a quick stop is the correct evasive maneuver for a deer suddenly springing into your path. Wouldn't it be better to either maintain speed so as not to startle the deer or speed up to get by sooner? Maintaining speed or increasing speed assumes you can predict what the animal—or the other driver—is going to do. Deer are notoriously unpredictable. Braking reduces forward energy, and a quick stop has a good chance of avoiding a collision if the other guy does get in your way.

When faced with a potential collision, would it be smart to toss the bike on its side and let it slide? For example, let's say I have just realized on a rainy morning that the pavement is coated with diesel oil just as an SUV driver changes lanes in front of me and slams on the brakes. Should I try to do a quick stop, or toss the bike on its side?

If you need to make a quick stop on a slippery surface, should you keep the bike on the tires or lay it down?

My experience with slick surfaces is that the situation will decide for you. I intend to always stay on the rubber and brake to a stop. My reasoning is that rubber has more traction than does metal or plastic, even on oil-slick wet pavement. In most situations, the bike will stop faster with the rubber side down. Once the bike is down and sliding, I've lost control. If I can keep the bike on the rubber, perhaps I can ease over between the vehicles for a little extra stopping distance.

I'm sure you could think of other scenarios in which the best tactic would be to gas it or to try swerving around the hazard. But there is only a limited amount of traction, so you shouldn't attempt to swerve and accelerate simultaneously. If you choose to accelerate, it pretty well cancels out the other options. Maintaining speed and attempting to swerve is sometimes the best option, but you need to guess right about which way to swerve. When faced with a deer leaping into the road, the odds are that you're not going to second guess which way it is going to leap.

Hard braking has several advantages over either accelerating or swerving. One big advantage of straight-line hard braking is the potential of stopping short of a collision. The brakes on today's motorcycles are typically more powerful than the engine. More often than not, a quick stop is your best collision-avoidance tactic.

If it isn't obvious, the first step in taking the panic out of quick stops is being prepared for them. A big part of that is actively searching the road for clues and predicting hazards that you can't see yet. When you are riding through a forest at dusk, you shouldn't be surprised when a deer or two leap out of the roadside bushes. In farm country, after you've noticed haying crews mowing, it shouldn't be a big shock when a hay truck snorts across the road on the way from the field to the silage pit. If you see a moose sign on that twisty New Hampshire road or an elk-crossing sign out in Washington, wouldn't it be clever to cover the brake lever and prepare for a quick stop? In city traffic, wouldn't it be a good idea to shake that tailgating cabby before you get to the next intersection?

Passing through a string of busy intersections in the big city, you shouldn't be amazed to encounter a few car drivers making quick left turns across traffic. Out in the suburbs, wouldn't you expect cars to back out of driveways, kids to ride skateboards out into the street, and dogs to chase motorcycles? If you've got your head in the ride, you'll not only be searching for problems, but you'll also be thinking well ahead of your front fender.

When you know you're riding into a hazardous situation, wouldn't it be clever to get prepared for a quick stop?

Once you recognize a hazardous situation, you can get yourself prepared for a quick stop. For example, as you round a blind turn with a barn roof in the background, you should already be covering the front brake lever and getting yourself psyched up for a quick stop.

The big mistake Roger Rider made was assuming that if he just kept his motorcycle under control, everyone else would stay out of his way. He didn't brake when his sight distance closed up approaching that corner because he assumed the road was the same ahead as behind, even though he couldn't see what was happening. And when he did finally spot the deer, he assumed it would stay put while he continued on by. He could just as easily have collided with a loose cow or a hay truck entering the road. It isn't sufficient to just keep your own vehicle under control and expect others to get out of your way. You've got to be prepared to get out of the way of other users, whether they are wild animals or other drivers.

So Why Did You Let Him Get You?

A couple of years ago, I was having a discussion with a young rider who was limping around in a leg cast. He'd been knocked down in a merging lane by a driver who didn't yield the right of way.

Rider: "I can't believe he hit me! He was supposed to yield!"
Me: "Did the driver get injured?"
Rider: "Heck no. But I got a broken leg!"
Me: "So why did you let him get you?"
Rider: "He should have stopped. I had the right-of-way!"
Me: "Does your leg hurt?"
Rider: "Sure it hurts."
Me: "So why did you let him get you?"

It doesn't make any difference whether a motorcyclist has the right-of-way or not, the rider is the one most likely to get hurt. The way to avoid the pain and expense is to get out of the way. My father used to repeat a little ditty on the subject:

He was right, dead right, as he sped along.
But he's just as dead as if he'd been wrong.

If you wait until the last second before making the decision to brake hard, whatever you do is going to be in a panic. It's important to get on the brakes early, when you first see or predict a potential collision. When sight distance closes up or another vehicle gets into a position where it could turn across your path, you should already be on the brakes, scrubbing off a bit of forward energy and heating up the discs.

If the other driver doesn't yield or makes a sudden swerve across your path, you can just squeeze a little harder and make a quick stop to avoid a smasho. If the other guy stops after all, you can ease off the brakes and get back up to speed without a lot of fuss. You don't have to make quick stops every time you see a problem, but you should be prepared.

OK, let's say you are riding a busy urban arterial with many confusing intersections and lots of cross-traffic. You are predicting the possibility of other drivers mak-

When you are approaching another vehicle that could turn left, you should already be on the brakes preparing for a quick stop.

ing sudden moves. You've passed that creeper car with the out-of-state plates, you've moved out from behind the view-blocking bus, and you've changed lanes to let that aggressive cabby get on by. You are scrutinizing the road surface for slick spots and edge traps, observing the hoods of oncoming cars for potential left turners, and glancing at the tops of front tires to get the first indication of cars beginning to pull out from side streets. What more can you do?

Veteran Quick Stop Tactics

Let's review six veteran techniques for making successful quick stops with a minimum of panic.

Stay in the habit of using the front brake every time you brake.

Get in the Front Brake Habit

Stay in the habit of using the front brake every time you brake, even if your machine has integrated front/rear brakes or antilock brakes. There is a reason why the front wheel has the big stoppers: in a quick stop, it is the front tire that gets pushed into the pavement. It is tempting to fall into the habit of just rolling off the throttle or just using the rear brake and believing that you can reach for the front brake on those rare occasions when a quick stop is needed. The trouble is very few of us can out-think our habits. In an emergency, we will do whatever we have been in the habit of doing and think about it after the fact. If you get in the front brake habit, you'll use the front brake in a crisis without even thinking about it.

Approaching Turns, Use Your Front Brake

Braking should be part of your cornering sequence. Sure, rolling off the throttle slows the bike, but remember that the engine compression functions as a rear-wheel brake only. Adding a touch of front brake to help decelerate prior to leaning over into corners makes two-wheel braking part of your habit pattern. If you're in the habit of braking approaching turns, you will automatically brake harder when a pedestrian steps off the sidewalk as you make your turn, when you spot a gravel spill at the apex, when you realize the curve ahead is a little tighter than you thought, or when the view suddenly gets blocked by roadside trees and bushes.

If you're in the habit of braking when approaching turns, you'll brake harder for a tight turn without having to think about it.

Brake Early

When you approach a hazardous situation such as a busy intersection, get on the front brake before you are faced with an impending collision to reduce both reaction time and stopping distance. All of us require a half second or more to make the decision to brake and another half second if we have to reach for the lever. Reaction time can eat up a lot more distance than you might think. At 40 mph, you are covering almost thirty feet every half second. And even if you are quick enough to reach for the brakes in only a half second, it takes at least another half second of progressive squeezing to get the front end loaded before you can get full on the brake. One wasted second at 40 mph eats up about sixty feet of critical road space—just about the same distance it takes to brake to a stop from that speed.

One wasted second at 40 mph eats up about sixty feet of critical road space. If you're already on the brake approaching an intersection, you can make a quick stop in a much shorter distance.

If you are already on the front brake lightly to get the discs heated up and to transfer a little weight onto the front tire, it shouldn't take more than a half second to squeeze harder and initiate a maximum-effort stop. Getting on the brakes early can make the difference between stopping five feet short of the car fender or bashing into it at 30 mph.

Slow Down by 10 for Problems

As you approach a hazardous area such as a busy intersection with a car waiting to turn left or a driveway with a bumper sticking out, ease on the brakes and decelerate just 10 mph, shifting down as needed to keep engine revs up. Typical urban intersection speeds are 30 to 40 mph. Slowing just 10 mph, from 40 mph to 30 mph, reduces forward energy by almost half. That means the same brakes and tires can stop the same load in half the distance.

At typical urban speeds, slowing just 10 mph cuts your stopping distance in half.

Reduce Speed to Sight Distance

There is a tendency to settle into a steady cruise speed rather than speeding up or slowing down for changing conditions. One accomplice to that is an engine with a narrow power band that encourages the rider to maintain speed comparable to the torque band rather than shift up and down constantly. But your view of the road ahead changes dramatically as you ride along. And when the view closes up, it is important to immediately shed speed, so you can always bring the bike to a complete stop within the roadway you can see.

What that really means is that when your view ahead is suddenly reduced, you should immediately get on the brakes and scrub off speed. That's especially important on any twisty road where you can't see around corners or over hills. And the faster your speed in the straights, the more important it is to brake hard approaching blind situations. The more you are assuming where the road goes, even though you can't see all of it, the more you are hanging yourself out. If you are interested in being quick on public roads, remember that crashing really ruins your average speed.

It's relaxing to motor along at a constant speed, but it's critically important to reduce speed quickly when sight distance closes up.

Practice

Reading is OK to improve your mind, but you've got to practice on the bike to hone your skills. If Roger had practiced a few quick stops this spring or practiced braking as part of his cornering, maybe he would have been able to stop short of that deer collision without dropping the bike. One good way to get more proficient at aggressive braking is to practice maximum-effort stops at least once each season.

The goal of quick stops is decelerating from traffic speed to zero in the shortest distance, without losing control. Even if your favorite road burner has integrated brakes or you spent the big bucks for ABS, don't excuse yourself from practicing the skills. You must still be able to quickly separate braking from swerving and be able to do a quick stop on dry pavement or in the rain, pointing uphill or down, in a straight or in a corner. All the veteran techniques we've suggested work equally well for riders of ABS machines.

Before attempting to practice hard braking on the street, I really urge you to practice quick stops away from traffic. Think about practicing your quick stops at least once each season and immediately after buying a different bike or when riding a machine you aren't familiar with.

If you intend to teach yourself how to brake more efficiently, be very wary of the skills of your instructor. Start your braking runs at a modest speed of 18 mph to 20 mph and try a few normal stops first, then gradually squeeze a little harder on the lever as you gain familiarity.

Practicing quick stops is one way to get more proficient at aggressive braking.

And, before trying any practice maneuvers, whether at a training course or on your own, do us both a favor and strap on your most durable riding gear. There is always the risk of taking a tumble if you're not as good as you think you are.

Less Panic

Once you make those veteran tactics part of your own riding habits, you may discover that you are encountering fewer and fewer "sudden" hazards, and it may seem that you have more time to deal with the problems that do occur. For instance, if you make a habit of using the front brake approaching turns and some day you need to brake harder to avoid a hazard, you'll just squeeze a little harder without any panic.

Most of those victims in the Hurt Report offered the excuse that they didn't have time to react, but that's really an admission that they weren't monitoring the road far enough ahead. By predicting hidden situations, looking farther ahead, being prepared, and practicing the right habits, the skilled rider will do a perfect quick stop without wasting any time and marvel about it afterward.

CHAPTER 3

Cornering Tactics

CORNERING HABITS

Interstate Al is motoring cross-country on his big touring machine. Al isn't one of those peg-scraping zoomie bikers who terrorize the canyons. He prefers to ease down the road in the center lane with the motorcycle vertical and the engine idling along in fifth gear. At such a modest pace he can smell the flowers, listen to the tape deck, and allow his mind to wander. Today his thoughts drift toward a question. Why do some riders get so embroiled in meaningless details of cornering? he ponders. Al has read about such concepts as delayed apex cornering lines and rolling on the throttle in turns, but frankly he thinks such stuff just isn't related to his riding style. Besides, his big touring bike is better suited to the superslabs where he doesn't have to worry about sharp turns.

It's time for a coffee break, and Al decides to take the next exit. But traffic in the right lane has suddenly closed up bumper to bumper, and he must somehow jockey through to get to the exit lane. Al doesn't like to dodge between cars. He breathes a sigh of relief when a space opens up in front of an old pickup truck. He signals, rolls on the throttle to rocket the bike forward, pulls in ahead of the truck with room to spare, and banks off onto the exit ramp a little fast, but under control for the curve he can see.

Al rolls off the gas as he leans into the off-ramp, but he is surprised when the ramp doesn't curve around in a nice constant circle as he assumed it would. About halfway around, it suddenly tightens up into a decreasing radius. Al had been pointing the bike toward the inside of the curve and suddenly he's headed for the outside. Al tries to heave the machine over, but can't seem to get the bike to turn as quickly as the pavement, and his scraping footboards limit how far he can lean. With the machine drifting toward the outside curb, his survival reactions take over: He snaps the throttle closed and stomps down on the brake pedal.

In a flash, the rear tire breaks loose, and the bike goes down. The centerstand hangs up just enough to flip the machine into the barrier, and Al is mercifully highsided into the bushes and beauty bark. Al is only bruised, but he will later discover that the bent metal and shattered plastic will add up to a total loss of his big road burner.

Consider this: If Al had trusted his tires and just pushed harder on the right grip to lean the machine over to its cornering limits, could he have made the turn without sliding out? If Al had entered the turn more from the outside and gotten the bike pointed more in the right direction, would he have had a better chance of turning it tighter as the road tightened up? And if Al had not jammed on the brakes while leaned over, would it have continued around the curve without sliding out?

It is hoped that Al will realize that his crash has answered his own questions. Serious motorcyclists get embroiled in the meaningless details of cornering because the world is full of strange corners, including superslab exit ramps. Good cornering habits are just as important for the touring rider as they are for those who seek out twisty roads for their sportbikes.

We've discussed the basics about how two-wheelers balance, turn, and stop. Now, we're ready to take the theory out to the public roads. First, I'd like you to answer, as honestly and realistically as you can, some questions about how you control your machine in corners. And if you aren't really sure what you do, take your bike out for a spin, and focus on your habits while cruising down your favorite twisty road.

- When turning, do you follow more or less in the center of the lane, do you follow one of the car wheel tracks, or do you follow a different motorcycle cornering line?
- Approaching a sharp turn, do you roll off the throttle, or do you also use the brakes?
- When you need to brake approaching a turn, do you brake before leaning the bike, or do you trail the brakes as you continue around the corner?
- When you brake approaching a corner, do you use both brakes, just the front brake, or only the rear brake?
- When rounding a turn, do you focus on the pavement in front of the bike, on the right edge of your lane, on the centerline, or on the pavement farther around the corner?
- Do you lean your head with the bike, or do you keep your eyes level with the horizon?
- Do you actually turn your head toward the curve, or do you just move your eyes?
- To lean the bike into a turn, do you just think "lean," do you consciously push on the grips, or do you press down on one of the foot pegs?
- As you lean the bike into the turn, do you hold a steady throttle, ease off the throttle, or ease on the throttle?

Now, some riders might think such questions are silly. If you've managed to get your motorcycle down the road for thousands of miles without having to think about such boring little details, why do you need to start now? Well, if you're happy with the way you ride and don't feel you could use any improvement, you can stop reading here and get back on the bike. But during your ride, you may start to notice other motorcyclists who wobble through turns, cross the centerline, or suddenly decelerate in corners—forcing you to take evasive action to keep from running up their backsides. You'll probably agree that those folks need some cornering help.

Of course, you might want to close the bathroom door, stare at that rider in the mirror, and see if he looks like one of those folks who can't quite put their bikes where they want to. However you perceive your skill level, let's see if we can help you improve your cornering tactics. And let's be clear that I'm talking about cornering on public roads, not on a racetrack.

You've probably seen a lot of riders who think that cornering is just a matter of stuffing the bike through the bends by grunt and feel and cranking on more throttle until the tires start to squeal. But improving your cornering control (and yes, your cornering speed) is mostly a matter of technique, not fearless throttle twisting. You need to be doing the right things at the right time. That's why I asked those personal questions back at the beginning. Now, obviously, a big sweeping curve like those on the freeway don't need any special tactics. But those twisty back roads really challenge your skills, and there are even a few tricky freeway ramps that tighten up or change direction. The tighter the curve, the more important it is to use the right tactics.

Slow, Look, Lean, and Roll

Different riding schools have different ways to describe the correct cornering techniques. Having a slogan helps you remember the details. One of the most concise descriptions is the slogan Slow, Look, Lean, and Roll that's been used over the years in rider training courses.

Slow

Approaching a curve, you need to decelerate to a speed at which you predict you can make the turn. Most of the time, you'll roll off the throttle approaching tighter curves. It's smart to decelerate with the bike vertical—while in a straight line—because that allows maximum-effort braking if needed, without the risks of a slideout. Ideally, you will squeeze on some front brake in addition to rolling off the gas.

Why brake? Because rolling off the throttle applies compression braking only to the rear wheel. To conserve traction, both brakes should be used. First, you should be prepared to brake harder for a turn that you discover is tighter than expected. If front braking is part of your cornering habits, your survival reaction will be to brake harder on the front, which helps avoid a rear wheel slideout. Second, if a hazard comes into view halfway around the corner, you should be prepared to brake aggressively without sliding out.

ROLL
As you lean, smoothly roll on the throttle

LEAN
Lean the bike

LOOK
Keep your eyes level
Select cornering line

SLOW
Brake to corner entry speed, then get off brakes

You may be called upon to brake aggressively during a curve, so braking on the front is a good habit to incorporate into your cornering techniques.

Look

Before you dive into a corner at full chat, you really ought to figure out where the road goes, scrutinize the surface for loose gravel and horse poop, and determine whether that's a deer about to leap out of the flickering shadows or just spotted leaves. Note that you'll get the best view of what's happening from the outside of the curve. So for a right-hander, you'll get the best view if you point the bike way over toward the centerline while you're still decelerating.

When you're ready to dive into the curve, swivel your head around to point your nose toward your intended line. Sure, it looks cool to just shift your eyes behind your blue aviator sunglasses, but turning your head actually helps provide directional control and a smooth entry into the turn.

Where does the road go, around the corner? Approaching a blind right-hand turn, you'll get the best view from way out close to the centerline.

Lean

With the bike slowed and positioned for best view and your nose pointed toward where you want to go, it's time to lean the bike over and roll on a little throttle. The most accurate way to lean any two-wheeler is by pressure on the handgrips. Push on the right grip to lean right. Hold enough pressure on the grip to get the bike leaned over and pointed where you're looking, then ease up on the pressure to stabilize the lean.

It's important to get both hands synchronized, and it's not uncommon for a rider to be subconsciously resisting the steering input with the opposite arm. If your bike feels reluctant to lean, concentrate on pressing both grips toward the curve. Or, try steering with one hand and relaxing the opposite arm, a technique included in Lee Parks' Total Control course; that is, in a right turn, steer with the right hand and relax your left arm.

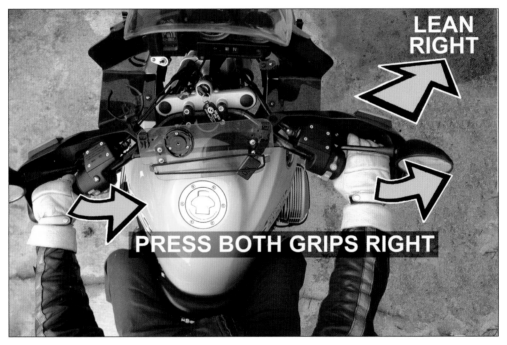

When rolling the bike into a lean, it's important to get both hands synchronized. To roll right, momentarily press both grips toward the right.

Roll

When the bike has leaned over to your desired lean angle, you need to arrest the roll. On a well-balanced bike, just relaxing your countersteering input will stabilize the lean angle. But easing on some throttle will also help stabilize the lean. Many riders think of the throttle as only a speed control, but how and when you twist the throttle has a lot to do with traction, stability, ground clearance, suspension, and steering. Conservative riders like Al may feel that a technique such as rolling on the throttle in corners is something that belongs only on the racetrack, but good throttle control is all about managing traction, and conserving traction is just as important on the road as on the racetrack.

Rolling on the throttle helps balance weight between front and rear, sets suspension in the middle of its travel, and maximizes leanover clearance. The throttle also controls which way the bike wants to go. I'm not suggesting you roll on a big handful of throttle while leaning. Rather, you should ease on just enough throttle to transfer some weight rearward but not enough to accelerate the bike. Some experts call this maintenance throttle.

What's wrong with just rolling off the gas and letting the bike slow down as it goes around the curve? Well, a trailing throttle not only uses up rear-wheel traction for engine braking, but it also causes most bikes to squat on the suspension, eating up leanover clearance. The best technique is to progressively ease on more throttle to keep the engine pulling smoothly all the way through the curve. As you gain skill, you may prefer to ease on the front brake deeper into corners (trail braking) and transition from brake to throttle as you pass the apex. Trail braking requires that you be very smooth at transitioning from brake to throttle to avoid upsetting the bike or sliding out. One big advantage of trail braking is that you are prepared to change speed while leaned over.

The Throttle Affects Traction

Think about this: acceleration and deceleration shift weight. Rolling on the gas shifts weight to the rear. Roll on enough throttle, and you can lift the front wheel off the surface. Rolling off the gas shifts weight forward. Since weight affects available traction on a tire, a weight shift toward the front reduces traction on the rear tire. When carrying a touring load or a passenger, there is plenty of weight and therefore traction on the rear. But when riding solo, any weight shift to the front takes away traction from the rear tire—traction that may be needed to push the bike around a turn. That's why it is important to avoid suddenly rolling off the gas or jamming on the rear brake while leaned over. Al had already rolled off the gas, so his bike had less leanover clearance. He didn't recognize the need to follow a delayed apex line, so he wasn't prepared for the decreasing-radius turn. Slamming the throttle closed withdrew more rear tire traction than he had in the bank. The combination of bad habits sealed his fate.

An unladen motorcycle at rest might have a 50/50 rear/front weight distribution (bias) on the tires. And since traction is related to the load on a tire, it might seem

Off throttle: rolling off the throttle transfers weight to the front wheel while the bike is leaned over, just as it occurs in a straight line.

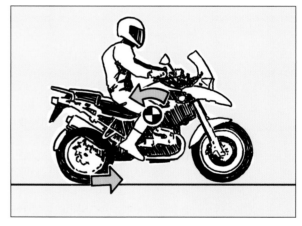

On throttle: rolling on the throttle transfers weight to the rear wheel. In a curve, that maintains more of a rear-wheel weight bias.

that coasting through corners would be ideal, balancing traction 50/50 between the tires. But that isn't ideal for several reasons. First, the rear wheel needs to keep pushing the bike around the corner as well as overpowering centrifugal force, so we really could use more traction on the rear, say a 60/40 weight bias. Second, just rolling off the throttle isn't coasting—engine compression adds drag on the rear tire that uses up traction.

Sure, you could try to match engine speed exactly to bike speed, but that's nearly impossible. Even if you squeezed the clutch and coasted, at some point you'd need to get back on the power, with a resulting wobble and possible slideout as traction transferred from front to rear. To achieve a wobble-free turn, to maintain that ideal weight bias, and to also conserve traction, the technique is to ease on the throttle as the bike is leaned over.

Rolling on a bit more throttle while leaned over happens to do some other helpful things. The added thrust from the rear tire helps keep the front end up on its suspension. On most shaft-drive machines and many chain-drive bikes, the torque reaction of power to the rear wheel causes the rear end of the bike to rise. The results are that staying on the throttle while leaned over helps lift the bike up on its suspension at both ends, which increases ground clearance and maximizes suspension travel.

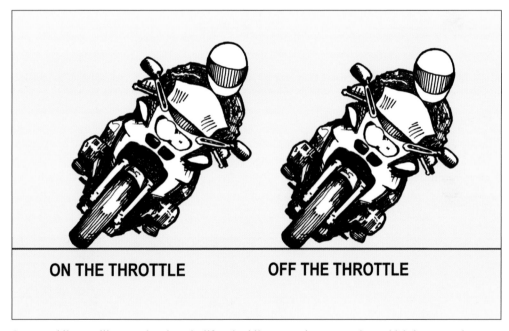

ON THE THROTTLE   **OFF THE THROTTLE**

On most bikes, rolling on the throttle lifts the bike up on its suspension, which increases leanover clearance.

Contact Ring Diameter

Oh, RIGHT! someone is thinking, *Speed up and run off the road!* Well, let's think about that. Rolling on the throttle does increase engine power, but does that always make the bike accelerate? Remember that the contact ring of a tire moves toward the sidewall as the bike is leaned over. When leaned over, the contact ring is smaller in diameter. What this means is that if you aren't rolling on a little throttle as you lean the bike, it's probably decelerating.

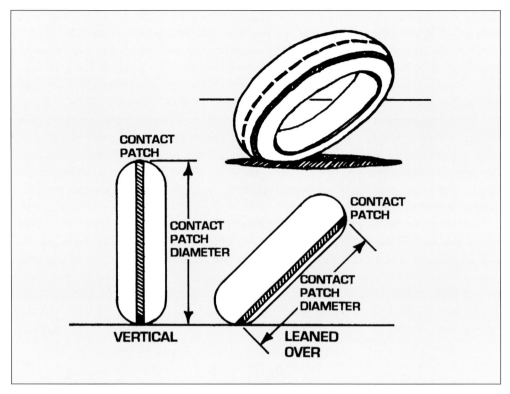

When the tires lean over, the contact ring moves toward the sidewall where the diameter is smaller. So as you lean the bike, you need to ease on some throttle just to maintain the same speed.

Throttle Steering

The throttle also helps steer the bike. Although it may appear that a wheel goes around a corner with the axle pointed exactly at the center of the turn, that's seldom the case. Rubber tires allow some side slip, so in a curve the wheel will typically be moving in a slightly different direction than where it's pointed. The difference between the centerline of the wheel and the path of travel of the tire is called slip angle. A front wheel must be pointed somewhat more toward the curve to compensate for side slip. A rear wheel will also have side slip, moving in a path more toward the outside of the curve. Since the front wheel can be steered away from the bike centerline, the two wheels may have slightly different slip angles. Since the throttle controls rear-tire slip angles, rolling on or off helps steer the bike. Rolling on more throttle steers the rear wheel wider, pointing the front end more toward the curve.

Because the position of the contact ring controls lean angle, increasing slide slip increases the lean angle of the bike.

Ruben Xaus demonstrates that the rear tire can be powered into extreme slip angles, steering the bike. This is an extreme example of tire slide slip, but it demonstrates that a wheel can be moving in a different direction than where it is pointed.

And because centrifugal force is a function of speed, rolling on more throttle tends to lift the bike toward vertical. The flip side is that rolling off the throttle tends to lean the bike more into the curve. So when turning into a curve, it may be helpful to lean the bike with the throttle closed, then ease back on the throttle to hold the lean angle through your turn apex. Smoothly easing on more throttle after the apex helps lift the bike upright and steers it toward a gradually increasing radius through the turn exit. The key word here is *smooth*, since throttle changes will steer the bike, and abrupt throttle changes can punch through the traction envelope.

Bumps and Dips

Suspension is also affected by throttle control. And how the suspension works is more than just a comfort consideration. Suspension allows the tires to maintain contact with the pavement when rolling over bumps and dips. If the suspension is bottomed out, it can't absorb a bump and will jolt that end of the machine upward. For example, when the front end is down on the stops under heavy braking, it can't absorb a bump. A bump can jolt the whole front end off the ground and cause the tire to skip. If the suspension is already topped out, the wheel can't extend any farther down into a dip, and that tire will momentarily lose traction with the surface. Best traction—and smoothest ride—will be with the motorcycle floating somewhere near the middle of its suspension travel.

When you roll on, both ends rise, and if you roll on hard enough, the suspension can actually top out—at least on the front. In a curve, the suspension is compressed by the pull of gravity and centrifugal force. Get the point? Easing on the gas while leaned over helps keep the shocks in the middle of their range, helping the tires maintain traction even when bouncing over bumps and dips.

Roll It on Through the Curve

So the ideal throttle technique while cornering is to smoothly ease on the throttle from the point where you stabilize lean angle, all the way through the turn. You will be decelerating approaching a curve. That makes the front end heavy and reduces ground clearance, but that's not a problem if you decelerate in a straight line toward your turn-in point. As the bike leans over to the desired angle, ease on the throttle to arrest the lean and continue easing on the gas all the way through the rest of the curve. That technique provides good turn-in traction, stabilizes the lean, maintains best ground clearance and suspension travel, and takes advantage of throttle steering.

Sure, there are situations in which you wouldn't be rolling on the throttle in a curve, such as this downhill turn in the rain. But even here, smooth throttle control is essential. Snapping the throttle closed could easily cause a rear wheel slideout. Throttle control in such situations is critically important.

Now, obviously, we can all think of situations in which rolling on the gas in a turn would be inappropriate. You wouldn't be gassing it during a steep downhill left-hander in the rain, for example. But correct throttle control is one of the keys to better cornering. It's the best technique for conserving traction, whether you corner leisurely or swiftly. And it's a skill that you can practice while riding.

Next time you're out on your favorite motorcycle, practice rolling on the throttle as you lean into a turn. When approaching an intersection where you intend to turn, lightly apply both brakes while in a straight line, then get off the brakes, look through the turn, lean the bike, and roll on a little throttle as you round the corner. If you panic and have to shut off the throttle before you're all the way through the turn, it means you didn't slow enough before leaning.

Getting more proficient with throttle control is more than a way to ride faster. Developing good throttle habits is one of the ways you can expand your safety envelope. And good habits are the key to survival when you are suddenly faced with an unexpected hazard while you're leaned over. Ask Interstate Al. He's a lot more interested in those "meaningless" details of cornering these days. He's thinking about better cornering lines now and learning to ease on the throttle while leaned over. And he's a little more cautious about bolting on highway boards that decrease the leanover clearance—on his new bike.

Corner Entry Speed

I usually get a chuckle from speed signs that say 25 mph when I know I can make the curve without a lot of drama at 35 or 40. OK, the signs are posted for everyone, including top-heavy hay trucks. So is there a rule of thumb for motorcyclists? Yep. But you won't find it posted on a sign. The ideal entry speed into a curve is *whatever speed will permit a gradual throttle roll-on through the rest of the curve.* You'll have to figure out what that speed is based on what you discover about the road. The

key is, if you couldn't gradually roll on the gas all the way through the last several turns, it means your entry speeds are generally too high. If you find yourself panicking in midcorner and snapping off the throttle, it's a message that you didn't decelerate enough before leaning the bike over. Sage advice about curves is go in slow, go out fast.

Eyes Level

Many riders find it helpful to tilt their heads to keep their eyes level with the horizon while cornering. It's not easy to calculate the curvature of the road at speed, and it's even more difficult if you're trying to triangulate everything at a slanty visual angle. Tilting your eyes level as you lean the bike seems to help keep things in perspective.

As you lean the bike, tilt your head to keep your eyes level with the horizon to help you triangulate the corner.

Pleasure and Risk

I think you'll enjoy motorcycling more if you master a few important cornering skills. It can be tremendously satisfying to have your motorcycle completely under your control, knowing how it performs and being able to make it do what you want it to do. But beyond the enjoyment, there is the matter of risk. Think about this: even if you ride at the same speed, on the same road, will certain cornering tactics increase or decrease the risks? Consider some risk concepts that relate to cornering lines:

- The largest radius of turn demands the least traction for a given speed and therefore keeps more traction in reserve for dealing with unknown hazards such as loose gravel or wild animals.
- The risk of riding into unseen hazards is reduced by following a line that enters blind curves at positions that provide the best view ahead.
- The risk of collision is reduced by following a line that achieves maximum separation from other traffic at critical locations.
- The risk of falling on surface hazards is reduced by making the sharpest part of the turn on pavement already within the rider's view.

It should be pretty clear that cornering lines have a lot to do with the relative risks, whether your riding style is to putt along serenely or to blitz the countryside at full chat.

Cornering Lines

Let's face it: riding the superslab cross-country is pretty much a no-brainer. Fill the tank, crank up the wick, keep it between the lines, and don't let anybody hit you. It's on the twisty roads where we separate proficient riders from those who merely own a motorcycle. If riding the superslab can be compared to line dancing at the local tavern, cornering on a twisty back road is more like Gene Kelly dancing in the rain: exactly the right speed for the action, powerful leaps forward at precisely the right time, dramatic lean angles, perfect balance, and an obvious enjoyment of the whole thing.

The View Ahead

Whether or not I can keep my two-wheeler upright often depends upon the condition of the road surface. I would prefer not to discover that the smooth dry pavement I'm riding on happens to be submerged in fresh diesel oil or cow poop halfway around the blind turn ahead. If the view is limited, it makes a lot of sense to plan the tightest part of the curve where I can see that the pavement is acceptable. Sure, there might be even better traction just around the corner. And, if the surface around the corner does happen to be smooth, clean, and tractable, I can use it for accelerating. But it's a poor gamble to plan on the condition of unseen surfaces being better than what is already in view.

A big part of cornering is to decide where the pavement goes, choose where to do your turn-in, and then plan the straightest line that smoothly arcs through the turns. This isn't easy because there aren't special motorcycle markings on the surface to give you any hints about where you should be doing what. We have to imagine our intended lines while also trying to practice that slow, look, lean, and roll technique I suggested earlier.

Doesn't it make sense to make the tightest part of your turn on pavement that's in view? There might be tractable pavement around the corner, but it's a poor gamble to bet on it.

I know lots of riders who are paranoid about leaning their machines over too far, sliding out, and dropping the bike. If you're concerned about slideouts, it's time to get serious about cornering lines. One of the unique advantages of two-wheelers is the ability to follow a path of travel or line that is different from the curve of the pavement. Think about this: side forces on the tires are least when the bike is traveling in a straight line. The straighter your curves, the less risk of a slideout. If you ride around a curve following a car line, your tires are using more traction than if your path of travel followed a straighter motorcycle line. Sudden steering inputs to change direction also demand more traction and eat up ground clearance. A smooth, gradual, stabilized arc is better than a line with constant corrections.

If you watch road racing on television, you'll get lots of views from above, and you'll notice that generally the racing lines curve as smoothly as possible from apex to apex, like a springy board bent around posts at the inside of each turn. Racing lines maximize both traction and speed. But trying to adapt road racing lines to public roads can be a big hazard for aggressive motorcyclists. On public roads, we must give priority to the unknown. On a strange road, we have no idea of the curve ahead or what hazard we might encounter just around the turn. So our cornering lines must be suitable for all manner of strange uphill/downhill/off-camber corners and also give us the best chance to avoid unannounced hazards as they pop into view.

Unlike the racetrack, public roads are very narrow. And when riding public roads, it's easy to point the bike toward the inside of the curve too early. Remember that people have a target fixation characteristic. We tend to point our vehicles where we are focusing, even if that's not where we think we're steering. On a bike, it's easy to get hypnotized by the inside edge (the fog line) as it rolls into view. That's one reason why novice riders tend to point the bike toward an early apex without even realizing it.

It's very easy to watch that hypnotic white line reeling into view and steer the bike toward the inside of the curve way too early.

Apexing too soon leads to the bike drifting wide about halfway around the corner. When you suddenly realize you're running out of road in the middle of a corner, there aren't many options available. You'll either have to risk an excursion into the oncoming lane and gamble that no one is coming around the corner, or squander all available traction swerving back into the right lane and risk a slideout.

If we look at a typical corner from an eagle's-eye view, we can see what the problem is. Pointing too soon toward the inside of the curve (the apex) points the bike too wide for the rest of the turn. It's important to focus on where you want the bike to go, not at that hypnotic inside edge.

If you point the bike toward the inside edge of the curve too soon, the bike is pointed the wrong way for the rest of the curve. Once you realize the bike is running wide, there aren't a lot of options to get back where you belong.

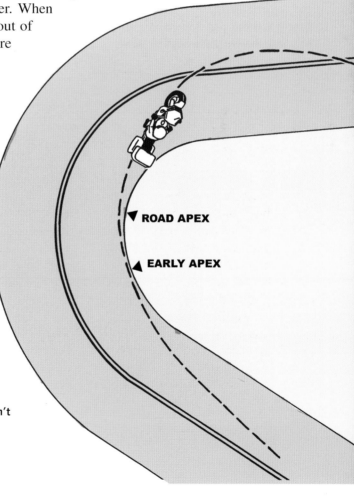

ROAD APEX

EARLY APEX

The Delayed Apex Line

The smart tactic for public roads is to delay your apex. In other words, plan on an apex farther around the curve. To reach an apex farther around the curve, you have to enter the turn more from the outside. The delayed apex line starts from the outside of the lane, turns tightest as the bike is leaned over, then follows a gradually increasing radius of turn, apexing about two-thirds of the way around the curve.

Visualizing Your Line

OK, let's assume you have a specific cornering line in mind. How do you decide what the line should look like down at motorcycle level, and how do you get the bike to follow it? One big difficulty with cornering lines is that we can't visualize them from the eagle's-eye view. On public roads, we're never quite sure how tight the next turn is, which way it is cambered, if it goes uphill or downhill, and whether there's loose gravel just beyond those bushes. It's especially tricky because we're trying to figure it all out from a viewpoint four feet off the pavement, with the world rushing toward us at warp speed.

One way to imagine a delayed apex line is to mentally slide the apex a little farther around the corner than you can see. In other words, as the corner rolls into view, decide about where you think the apex should be, then mentally push that apex farther around the corner. In a blind curve obscured by trees or rocks, you may not actually be able to see where that delayed apex is on the pavement, but that's not important. What is important is that you'll have to enter the turn wider to reach your imagined delayed apex. With your attention focused on a delayed apex rather than on the fog line, you're more likely to point the bike in the right direction.

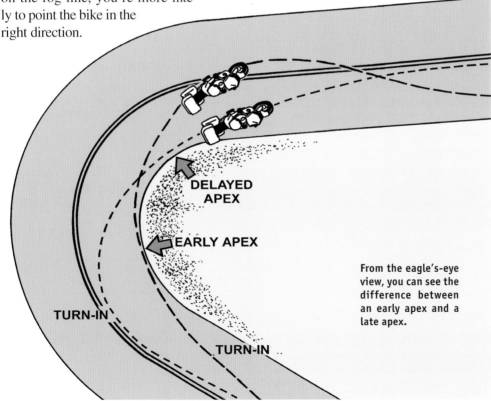

DELAYED APEX

EARLY APEX

TURN-IN

TURN-IN

From the eagle's-eye view, you can see the difference between an early apex and a late apex.

To reach your imagined delayed apex in this blind right-hander, you must turn in from closer to the centerline.

Critical Windows

Many riders also find it helpful to imagine locations, or "windows," on the pavement through which the bike must pass. For example, when approaching a right-hander, you might imagine an entry window way over toward the centerline. The entry window is the point where you actually start to lean the bike, roll on the gas, and get the machine stabilized in a smooth arc toward that delayed apex. Of course, if the entry window is where you actually lean the bike, you should also imagine the other steps that precede it. Critical windows include getting off the brakes (Slow), looking as far through the corner as possible (Look), leaning the bike over to make it turn (Lean),

You might find it helpful to imagine "windows" on the road where you'll complete the cornering steps.

and easing on the throttle as you lean over (Roll). Try to imagine where these windows are as you approach a corner, and then visualize a continuous ribbon passing through them all.

If you're just in the process of improving your cornering skills, I suggest you avoid braking while leaning. Squeeze on some front brake as well as roll off the throttle while slowing. Consider the slow window as where you should be off the brakes, not where you roll off the gas and start squeezing the lever. Remember, the point of being off the brakes before you initiate any serious leaning is so that you're not using traction for braking when it's needed for pushing the bike around the corner.

Making Sparks

If your cruiser or tourer has limited leanover clearance, you'll need to be a little more clever about turns. The giveaway is that your machine makes grinding sounds and leaves trails of sparks in every sharp curve. First off, when you get back from a sparkly ride, check your suspension. Ideally, your suspension should be in the middle of its travel with the bike loaded as you normally ride. The best way to check suspension travel is to sit on the loaded bike and have someone else do some measurements. If you normally carry a passenger, get the passenger on board, too. You want to measure the elevation of the bike with no load and then the elevation when loaded to determine how far it sags.

If you discover that your machine sits too low when loaded, first jack up the shock springs to maximum preload, and if that doesn't do it, figure on replacing the springs with stronger ones. Weak front fork springs may be acceptable with added spacers to increase the preload. If your suspension has air, carefully add a bit of pressure. Adjusting suspension toward the middle of its travel not only increases leanover clearance but also helps keep the tires in contact with the pavement. If you've jacked up the shock springs but your low-slung cruiser still makes sparks, you can either lose some weight, learn to hang off, or modify your cornering lines.

Right Pace, Right Place

A few years ago, I was getting a quick tour of the back roads north and south of San Francisco with a group of skilled riders. A local motorcyclist was showing us some really fun secondary roads that snaked over the hills and down into canyons shaded by giant redwoods. We even stopped for lunch at Alice's Restaurant, the famous biker hangout on Skyline Boulevard, and checked out the fancy sportbikes in the parking lot. Every sunny weekend, the Skyline is a steady toccata of high-strung motorcycles.

And tow trucks. We passed by one shiny yellow Ducati being winched uphill out of the trees. All we could see of the bike was the rear end being hoisted back over the edge, but we could recognize the exhaust pipes sticking out under the stylish tail cone.

There was no obvious reason why the rider should have crashed at that location. It wasn't a blind intersection or a decreasing-radius sucker corner. The pavement wasn't littered with tree needles or wet leaves. It wasn't raining. We didn't see any deer. There were no cars nearby with dented passenger doors. As nearly as I could figure, the Duck rider had been flirting with the laws of physics and gotten slapped.

We can imagine the scenario. The rider is pushing his limits, his head swimming in adrenaline but dry on high-speed skills. He goes into the curve a little too hot, and somewhere in the middle of that sweeper his brain registers that those trees are approaching awfully fast and the bike isn't turning as tight as the road. He panics. His right hand slams the throttle closed, and his right foot nails the rear brake pedal. Adios, baby.

He'd probably been a little hot, started to drift wide, panicked, did something dumb, and sailed over the edge into some heavy-duty tree trunks. We didn't stop—this sort of thing happens all the time up on the Skyline.

Cranial Computer Speed

On a twisty road where one turn leads into the next, it is important to keep your cranial computer working as fast as your speedometer. Once you've plotted the critical windows in the approaching corner, start scanning ahead toward the next turn and deciding where the next windows should be long before you get there. The sooner you select your line ahead, the smoother you can be. If you don't think far enough ahead, you'll be making quick panic corrections as you suddenly awake to where the line should have gone. And quick corrections gobble traction. If you can't get your between-the-ears computer up to bike speed, the smart option is to slow down the bike to your processing capacity.

If you find that your bike often seems to have a mind of its own, or if you often get a panicky feeling that you aren't really in control of the situation, those are clues

For a fun ride in the twisties, don't overlook dual sport machines in the 350cc to 650cc range.

that the bike is too much in control of the ride and you're just going along as baggage. There are a couple of messages here, if you choose to listen. First, think about your machinery. Those shiny 100-horse sportbikes are sinfully seductive parked in front of Alice's Restaurant, but attempting to keep a 170-mph race replica bike under control on public roads is a challenge few of us are up to.

The Right Machine for the Ride

Today, lots of riders buy big machines. Even for a first bike, some folks would suggest nothing smaller than a 750cc. My first motorcycle was a 150cc. A year later, I moved up to a 305, then a 450, followed by various 500, 750, 800, 850, 900, 1,000, and 1,150 cc motorcycles. At one point, I added a 350cc dual sport to my stable and rediscovered how much fun a smaller motorcycle can be, on pavement as well as on unpaved roads. On that San Francisco trip, I took the 350, and it turned out to be the right machine for those twisty back roads north and south of San Francisco as well as for slipping through downtown traffic. *A little 350?* you might be wondering, *running with the big dogs in the canyons of California? Didn't you get blown into the weeds?*

Well, I did get some funny looks from the other riders before the ride. The leader asked about maximum speed and fuel range. I'm not sure he believed me when I said it would cruise at 70 mph, with a fuel range of at least 250 miles. What was more surprising to the other riders was that once we hit the twisty back roads the 350 could maintain the same pace as the group and even leave some bigger bikes behind. There's no trick to this: a lighter bike can corner much more easily than a heavier bike can and with less risk of making a mistake. The 350 was a lot of fun to ride on the twisty little roads and highways. I'm not sorry I didn't take my 1,150cc firebreather on that trip.

If you're thinking about buying a different machine or adding another bike to your fleet, don't overlook the dual sport or street bikes in the 350cc to 650cc range. Sure, if you normally carry a passenger, cruise the superslabs from coast to coast, or carry big loads of camping gear, a big 1200 or 1800 tourer is the right tool. Just don't forget that midsize bikes can be a lot of fun.

Whatever your choice of machine, the same general riding skills apply. Let's consider some cornering tactics that will help you stay out of trouble and allow you to enjoy the ride more.

The Pace

Most of us enjoy the performance of a high-powered bike. We like the feel of leaning a massive machine over into curves and the kick in our pants as we accelerate down the straights. But, somewhere between road racer and plonker, there's room for spirited riding, and if we do it right we don't have to jack up the risks to unacceptable levels. That's really what *Proficient Motorcycling* is all about. Most of the time, we're talking about techniques such as steering, braking, throttle control, and cornering lines. But motorcycling also involves rhythm. A large part of the enjoyment of motorcycling comes from setting the right pace for the right place.

Consider a musician who plays every piece the same way: loud and fast. A galloping allegro tempo might be fun for something like *The Flight of the Bumblebee*, but it would be silly to rush through the blues, or country-western, or an anthem. The mood of the piece determines an appropriate tempo. That's the way it should be with motorcycling. The road, the situation, the bike, your companions, the weather, and your attitude all help determine an appropriate riding pace. It's up to you to find the pace—the right tempo—for today's ride. That's not a matter simply of road speed but of the rhythm at which you approach a corner, apply the brakes, lean the bike, or roll the throttle.

For example, the force you apply at the grips determines how quickly your motorcycle leans into a turn. Shove hard on the inside grip, and the motorcycle snaps over. Push gently, and it eases over. Push too lazily, and you can run into the ditch before you get the bike turned. Push too aggressively, and you can slide the front tire out from under you. Different corners demand different paces. As you experiment with different cornering lines, you also need to adjust the tempo.

Braking Tempo

Out on a twisty road, the number-one survival skill is being able to set an appropriate corner entry speed without having to brake hard or late. When braking, how quickly do you squeeze the lever? How firmly do you squeeze? How quickly do you release the lever? Isn't the tempo for getting off the brakes just as important as how you apply them? If you are full on the front brake with the suspension compressed and you suddenly let go of the lever, the front end will jump back up, upsetting the bike and changing the traction equation. Smooth on the brakes; smooth off the brakes. Remember, you should be squeezing progressively harder over one full second as weight transfers onto the front wheel. It's just as important to "unsqueeze" the brake over one full second.

At this point, you might be wondering what's wrong with just riding along at a modest pace and controlling speed with the throttle. Lots of riders do that. But then lots of riders end up bashing into hazards because their survival habits didn't include braking in corners. If you expect to be able to brake hard someday to avoid a hazard that suddenly pops into view, you should stay in the front brake habit and use both brakes as part of your cornering sequence, even if you just lightly touch the levers.

Cornering Tempo

I've suggested the importance of finding the right entry speed for corners. The only good guideline for entry speed is what happened in the last corner. If you had to roll the throttle closed after you leaned over, you didn't go in slowly enough. Your target entry speed should be whatever speed will allow you to ease on the throttle smoothly through the rest of the curve. You'll also get some clues from a series of bends. If you discover that you were a little late and a little wide in turn two, then drifted even wider in turn three and headed toward the gravel in turn four, that means bike speed is faster than your thinking speed. Slow down a bit more entering corners, get the bike under control, and enjoy the ride at a more relaxed tempo that matches your thinking pace.

Throttle Tempo

Do you roll off the gas and let engine compression slow the bike all the way to the apex? Do you wait until you lift the bike up again before rolling on the gas? Or do you ease on the throttle as you lean the bike over? Unless it's a really strange downhill turn, the correct time to ease on the throttle is when you lean the bike over, long before you pass the apex. If you get the bike slowed to the right entry speed, then lean the bike over into a nice stable arc and simultaneously roll on a little throttle, everything will feel a lot smoother and more enjoyable. I'm not talking a sudden burst of power here, just smoothly sneaking on the throttle all the way through the turn. If you find yourself panicking in the middle of curves because the bike is drifting wide, think about your cornering lines and what you're doing with the throttle.

An important part of your throttle tempo is how smoothly you roll on or roll off. Herky-jerky throttle control leads to sudden traction demands. As with braking, you should roll the throttle closed as smoothly as you roll it on.

Leaning Tempo

You don't want to lean the bike too early because that points the bike toward the inside, and then it's pointed too wide at the apex. Delay the turn-in slightly, keeping the bike closer to the outside of your lane, then smoothly and forcefully lean the bike over, pointing toward a delayed apex. It's better to push firmly on the low grip and hold it a little longer than to slam the bike down with a quick, hard push because a smoother, longer push results in less chassis wobble as the machine settles into its cornering line. The smoother you are at leaning the bike, the more traction you'll have for cornering, with the least risk of a slideout.

At the tail end of the corner, it's time to straighten the bike up. There is no advantage in pushing hard on the up grip to suddenly straighten the bike unless you have to swerve around a hazard. Just roll on a little more throttle, and let the bike lift itself up as it follows a smooth arc toward the outside of the curve. Unless there's another vehicle in the way or a surface problem, you can use your entire lane for the exit.

OK, let's put it all together, riding through a series of corners.

Your turn-in approaching a left-hander should be from the far right side of the lane. Turn your head to look toward your intended apex, and ease on some throttle as you lean the bike over. Remember to keep your eyes level with the horizon.

Choose your turn-in point for the right-hander, and adjust your speed for the corner ahead, smoothly easing off the throttle and sneaking on a little front brake.

At the turn-in point, turn your head to look toward your intended apex, then ease on a little throttle as you lean the bike.

To set up for the left-hander ahead, point the bike toward the outside edge of the lane. Adjust speed as needed by smoothly transitioning from throttle to brake.

At the turn-in point for the left-hander, point your nose toward your intended apex, lean the bike over, and smoothly transition from brake back to throttle.

Look toward your intended apex, and plan your turn-in point for the upcoming right-hander.

Homework

If you verified that your habits are good, you're well on the right track to faster, more controlled corners with less risk of slideouts. But if your habits aren't anything like what I've suggested, it's time to practice some specific skills. Why not find some twisty road that's not too busy and focus on the techniques I've outlined? Slow down to give yourself more time to think about each of the actions. For example, if you know you can stuff the old road rocket down Twisty Hollow Canyon at 50 mph, slow down to 35 and concentrate on doing the right actions at the right location and the right time. If you have trouble getting it right, slow down even more until you can do all the steps in sequence, including swiveling your chin around toward the curve, easing on the front brake, and then sneaking on the gas all the way around the turn. Remember that it's the techniques, not just bravado, that lead to better cornering habits. And if you're looking for higher speeds, the correct techniques are essential.

All right—get those tires pumped up to correct pressures, make sure your brakes are functional, and zip on your most durable crash padding. Find a really twisty road and practice following the delayed apex line I've talked about. Maintain a modest pace and concentrate on the techniques. First, concentrate on braking lightly prior to the turn-in point, and then smoothly transition back to throttle. Turn your head to look where you want the bike to go. Consciously *countersteer* to lean the bike over and follow a smooth continuous line through the windows. Then focus on entering turns way out toward the edge of your lane and finding that delayed apex line. Practice easing on the gas as you lean over and rolling on more throttle to lift the bike up out of the corner. In a series of turns, start thinking about the best line for the next corner while still passing through the windows of this one.

Cornering Problems

You Find Yourself Drifting Wide in Midturn
Concentrate on slowing more prior to lean-in, move your lean-in point to the side of the lane opposite the turn, and press hard enough on the low grip to lean the machine over.

You Find Yourself Making Sudden Steering Corrections in Midcorner
Get your eyes up and looking toward the next turn, not down at the pavement rolling under your front wheel. Ease on the throttle as you lean the bike, and gradually ease on more throttle as you round the curve.

The Bike Wobbles When You Try to Get on the Gas While Leaned Over
Ease on the throttle as you lean over, not halfway around the turn. If the bike is going too fast to allow easing on more throttle, focus on getting the bike down to a slower speed at the turn-in point.

You Can't Seem to Get the Bike to Follow a Consistent Line
Visualize your line toward the next corner before you lean the bike over. Consciously keep your eyes up and point your nose toward your intended line. Tilt your head to keep your eyes level with the horizon.

Enjoy the Ride

The point of all this is that you will probably enjoy the ride more when the emphasis is on perfect control of the motorcycle rather than on what the speedometer says. As you master accurate countersteering, smart cornering lines, and proper timing of the critical windows, you'll probably discover that you can corner much more swiftly than before, yet still keep your risks within your tolerance level. The big payoff is that smarter cornering tactics give you a greater margin for handling whatever surprises you may encounter, whether you choose to dawdle along or engage warp drive.

CHAPTER 4

Urban Traffic Survival

CITY TRAFFIC

Occasionally, I get the opportunity to go motorcycling through some far-away places. The travels have always been great, but I'm constantly surprised at what the folks back home think about the relative dangers of riding around a foreign country on a motorcycle. A few years ago, I had the opportunity to join a tour across South Africa on a BMW GS Dual Sport. The most frequent question my co-workers asked about the trip was, Aren't you concerned about your personal safety? Well, sure, I was concerned about my safety. After all, I had to get through New York City. But I wasn't as concerned about getting caught up in a race riot as I was concerned about surviving South African traffic. Let's face it: riding around in traffic on a motorcycle involves some big risks, no matter what country you're in.

Sure, you could get assassinated in Afghanistan or firebombed in Bloemfontein. But you are more likely to get crunched by a cabbie in Cincinnati or totaled by a truck in Toledo. In other words, getting mugged, shot, torched, or blown to bits by some fanatical terrorist isn't the traveler's worst nightmare. The traveling motorcyclist's greatest hazard—almost anywhere in the world—is motor vehicle traffic.

Best Advice for Travelers

So if you are really, really concerned about personal safety, my absolutely, positively best advice about travel is: (drum roll please) STAY OUT OF CITIES. Go anywhere you want, but just don't ride into big cities. Ireland is great, just stay out of Dublin. Cities are a combat zone of cars, trucks, busses, trains, trolleys, donkey carts, bicycles, skateboards, and other assorted wheeled vehicles, all seemingly trying to smash into each other at high velocities. It's not the sort of environment a clever person would choose to ride into on a motorcycle.

But You're Going to Do It Anyway, Right?

OK, I know you're going to ignore my advice and ride into cities anyway. Maybe you live in the city. Or maybe you live in the suburbs but you ride into the big city because a motorcycle is the only vehicle you can find a parking place for. Or maybe you have a burning desire to snap a photo of your motorcycle with the Statue of

Liberty in the background, or you're headed for Disneyland and you've got to get through San Bernardino, or you are headed for Sturgis and somehow end up on a one-way street into downtown Chicago.

Maybe, like me, you get really nutzo and choose a motorcycle for the daily commute to work.

Whatever the reasons for zooming into the city on motorcycles, we'd be wise to work on our traffic survival skills. So park your scooter outside the garage door there, pour yourself a cup of your favorite beverage, pull up that creaky chair, and let's get started.

"Sudden" Collisions

The first thing to realize about collisions is that they seldom occur as suddenly as most crashees think. Now, if you suddenly realize that you are on a collision course with a Chicago cab just a second away from impact, the rest of the crash may seem awfully quick. But the suddenness is often a matter of not observing what is happening until too late in the process, typically the last second or two. If you know where to look, how to look, and what to look for, you can almost always spot a potential collision several seconds before the point of impact. And, once you understand what is happening, you can usually make a little correction to avoid riding into the problem.

One of the reasons cities are so hazardous is just the amount of stuff going on all at once. We've got multiple lanes of traffic, vehicles weaving around in all directions, cross-traffic squirting out at intersections, double-parked cars, jaywalking pedestrians, aggressive bicyclists, roaring trucks, oil-dripping busses, slick plastic arrows, sunken railroad tracks, grated bridge decks, man-eating potholes, and millions of traffic signs and signals (most of which are confusing)—and that's just the good stuff. Whatever is out there demands your attention at once, and any one problem is capable of causing you grief. The paradox is that you've somehow got to be aware of all the hazards at once, but there are usually too many hazards to keep track of at any one moment. Let's share a few ideas on how to deal with this paradox.

Separating the Hazards

The first important idea is to separate the hazards. Of course you can't make the other guys move farther apart or go more slowly, but you can observe them over more distance or more time by looking farther ahead. Although it often seems as if everything is demanding your attention at once, it is possible to separate your awareness of the hazards, if only by a few feet or a few milliseconds.

One trick is to get in the habit of scrutinizing stuff w-a-a-a-ay down the road. The farther ahead you spot trouble, the more time you will have to observe it, make a decision about it, and deal with it. You won't have to do any sudden panic maneuvers because you will make a few simple adjustments early on and just stay out of harm's way. The safety experts often use the yardstick of twelve seconds when describing how far ahead to look. That's the distance you will be covering during the next twelve seconds, which translates into about as far ahead as you can see any details. To put this another way, you want to spot any problems twelve seconds before they get close enough to become a hazard to you.

Try to maintain your awareness of the situation within the next twelve seconds, so you'll have time to deal with any problems.

Just as you can mentally separate your observations of what is happening around you, you can physically separate yourself from hazards. You can move the motorcycle farther away from a bad situation, and you can separate one hazard from another by changing lane position or speed. For example, if that rattling car transporter is too much of a distraction being so close, you can speed up, slow down, or change lanes to get farther away. Likewise, you can move away from a slow-moving car that's in the process of collecting a gaggle of trouble around it or change lanes to move farther away from a car that's poking its nose out of an alley.

Since intersections are trouble enough, I try to separate myself from other hazards before I get to an intersection. If I am being tailgated by an aggressive driver or paced by someone in an adjacent lane, I take steps to move farther away. If at all possible, I move away from trucks or busses, primarily because they block the view. I'd rather not allow myself to be a victim of whatever happens, and I prefer not to let the hazards multiply. I suggest you do the same. Take control of the situation to continuously improve the odds in your favor. Don't be squeezed into a corner or boxed into a trap if you can help it.

Observing Twelve Seconds Ahead

Looking twelve seconds ahead is a good habit, but I'm talking about more than just staring ahead with glazed eyeballs. You need to be a good observer. And by *observe* I mean really keeping your eyes moving to take in as much as possible and making some judgment calls about what's happening.

Try this exercise right now: Go back and read the previous paragraph again, but this time read one line at a time and spend two seconds scrutinizing the world around you before reading the next line. See if you can remember what you're reading while also observing details of what's happening around you—the current time,

Don't let yourself be squeezed into a corner. Move away from view-blocking trucks or busses.

what TV channel is on, who else is in the room, the color of the car driving by, what pictures are on the wall behind you, and so forth.

It's not easy, is it? The temptation is to either look around and stop reading or continue reading and ignore the observing. But don't you do something very similar as you simultaneously ride the bike and observe traffic around you? And consider this: once you record in your memory what time it is or who else is in the room, you have a pretty good idea of what's going on. The only items you need to study on subsequent glances are things that have changed.

It's the same way in traffic. You need to be aware of everything, but you can focus momentarily on those things that are in the process of becoming potential hazards. For example, the big rattling car transporter rolling along in the next lane may scream for attention, but one or two glances may confirm that it's not really a problem. That oncoming car approaching the intersection ahead isn't demanding attention, but you know that left-turners are a frequent hazard for motorcyclists, so you need to focus on that car, not on the noisy truck.

Danger Zones

Intersections are danger zones where we especially need to focus our attention. Folks with poor judgment are very likely to make mistakes at intersections, pulling out in front of other drivers, making quick turns, jamming on the brakes, or motoring through red lights. Recognize that "intersections" include anywhere vehicles can cross paths, whether on divided eight-lane arterials or where two lanes cross in the shopping mall parking lot.

Intersections include anywhere vehicles can cross paths, including shopping mall parking lots.

Move It or Lose It

Back at the beginning, I suggested that the wise rider could learn to make simple adjustments to avoid hazards that appear ahead and never have to make rapid evasive maneuvers. OK, I wasn't quite honest about that. You can learn to avoid almost all accidents, but once in a while you really do get a sudden hazard you had no way of seeing or predicting. For example, a large rock suddenly tumbles down onto the road just as you come along, or a black horse escapes his corral on a rainy night and stands in the middle of the road. When you suddenly realize you're two seconds from impact, you'll do whatever you're in the habit of doing and think about it later.

Left-turning vehicles at intersections are a frequent hazard for motorcyclists.

If you're in the habit of using the front brake to the limits of traction, you'll squeeze the brake lever without thinking about it. If you're in the habit of pushing on the grips to quickly lean the bike, you'll do a quick swerve without wasting any time.

That's why I keep repeating the same advice: to practice emergency avoidance maneuvers such as quick stops at least once each season and to practice all the right cornering techniques even when you don't have to.

Snap-Jawed Intersections

Cities are full of booby traps lying around waiting to snap shut on the unwary motorcyclist. Collisions with other vehicles should be high on the danger list. Novice street riders may assume that keeping the rubber side down is simply a matter of learning skills such as balancing, shifting, and throttle control. Experience soon teaches that avoiding motorcycle accidents involves outsmarting as well as outmaneuvering other motorists.

Let's define *intersection* so we're all thinking about the same situations. An intersection is anywhere two traffic lanes connect, and that includes not only the obvious places where two streets cross, but also entrances to gas stations, alleys, driveways, traffic lanes in shopping malls, and anywhere else two vehicles are likely to cross paths. The diagram at right, based on the Hurt Report, shows the relative percentages of accidents and fatalities that occurred at different types of intersections.

A whopping 28 percent of collisions between cars and motorcycles listed in the Hurt Report occurred when the motorist made a left turn. Typically, the driver turned left in front of the motorcyclist, and the bike slammed into the side of the car. But let's not forget about those other situations. It's informative to note that only 13 percent of accidents happened at alleys, but alley collisions generated 17 percent of all motorcycle fatalities. Obviously, we need to pay more attention to vehicles coming out

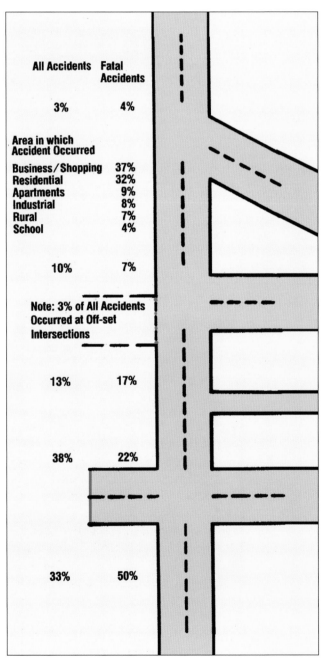

All Accidents	Fatal Accidents
3%	4%

Area in which Accident Occurred

Business/Shopping	37%
Residential	32%
Apartments	9%
Industrial	8%
Rural	7%
School	4%

10%	7%

Note: 3% of All Accidents Occurred at Off-set Intersections

13%	17%
38%	22%
33%	50%

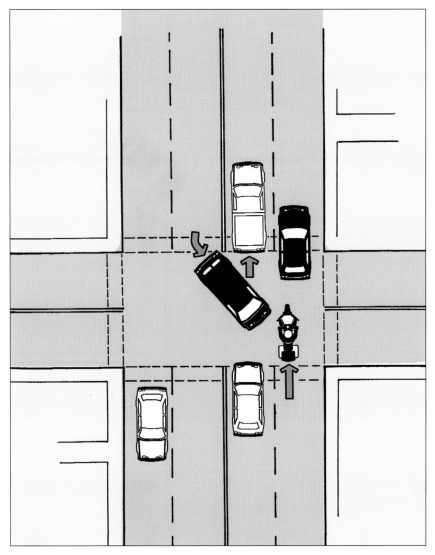

The classic left-turner, top view

of alleys and driveways. Today, roughly half of all motorcycle crashes are collisions, often with a car or SUV driver violating the motorcyclist's right of way. Four-way intersections generate the majority of collisions and account for 22 percent of fatalities, so let's first consider how crashes occur at such locations.

While most left-turn collisions are with a vehicle approaching from the opposite direction, there are several variations we need to watch for. A driver can turn left from side streets either from your left or from your right. When such vehicles are hidden behind busses, trucks, or parked cars, they can appear in your path suddenly. One scenario that catches a few surprised riders is the driver in the right lane of a one-way street who suddenly turns left across the path of the motorcyclist. As we try to figure out some collision-avoidance strategies, let's note that crashes are sudden only when neither motorist has looked far enough ahead to spot the problem. Riders who report a mere two seconds between the time they saw the offending driver and the time they hit the door are simply admitting they weren't looking far enough ahead, didn't know what to look for, or didn't believe there was a potential for a crash.

Large vehicles can really limit your view ahead and also prevent other drivers from seeing you, so it's a good idea to stay well away from them. Be very wary of passing trucks or busses waiting to make a turn. The problem isn't just that you can't see what's happening ahead, it's that other drivers can't see you hidden behind the truck or bus. The driver in the opposite lane who is waiting for a chance to turn left may think that space behind the bus would provide just enough room to zip across traffic. Wise riders don't follow immediately behind big obstructions such as busses. It's usually a big surprise to both the motorcyclist and the left-turner when the driver suddenly swerves behind the bus and takes out the bike.

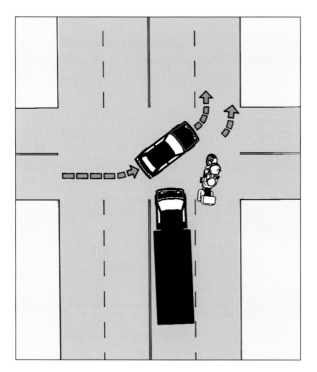

Be cautious about passing a large vehicle waiting to turn left. A car pulling out from the side street on your left can't see you.

A driver can also make a left turn from a street on your right. Moving to the left wheel track will give you more time to react to such a situation.

A driver in the right lane of a one-way street may momentarily think it's a two-way street with no oncoming traffic and make a left turn without looking behind. It's seldom smart to ride through an intersection alongside another vehicle. You should either pass or drop back.

It's usually a big surprise to both the motorcyclist and the left-turner when the driver suddenly swerves behind the bus and takes out the bike.

Clues and Rumors

Previously, I discussed looking twelve seconds ahead, or scrutinizing the road over which you will be traveling in the next twelve seconds. At a street speed of 40 mph, twelve seconds covers more than 700 feet! If you can't see that far ahead because of other traffic or obstructions, slowing down will give you more time to react to whatever suddenly pops into view. Of course, the driver could be signaling a turn, but that doesn't tell you *when* the vehicle might actually pull into your path. Some naïve riders suggest establishing eye contact with the driver, but eye contact is no guarantee he or she won't make the turn anyway. The driver could actually see you but not comprehend you have the right-of-way. Once you identify a car that *could* turn in front of you, you need to know if it is actually starting to move into your path.

To identify potential left-turners approaching from the opposite direction, watch for some important clues:

- The vehicle begins to slow as it approaches the intersection.
- The hood dips slightly as the driver begins to brake.
- The car enters a left-turn lane or eases over close to the centerline.
- The front wheel begins to turn in your direction.

Why do alleys and driveways produce a disproportionate share of fatalities? Very likely it's because we get complacent about them. Alleys are narrow and often hidden between buildings, so they are easy to ignore. You need to search aggressively for evidence of a vehicle about to pull out. Clues may be as subtle as a flicker of light reflected from a chrome bumper or the momentary glance of a pedestrian on the sidewalk. Streets, alleys, and driveways on your right are more of a danger because vehicles emerging from them are closer to your path of travel. Moving farther away from alleys definitely improves your odds of avoiding a collision with a car that suddenly pulls out onto the street.

When observing vehicles on side streets, watch the top of the front wheel. The top of the wheel moves twice as fast as the bumper, so the top of the tire starting to roll is your first clue that the vehicle is starting to move.

Sure, you may have the legal right-of-way at intersections, but having the legal right-of-way is little consolation when you're looking up at the trauma doctor. When you can't see what's going to happen in the next twelve seconds, what are the smart tactics? Right—slow down to give yourself time to react to the unknown, move to a lane position that maximizes your view, and be prepared to take evasive action to get out of the way.

SUVs and LTVs

Since around 1987, there has been a noticeable increase in the number of sport utility vehicles (SUVs) and light trucks and vans (LTVs) in the traffic mix. Today, LTVs account for over one-third of registered U.S. passenger vehicles and generally include the subcategory of SUVs. When collisions occur between LTVs and smaller, lighter vehicles, the weight and higher CoG of the LTVs puts smaller vehicles at a disadvantage. This is nothing new to motorcyclists, who understand the importance of getting out of the way of automobiles; but it's new to automobile drivers, who have yet to learn to get out of the way of LTVs. According to the NHTSA, there were 5,259 fatalities in LTV/car crashes, with 81 percent of the fatalities incurred by the car occupants.

Even a midsize four-wheel drive SUV or pickup truck weighs in the neighborhood of 4,500 lbs, so colliding with one is like running into the proverbial brick wall.

In a collision with a pickup truck, the motorcyclist isn't likely to fly over the top. Therefore, injuries are more severe than when colliding with a smaller passenger car.

NHTSA has been studying the problems of LTVs and has been wondering out loud whether they are fundamentally incompatible with cars in highway crashes. The buzzword is *aggressive vehicles*, which refers not to a driver's habits but rather to the ability of a larger, taller, heavier vehicle to severely damage a smaller, lighter vehicle. Aggressive vehicles are even more of a danger to motorcyclists. In a collision with another vehicle, the motorcyclist is typically thrown forward over the handlebars, and if it's a typical automobile, the rider is thrown over the top of the car. But in a collision with an LTV, the rider is much more likely to body slam into the side. The increase in the number of LTVs correlates to the increase in motorcycle fatalities in recent years.

Aggressive LTVs

The NHTSA has ranked the top LTVs in order of aggressiveness. The numbers are fatalities in the struck vehicle per 1000 police-reported crashes. Other aggressive vehicles include Dodge Dakota, Colt, Ram, and pickup models. File these LTVs away in your mental hard drive, and go on high alert when they are in proximity.

Dodge B series van	6.67	GMC/Jimmy/S-15	3.07
Chevrolet S-10 Blazer	5.70	Ford F-series pickup	2.92
Chevrolet Blazer, full size	4.17	Ford E-series van	2.66
Toyota 4-Runner	3.73	Ford Explorer/Bronco II	2.63
Mazda MPV	3.50	Chevrolet/GMC G-series van	2.62

Source: NHTSA report 98098, The Aggressivity of Light Trucks and Vans in Traffic Crashes, 2007.

The lesson for motorcyclists is to be especially aware of LTVs in traffic. If you find yourself in a situation where there is any question over who should go first, yield to the LTV driver.

Intersection Approach Tactics

When you are approaching an intersection where you predict the possibility of a collision, prepare yourself for avoidance maneuvers. Consider that stopping distance depends on your speed, your reaction time, and your skill, as well as your equipment. Position yourself for the best view and for maximum separation from other vehicles. For example, if buildings or large vehicles block your view of traffic on streets to your right, you can get a better view by moving to the left side of the lane or moving to the left lane. That same tactic works for narrow alleys.

The higher your speed, the greater the distance required to stop, even with quick reaction and perfect braking technique. At typical street speeds, stopping distance almost doubles for every 10 mph increase. For example, if it takes you 65 feet to stop from 30 mph, it will take you more than 100 feet to stop from 40 mph. The moral is, slowing down just 10 mph can cut 40 feet off your stopping distance at typical urban street speeds. You don't have to putter along urban arterials at 30, but if you're approaching a busy intersection with multiple left-turners, slowing down 10 mph could make the difference between a quick stop and a collision. Even slowing from 40 to 35 will reduce your stopping distance enough to matter.

But remember, you've got to squeeze the lever before the brakes can do anything. Even at 30 mph, your reaction time to get on the brakes might eat up 30 feet—or more if you don't already have your fingers squeezing the brake lever. And, regardless of when you manage to get on the brakes, your actual stopping distance depends greatly upon your braking skill as well as your equipment. Riders who haven't actually practiced quick stops from 30 to 0 typically can't pull off a quick stop successfully. In rider training courses for experienced motorcyclists, even veteran riders often can't stop quickly without sliding the rear tire or don't know how to do a quick stop in a curve without losing control. If the thought of practicing quick stops makes you nervous, that's probably something you should take care of before you get the big test out in traffic.

Once more, I'll remind you that in a panic situation, your muscles will follow your habits. Too many riders don't use enough front brake or don't use the front brake at all. That's why some machines have integrated brake systems that automatically activate both front and rear brakes and ABS to help prevent skids. But the quickest stop still requires proficient use of the front brake lever in addition to the pedal.

Riders who have spent the big bucks for antilock brake systems are sometimes under the delusion that they don't need to be proficient at braking, since the ABS will save them from a spill. Yes, ABS can help avoid a spill if you overbrake on a rain-slicked surface, but ABS won't prevent the tires from sliding out if you snap the throttle closed while leaned over in a curve. And even with ABS, shortest stops can be made if the rider brakes to a maximum just short of where the ABS activates. ABS doesn't stand for *automatic brake system*. So whether your bike has interlocked brakes, ABS, or independent brakes, you need to be proficient at both comprehending the situation and making quick stops, whether in a straight line or in a curve.

The Possibilities

Let's add up the tactics and see what they mean in terms of straight-line stopping distance:

Tactic	Effect	
Reaction, already on brake lever	+30 ft	↑
Reaction, reaching for brake lever	+54 ft	↑
Marginal braking technique at 40 mph	+75 ft	
Proficient braking technique at 30 mph	+33 ft	
Potential difference in braking distance:	129 feet versus 63 ft	↑

Looking Good

It may sound odd, but your motorcycle tends to go wherever you are looking. That's why you're more likely to hit a pothole if you keep staring at it. If you'd rather ride over the pavement on one side of the pothole, the trick is to focus on the good pavement, not on the problem. If you stare at the side of a left-turning truck, that's where the bike will go. More correctly, your motorcycle goes where your nose is pointed. So actually turn your head and look where you want the bike to go. If you'd rather avoid a collision, focus on the open street where you want the motorcycle to go. Wouldn't it make sense to focus on the pavement in front of the car where you intend to stop short of a collision, not on the side of the car?

Whether you've taken a training course or practiced braking by yourself, it's important to stay in the habit of using the front brake during every stop and to include braking as part of your cornering sequence. When the chips are down, you'll do whatever you've been in the habit of doing.

Suburb Survival

Bigdawg Dan has been fidgety ever since he watched the European road racing on TV last Tuesday. His right hand has been twitching, and his soul is itching for a twisty road fix. As the week unfolds, Dan checks his tires, tops off the oil, runs a rag over the chrome, oils up his leathers, and polishes his face shield one more time.

The weather report Thursday night promises sunny on Friday, rain by Saturday. While he's been futzing with the bike, Dan has been formulating a believable medical excuse for the boss. The weather report clinches the decision: Friday morning, instead of heading for work, Dan calls in sick, suits up, and

Suburbs may look benign, but they can generate lots of motorcycle crashes.

points the bike through commuter traffic toward his favorite back road. Even as he carves through frustratingly slow traffic, he's slicing through those turns in his mind. To make better time, Dan cuts over to the side streets he knows so well.

But before Bigdawg can get out of Dodge City, a posse of sleepy commuters pulls a hold-up. With no warning, a car zips out of an alley, directly into Dan's path. Like the sleepy driver, it takes Dan a moment to wake up to what's happening, and that extra reaction time seals his fate. Too late getting on the brake, Dan slams into the driver's door and catapults over the roof. Luckily, he isn't seriously injured, thanks to the serious riding gear he decided to wear today. But the bike's front end is wrapped back under the engine, and this machine isn't going to go anywhere soon. The ride is over. Now Dan can honestly fulfill his sick-leave prophesy with a sprained shoulder.

I bump into a lot of veteran riders in my travels. And I get a pretty good idea of what's on their collective minds. One top-level priority seems to be riding the twisty back roads as quickly as possible. Yes, drifting through the twisties is exciting. We're basically trying to emulate the road racers without having to buy track time or get serious about skills or leathers. In my opinion, there's nothing wrong with enjoying quick riding, but there's a lot more to motorcycling than emulating the racers. Remember, a lot of your riding time is in urban traffic. Even if you're headed out to the country, you've got to get through the suburbs first. And what many motorcyclists seem to overlook is that suburbs generate a lot of motorcycle crashes.

Freeways might appear to be a hazardous riding environment, what with the big volumes of traffic and the higher speeds, but the statistics hint that freeways are safer than undivided highways. And of course there are some nasty accidents on twisty roads favored by weekend riders. Most motorcyclists have figured out that urban (city) intersections are our biggest nightmare, complete with cross-traffic, multiple lanes, strange intersections, confusing signals, pedestrians, taxi cabs, delivery trucks, busses, and lots of aggressive driving as frustrated motorists attempt to get somewhere faster than everyone else. Sometimes just getting through a busy parking lot can be a major skirmish. When you can escape from the freeways, busy arterials, and heavy traffic and cruise down a quiet side street, it's easy to let your guard down.

Familiarity Breeds Complacency

You probably already know that the majority of motorcycle accidents occur in business or shopping areas; on sunny days; on straight, level, dry roads; and at speeds below 40 mph; and you know that about half of all motorcycle crashes are collisions with cars, pickup trucks, and SUVs. One of the interesting statistics from the Hurt Report is that most accidents occurred within the first twelve minutes of the intended trip or on trips of less than five miles.

Think about that. When you're close to home, you are familiar with your surroundings. *I've traveled this street a thousand times and have never had a car pull out of that alley before. I've ridden past these same parked cars on this residential side street for five years and have never had anyone back out of a driveway into my path. I've never had someone swerve into my lane to get around a bicyclist.* Familiarity tends to breed complacency. Obviously, it's a lot quieter on the side streets. But if you happen along at the same instant when someone else suddenly gets in your way, you need to be just as prepared to avoid a crash as you would be on the busier arterials.

Timing, Timing, Timing

You might be amazed that there are significant differences in the accident and fatality numbers depending on time of day. The time frames when frustrated workers head home from the job and when the drunks head home from the bars on weekends are especially hazardous. Be aware that afternoons between 3 p.m. and 6 p.m. generate about one-fourth of all motorcycle crashes and fatalities. There is also a surge in accidents around midnight on Friday and Saturday nights. By comparison, early mornings between 3 a.m. and 6 a.m. have a very low accident frequency, even on weekends. So Bigdawg Dan actually faced a much lower collision risk heading out on a Friday morning than if he'd waited until Saturday afternoon. That ought to be useful information when you're scrambling for an excuse to slip away from the job for a day of riding in the canyons. But, whatever the time of day or week, the risk of a smasho never drops to zero. Those suburban side streets have some peculiar hazards we need to understand.

Do you see there's a driver in the station wagon and the front wheel is pointed toward the street? It shouldn't be a surprise when the driver pulls out in front of you without looking.

Parked Cars

With all those parked cars lining the side streets, it's easy to start thinking of them as permanently fixed objects. Just remember that most of them are auto*mobiles*. They move occasionally. The clever rider looks for clues that a parked car is about to go mobile. For cars parked parallel along the curb, watch for a driver behind the wheel or eyes reflected in a side mirror. Look for exhaust emanating from the tailpipe, for a brake light illuminated, or for a flickering backup light as the driver shifts into drive. Beware a front wheel turned toward the street, and remember that the top of a wheel moves twice as fast as the bumper.

Don't ignore cars parked in narrow driveways just off the street. A driver backing into the street isn't likely to have a good view of a motorcycle zipping along. This is especially important where cars are parked on steep inclines or partially hidden behind retaining walls, hedges, or fences. When you do spot any clues that a vehicle might move, get prepared for evasive action, preferably a quick stop.

Pedestrians, Bicycles, and Skateboarders

You're more likely to encounter kids and animals dodging into the street near residences. Kids who are playing along side streets also become complacent about traffic and might chase a bouncing ball into your path without thinking about the consequences.

Bicyclists, in-line skaters, and skateboarders are also very common these days on suburban streets. For whatever reason, many of these folks seem to believe that the traffic laws don't apply to them. It's fairly common to encounter an adult bicyclist or skater zipping through an intersection against a red light or sailing off the sidewalk and into the street against the flow of traffic. And remember that a vehicle in the opposing lane may swerve across the line to avoid a skater or bicyclist. Young children can be excused for not really understanding the risks, but adults who should know better are just as likely to be the victims; 60 percent of bicyclist fatalities are in the over-15 age bracket.

Darting into the road is the single largest contributor to pedestrian accidents. Of the 4,749 pedestrians killed in the United States in 2003, 79 percent of the fatalities happened at locations other than intersections. It may also be helpful to know that 65 percent of pedestrian fatalities occurred at night in normal weather conditions. You probably won't be surprised that five- to nine-year-old males and ten- to fifteen-year-old females have the top injury rates. But the highest fatality rate belongs to the fifty-five- to sixty-four-year-old males. It may also be helpful to note that 37 percent of total pedestrian fatalities occurred between 8:00 p.m. and midnight on weekends. Top states for pedestrian fatalities (per 100,000 population) are:

STATE	FATALITIES
District of Columbia	3.19
Florida	2.94
Nevada	2.90
New Mexico	2.72
Arizona	2.17

Source: NHTSA Traffic Safety Facts, 2003

In a motorcycle versus pedestrian or motorcycle versus skateboarder collision, the motorcyclist is more likely to come out on top. But even if you aren't hurt and you had the green light, the sympathy of the court is more likely to lean toward the pedestrian than toward the motorcyclist. And your insurance company won't like the deal either. So even if you have the right-of-way, consider all pedestrians and human-powered vehicles as moving targets to avoid.

Evasive Action

The first step in avoiding any of these suburban hazards is planning ahead. The basic evasive maneuver (for everything except loose dogs) is a quick stop. Whether you are riding a freeway or a side street, you should always be able to stop within your sight distance. The big problem with narrow residential streets is that your sight distance may be only to the end of the car you are riding by or to that overgrown hedge at the next corner. A child could be ready to dart out from between the cars, for example, or a skateboarder could come zipping out from behind the hedge. So your speed through residential neighborhoods must be slow enough that you can make quick stops with very little warning. That's why it is unwise to hurry along side streets, as Bigdawg Dan was doing.

Plan to stop when approaching a blind intersection where you can't see traffic on the side street.

When approaching a blind intersection where you can't see traffic on the side street, plan to stop to look, just as if there were a stop sign. Assuming you have the right-of-way is an invitation to an embarrassing get-together. And when you do encounter a stop sign, get in the habit of making a complete left-foot-down stop. Lots of riders who intended only a slowdown when rolling by a stop sign or blind intersection have been surprised by cross-traffic and ended up stopping their machines horizontally.

Surface Hazards

Side streets often have more surface hazards than busier arterials do. Street crews tend to ignore problems such as pavement ripples or sunken drains on little-used side streets. So while you're scrutinizing the situation for the usual vehicle, child, and animal hazards, don't ignore the road surface.

In older cities, there are still streets with brick paving and bridges with wooden decking. Bricks or wood may seem to have good traction when dry but can be amazingly slippery when wet. What happens is that the brick dust or wood fibers mix with water to form a slimy lubricant that is the same color as the surrounding surface. You can't see the slippery stuff, so just remember that wood or brick surfaces can be treacherous when wet, even from a little dew.

You're also more likely to encounter pavement ripples or grooves on side streets. Where there are mature trees alongside, expect ripples from tree roots growing under the paving. There are also

On shady side streets, watch for tree root bumps in the pavement that could cause your suspension to bounce just when you're trying to brake.

Both wood and brick surfaces can be treacherous in the rain.

lots of side streets where the paving suddenly changes to gravel, the road narrows, or the sidewalks disappear.

In newer neighborhoods, you can expect edge traps, dips, and bumps created by the installation of underground pipes and wires as new houses are constructed. Expect manhole covers or drain grates that didn't work out to be the right elevation for the paving but never got fixed. Remember that manholes and grates are usually located at intersections, right where your attention is demanded for the moving targets.

Slip in Spring and Fall

In climates where the temperature dips below freezing in the winter, expect loose sand at the edges of the wheel tracks each spring. Wintertime street sanding operations often leave sandy berms that are most obvious for a month or two after the spring thaw. Watch carefully at intersections where the sand berms collect near the curb and close to the centerline.

You may want to think twice about blasting through a big pile of leaves in the gutter that could be hiding a sunken grate or collection of acorns.

In autumn, treat fallen leaves with respect. You may get this creative idea to go blasting through a big pile of leaves in the gutter, but think twice about that. Even if the leaves are dry on top, there is often a soggy-slippery layer of rotten vegetation on the bottom, down where your tires are looking for a grip. Or perhaps there are some hidden "ball bearings" in the form of acorns or chestnuts. Maybe there is a loose brick or a sunken drain grate hiding under the leaves, waiting to bend your wheel rim. You can chance the leaf blast if you want, but let's not hear any sniveling if it doesn't work out as creatively as it did in your imagination.

Wear Your Gear

One important admonition about riding familiar streets: wear your riding gear, especially when you don't think the situation demands the precaution. Like Bigdawg Dan, you know there are hazards of taking a soil sample when you're blitzing a twisty road at warp speeds, so it's a no-brainer to suit up for the good stuff. But hey, for a one-mile trip to the convenience store, it's a lot of bother to zip on the armored pants and jacket, right? Just remember that those quiet, innocent-looking side streets and alleys can spring sudden hazards on you just as quickly as your favorite twisty road, and a collision with an SUV can be just as violent as sliding off a curve.

Superslab Tactics

I happen to live out in the country where I can ease out of my driveway onto a quiet farm road, miles from city traffic. I realize I'm in the privileged minority. Most motorcyclists find themselves riding busy urban arterials and multilane superhighways more often than not. Even if you're just headed out into the country to get to your favorite twisty road, it's usually a lot easier and quicker to get on the nearest freeway and make an end run around urban traffic. And if you're making a cross-country transit on a limited time schedule, you'll be spending most of your time on the interstates.

It's pretty hard to avoid the superslab these days.

Let's consider some tactics for surviving those high-speed multilane highways we call freeways, parkways, tollways, or expressways. For purposes of this chapter, we'll call them all superslabs.

Statistically, divided multilane superslabs have far fewer crashes than city streets or two-lane highways do.

Take a look at the difference between a two-lane undivided road (a typical secondary highway with a painted centerline) and a divided four-lane highway (a typ-

Number of Lanes	Not Divided	Divided	One-Way
One	27	23	119
Two	1,907	603	66
Three	210	426	41
Four	377	221	16
More than four	486	120	4
Unknown	383	118	31

Source: US Motor Vehicle Crashes, All Vehicles, thousands of crashes, *NHTSA Traffic Safety Facts, 2003*

ical superslab with a grassy median or a cable barrier separating opposing traffic). Run the numbers through your calculator, and you can see that there are about twelve fatal crashes on a secondary highway for every one fatal crash on a divided superslab, mile per mile.

Now, while the superslab does look like a pretty safe environment compared with those dangerous two-laners, people do get killed and seriously injured in superslab accidents. To help you avoid becoming some statistic on the BTS hard drive (not to mention an odd stain on I-80), let's ramble through a bit of philosophy about superslab riding and then get down to some nitty-gritty tactics.

The Times They Are A-Changing

Back in the good old days when American traffic and drivers' thinking were much more sedate, it was fairly obvious that traffic in Europe was faster and European drivers more aggressive. An English friend who flew across the "pond" to Seattle in 1982 to tour the West Coast by motorcycle described American traffic as moving in slow motion. Things have changed a lot over the last couple of decades. Today, traffic in America is zipping along just as fast as in parts of Europe, and in some big mega-cities, drivers are just as aggressive as their European counterparts.

Twenty years ago, motorcycles had the performance advantage. Even on the bikes of yesteryear, we could out-accelerate, out-corner, and out-brake the average passenger sedan. Thanks to competition from the Japanese and German auto industries, just about every midsize passenger car today has performance that whittles away most of the advantages of motorcycles. Sure, there are lots of superbikes that can out-accelerate cars, but today's higher traffic speeds are getting faster than many riders can process information. On top of that, we've still got our thinking, vision, and hearing being buffeted by the windstream. And there does seem to be an increasing problem with road rage.

Thinking Skills

Where we might have held our own with performance back in the good old days, staying out of trouble in today's traffic environment requires that we get smarter rather than just quicker. Obviously, you need to be really proficient at skills such as cornering on slick or grooved surfaces, swerving to avoid debris, and hard braking. But you also need to be mentally sharp enough to plan your moves well ahead and predict what's going to happen before it happens. Sudden, unplanned moves encourage crashes. Indications that your planning skills need a tune-up are finding yourself making sudden, impulsive moves, such as frequently accelerating and decelerating, making unplanned lane changes, or diving across four lanes at the last second to peel off onto your exit.

It is essential to focus on today's ride, even if you've done the same trip every day for the last twenty-four months. When you snap up the sidestand, click your brain in gear before you ease out the clutch. If you're traveling cross-country, you need a better plan than when you're close to home. You can't afford to glance down at a map while you're also attempting to negotiate a decreasing-radius cloverleaf that slam dunks you directly into a warp 7 through-lane clogged with eighteen-wheelers. One veteran long-distance tactic is to pull out the map before hitting the road and write down the names of the next big towns and the highway numbers on a slip of paper clipped to the windshield or in the map pocket of a tankbag. Just before getting into a confusing interchange, glance down at the names and numbers to refresh your memory.

When traveling, you should expect lots of very strange intersections that don't look anything like the road map and fraudulent signs pointing to lane 5 when the local commuters all know you should be in lane 1 just around that curve ahead. What's important is to not panic and jam on the brakes or make quick lane changes when you realize you've taken the wrong road or can't get to the exit lane in time. Take the next exit, get out the map, plot a course back in the right direction, and make another short list. There are also some electronic devices to help you navigate, including GPS receivers that can show you exactly where you are and highlight the route to your destination with or without voice prompts.

Get Your Head in the Ride

Consider Bigdawg Dan's mental state at the time of his crash. He was squandering his thoughts on the ride to come, which in his mind would commence when he got to his favorite road. He wasn't focusing on the ride already in progress or the situation immediately in front of his machine. For Dan, getting through city traffic was just an inconvenience prior to the real ride of the day. It is important to get your head in the ride before you ease out the clutch, whether you're shifting down for that first of a hundred fun curves on the coast highway, heading out on the next leg of a cross-country trip, or just zipping down to the local coffee shop for breakfast.

And while we're thinking about thinking, let's note the importance of keeping your brain fed and free of toxins or dizzying drugs. Little of my advice will help if you're preoccupied with social problems, woozy from prescriptions, or bullet-proofed by alcohol. Nor can you expect your brain to function correctly without some food in the core. Have a good breakfast before a morning ride, or at least stop for some healthy food early in the day. If you're on any pills that make you drowsy or light-headed, I strongly urge you to scrub the mission and leave the bike in the garage.

Most important, avoid alcohol while you're riding a motorcycle. Yeah, alcohol has a bad reputation for being involved in fatal accidents, and it deserves it. Alcohol degrades most of the physical and mental functions you need to operate a motorcycle. Automobile drivers seem to be getting smarter about not driving under the influence, but too many motorcyclists don't seem to be paying attention, even though riding a bike requires greater skill and judgment than driving a car does.

Way too many riders seem willing to risk a cocktail of booze and bikes.

Lane Positioning

You'll hear all sorts of advice about superslab riding that begins with *always* or *never:* Never ride in the center lane. Always ride in the left wheel track. Always ride in the left lane. The trouble with such all-knowing advice is that the superslab environment is constantly changing, which means you should continuously reevaluate what you're doing. Which lane you ride in, or which wheel track, depends on conditions at the moment, including surface hazards. One "never" rule that does make sense is to never ride in the blind spots of other vehicles. If you can't see a driver's face in his mirror, he probably can't see you either. More than a few fatal crashes have resulted from a driver changing lanes on top of a motorcyclist who was riding alongside the car's right rear quarter.

Drivers tend to flock together into gaggles, leaving open spaces in between.

Traffic Gaggles

You might be amazed at how much open space there is on a busy highway. Sure, the superslabs around cities are often clogged bumper to bumper during the rush hours. But between cities you'll find more open space than you might have suspected. One of these days, park your scooter and walk out onto an overpass (one with a sidewalk, eh?) where you can study traffic for a few minutes. One phenomenon you can observe is that drivers tend to flock together into gaggles. Often you'll see a gaggle of ten or fifteen cars all elbowing for position, then a clear space with no vehicles, then another gaggle of cars.

The smart motorcyclist stays away from the flock, either intentionally dropping back into a clear space or aggressively moving on by a congested gaggle of creeper cars and motoring into the next clear space. I've met some experienced riders who prefer to ride at a slightly higher speed than traffic, but that means you will be working your way past many other drivers. Your risk is lowest when you are riding at the average speed of traffic but not getting entangled with other vehicles.

Sudden Problems

One essential mental skill for superslab riding is to look far enough ahead to predict what's going to happen in time to do something about it. You've probably seen this situation many times: you spot a few brake lights coming on ten or twenty cars ahead, ease off the throttle, squeeze on some brakes, and start looking for an escape route. But the driver in front of you doesn't seem to be aware of anything except the back of the next car. You feel like shouting, "Hey, Particle-Board-Brain! Wake up and get off the gas! Don't you see the brake lights ahead?" As you see the brake lights coming on in a wave traveling backwards, you head for the shoulder, clamp on the binders, and consider jumping over the guardrail for a little extra protection.

Sure enough, old PB-brain is so dense that he doesn't do anything until the brake lights of the car ahead suddenly light up in a blaze of red. You don't have to multiply this scenario by more than a few vehicles to have a whammo-bammo-slammo chain reaction with a hundred vehicles involved.

So what was the obvious difference between you and old PBB? First off, you were looking over the tops of cars and around trucks to scrutinize the situation wa-a-a-ay down the road. Second, when you saw the flicker of brake lights ahead, your mental hazard buzzer went off. You predicted that it wouldn't be long before whatever was happening up ahead would affect you up close and personal. By looking ahead and predicting what would occur, you could take some evasive action to get out of the way before you got caught up in the mayhem.

Scrutinizing the Road Ahead

We've discussed looking ahead twelve seconds, the distance you'll be covering in the next twelve seconds. As the speedometer climbs up the dial on the 'slab, that twelve seconds stretches way out toward the horizon, and that's a lot more territory than most of us have the mental capacity to monitor. The trick is to summarize what's happening. You don't need to study every vehicle in detail; just look for certain patterns or ripples in the flow of traffic ahead, similar to predicting treacherous rocks under the surface of a river by observing the swirl of the water over them. You're looking for the big picture, not small details, so you can use your peripheral vision more. It's sort of a Zen thing.

You can practice this right now. Focus on the middle of the wall on the other side of the room. Now, without changing your focus, become aware of the line where the wall meets the ceiling. Now become aware of the lower left-hand corner of the room, the number of windows, what's on the TV, who is in the room, and so on. You can keep track of what's happening without having to focus on specific objects.

Here are some common traffic ripples that often lead to accidents:
- A vehicle traveling either much faster or much slower than others
- A vehicle making sudden, erratic speed or lane changes
- A car in a "turn only" lane suddenly slowing
- A vehicle with an out-of-state license moving slower than traffic
- Traffic in one lane suddenly slowing for no apparent reason
- The second car on an on-ramp charging faster than the first
- A driver ahead using a cell phone, reading the newspaper, putting on makeup, or lighting a smoke
- A poorly maintained vehicle or a truck with a loose load
- A crash or emergency vehicles in the opposing lanes

When you observe such traffic ripples, take some action to move away from the problem. Change lanes, accelerate, decelerate, or head for an off-ramp. Don't just hang in there hoping the problem will go away by itself.

The Two-Second Bubble

To help maintain awareness of all those other cars, trucks, busses, and bikes around me in traffic, I find it helpful to visualize a two-second trajectory bubble circling me.

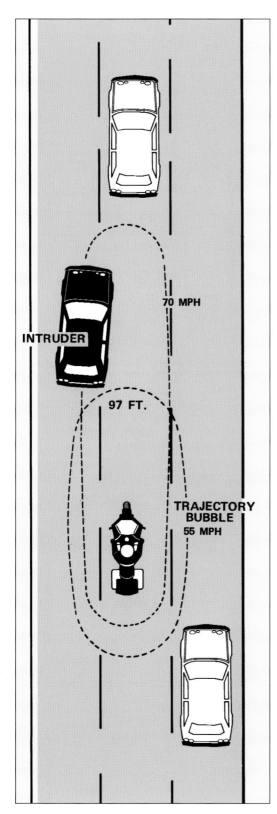

70 MPH

INTRUDER

97 FT.

TRAJECTORY
BUBBLE
55 MPH

The trajectory bubble concept

Sure, I'm looking for ripples in the traffic stream within the next twelve seconds ahead, but I'm especially interested in intruders who are closing in on my two-second bubble. Anyone who intrudes on the bubble (anyone closer than two seconds away) gets my immediate attention. At slower speeds, the bubble is shorter but wider. As speed increases, it stretches farther and farther out in front.

Same Dumb Stunts

While cars may be faster and more controllable these days, people still pull many of the same dumb stunts as their ancestors did, even at higher speeds. And some locations generate a lion's share of the accidents. Curves, on-ramps, off-ramps, and merging lanes are all locations where we can expect people to make last-second decisions and sudden changes of speed or direction. Next

When you are passing an on-ramp, watch for the on-ramp dodger who might swerve across several lanes of traffic as he bulls his way through.

time you're out riding, take a close look at dividers and walls in curving off-ramps, and you'll often see tire tracks halfway up the sides that are proof of some scary moves.

And while we're on the subject of ramps, make a point of positioning yourself in traffic so you aren't between another vehicle and a merging lane. That driver coming up fast on your left may just be in a hurry to pass. Or he could be an off-ramp dodger desperate to make this exit, even if it's over your dead body. And if you see an on-ramp dodger coming up fast on an on-ramp, you'd be wise to get out of the way.

Lane Crunching

When you are changing lanes, not only consider the space in the next lane but also think about other drivers who might be deciding to jump into the same space you are ogling. If you have decided to change lanes, why not turn on your blinkers first and then check for other vehicles parallel to your position? If you spot nervous head turns in your peripheral vision, that's a clue a lane cruncher is about to make a move. If there is any question about who might get to the space first, either move ahead or move back so it's harder to have a get-together.

Road Sharks

If you haven't encountered road sharks, let's introduce them. You know, those folks in fast cars with dark windows, racing through traffic about 30 knots faster than everyone else, zipping from lane 1 to lane 4 and back in one big swoop like some computer game. You'll know 'em when you see 'em. Road sharks are one good reason to maintain your awareness of what's coming up in adjacent lanes behind you.

I know a few riders with big dog attitudes who feel they can hold their own with the road sharks. *Think he could push me around, did he? He didn't know who the @#$% he was dealing with. I passed that jerk at a hun-nert and twenty going through the S-curves. I guess I showed him a thing or two.* Look, the reality is that in skirmishes between aggressive drivers and aggressive bikers, the biker almost always lands at the bottom of the heap. If you're a gambler, the odds are just about 115 to 1 that the biker wins the ride in the coroner's wagon.

Road sharks can really sucker you into stupid behavior. Over the years, I've been suckered into more dumb stunts than I'd care to remember. We all need to

When changing lanes, watch for that guy who has the same idea two lanes over.

Before you make a lane change, make sure there isn't a road shark behind you about to do the same.

file this important message away in the back of our brains for future use: if someone makes you mad, it is very important to take a break and cool off. Don't get mad. Don't get even. Don't get stupid. Most important, don't keep riding. Take a break until you get over the anger and can think clearly again. If you want to avoid getting scrunched in a superslab accident, it doesn't seem smart to challenge other drivers for road space.

Rear-Enders

You might also be getting a little paranoid about being rear-ended. Yes, there are crashes in which a car rear-ends the bike. But the most likely scenario is that the rider rear-ends another vehicle. The majority of all motorcyclist fatalities involved the motorcycle crashing head-on into something. When I checked the numbers a few years ago, the score was 1,540 front-of-bike fatalities versus 76 rear-of-bike. In other words, be aware of vehicles behind you, but pay primary attention to what's happening ahead of you. If you're really concerned about getting hit from the rear, make a point of leaving more space between you and the vehicle ahead to give yourself some maneuvering room. If you see someone approaching from your rear who doesn't seem to be slowing quickly enough, you could take evasive action—say pulling up alongside the car ahead.

You might consider adding lights or reflectors to the back of your bike. There are light-emitting diode (LED) taillights that can be programmed to flash for two or three seconds when you apply the brake and then glow steadily. One big advantage of LED lights is that they are extremely reliable. A standard bulb can burn out instantly without warning, leaving the back of your bike dark. The LED taillight array can lose one or two LEDs without much of a visual change.

Pedestrians on the Superslab

On a trip to Tennessee, I was surprised to encounter a man in dark clothing wandering across an unlit freeway cloverleaf at night, but apparently this is a common scenario. Pedestrian deaths on the super-slabs are on the rise. In 2003, 4,749 pedestrians were killed nationwide—compared with 3,714 motorcy-clists. Pedestrian deaths now comprise 12 percent of all fatalities on interstate highways. Most of these pedestrian fatalities occurred at night. Typically, the victims are males in the twenty-five to thirty-four age group. More than 90 percent of highway pedestrian fatalities involved walking in the roadway, standing on the shoulder, or attempting to run across a busy highway. The top states for highway pedestrian fatalities are (in order) Texas, New Mexico, Delaware, Nevada, Missouri, and Louisiana. California has a high number of highway pedestrian fatalities but also has more interstate miles (*NHTSA Traffic Safety Facts*, 2003).

The moral here is to be especially watchful for pedestrians on the road after dark. Be alert for pedestrians near interchanges or near a vehicle stopped on the shoulder. And if you are ever stranded by a motorcycle problem, be aware that more than 15 percent of fatalities involved someone working on or pushing a vehicle. It's not uncommon for an inattentive or sleepy driver to wander over onto the shoulder at night.

Serious Maintenance

Let's not leave the subject of superslabs without mentioning bike maintenance. Today's serious traffic on the superslab puts serious demands on your motorcycle. You can't afford to have a failure while you're zipping along in heavy traffic at warp speeds. At today's higher speeds and increased traffic aggressiveness, there isn't much extra slack for coddling tires that have been damaged from under-inflation, sacked shocks, spongy brakes, or loose wheel bearings. If you're going to go play with the big boys on the superslab, it's important that your motorcycle be up to the task.

Aggressive Drivers

I've suggested that motorcyclists face a variety of booby traps. The pavement may have a groove that snags your front tire and upsets the bike, the road may tighten up or change camber halfway through a blind corner, someone may have dribbled a puddle of diesel oil onto an off-ramp, or there may be a railroad crossing in an S-turn with slippery plastic aprons surrounding the rails. Sure, the road itself can have hidden hazards. But other motorists can also create booby traps. Let's consider overly aggressive drivers who often send others into road rage.

As traffic gets more congested, drivers get more impatient and resort to self-centered tactics. Remember that drivers are people, and most people take out their frustrations and aggression in their driving. Around big cities, we must expect more drivers to be zooming along at superlegal speeds, darting from lane to lane without signaling, and accelerating through intersections while the signal light turns from yellow to red. But a growing number of frustrated drivers go over the edge, carving through traffic with total disregard for laws and even threatening other drivers with collisions if they don't get out of the way.

A common estimate among psychology professionals is that one out of every ten people has some sort of mental health problem, from depression all the way to schizophrenia. That's something to think about as you motor down the road minding your own business. Of course, there are also lots of people out there who are more or less normal but are in a big hurry today, are angry at their significant other, or happen to be angry about motorcycles. And of course there are druggies and drunks weaving along, drivers with cellphoneitis, and others with 400 CI engines and 40 IQ social

The best way to protect yourself from an aggressive driver is to get out of the way.

skills. It's no wonder that car-motorcycle collisions account for so many motor-cyclist accidents and fatalities.

"Though this be madness, yet there is method in't."
(Shakespeare, *Hamlet*)

Here's Rider Ralph, who has been following a creeper car for too long on a narrow highway. The driver is apparently unwilling to exceed the speed limit and slows down below the limit for intersections and tighter corners where Ralph feels he should maintain speed. With a steady stream of oncoming traffic, Ralph can't get around, so he closes up behind the slower driver and flicks his high beam to encourage the driver to speed up or move over. Finally, Ralph has had it. He swings halfway over the double-yellow centerline, rolls on the gas, and passes. Ralph snickers as his right handlebar barely ticks the driver's mirror on the way by, before he swerves the bike back into the right lane inches ahead of the car.

But the other driver suddenly goes bonkers, zooming up behind Ralph, beeping the horn, shaking a fist, shouting, and weaving from side to side. Ralph accelerates, but the crazy driver jams the accelerator to the floor and roars around Ralph, forcing an oncoming school bus onto the shoulder, then cuts right in front of the motorcycle and slams on the brakes.

Now Ralph is enraged. First this creeper jerko held him up, and now he wants to start a fight. Ralph's first urge is to zoom alongside and kick a dent in the driver's door. Fortunately, Ralph has just enough survival instinct left to realize that he could get seriously hurt in a car-bike confrontation. His fight or flight response flickers over to flight, and he backs off to separate himself from the angry driver.

So what do you think? Did Ralph just happen to stumble on one of those 10 percent with serious mental problems, or did he do something to trigger the road rage? Let's note that motorcyclists can stimulate aggressive situations without realizing it or create a brewing anger that affects others later. For example, Ralph had no way of knowing that the "crazy" driver's next door neighbor had stayed up late last night tuning the carbs on his unmuffled cruiser, or that a few miles back two thoughtless riders had been motoring along side by side, carrying on a rolling conversation and holding up traffic. Then Ralph came along and tailgated the driver, blinding him with the high beam, passing in a no passing zone, scaring him with a blast of noise, and even hitting the car's mirror.

It didn't help that Ralph is one of those loud-pipes-save-lives guys. The noise had been annoying the driver for miles, and when Ralph roared on by with his screaming turkey straight pipes barking, the driver finally snapped. In this scenario, the driver wasn't someone with a serious psychological problem—he was just a guy who had been angered by one too many motorcyclists, and Ralph's behavior pushed him over the edge.

"Whom the gods wish to destroy, they first make mad."
(Euripides)
Remember, we can encounter aggression for a wide variety of reasons, and those drivers around us can come in all grades of mental health. Someone who is already angry or frustrated could be triggered into rage by a single thoughtless act. Worse yet, someone with a serious mental problem such as schizophrenia might initiate aggression for no apparent reason. Maybe the extraterrestrial voice in her brain demanded, *Whack that motorcyclist.*

To help you avoid getting snared by an aggressive driver, let's think through the drill. First of all, did Ralph do the right thing by backing off when the other driver showed aggression, or should he have attempted to fight back? I know of a rider who got a pushy driver to back off by pulling a handgun out of his fairing pocket. I've talked with macho riders who carry heavy steel ball bearings or lug nuts to toss over their shoulders to help educate tailgaters. I once knew a rider who was very proud that he had punched an overly aggressive driver in the face, right through the car's side window.

When someone cuts me off, I get mad, too. I used to think it was my job to educate drivers about their transgressions against motorcyclists. Once I put my bike on the sidestand in the middle of the street and marched back to explain sarcastically to an errant driver: "Apparently, you haven't discovered this little shiny thing on the outside of your door. It's called a mirror. Why, some drivers even glance in it before they change lanes."

Trying to Educate Other Drivers
But trying to educate other drivers on the road might be a little nutso. In the first place, an unstable driver could easily be triggered into something really dangerous by a simple act such as a rude gesture. You can create a bigger problem than you expected or get an innocent bystander injured.

Once, I almost caused an accident. A car had been tailgating me on the freeway. Traffic was light, but the other driver didn't want to pass me. I was thinking about pulling over onto the shoulder when the driver suddenly swerved halfway over into the passing lane and tromped on the gas. I swerved over to avoid getting sideswiped and then had to brake as the silver-haired woman pulled back into the right lane inches in front of me.

I took her aggressive pass as an affront, and I thought it would be clever to give her a demonstration of her rudeness. I accelerated up behind her, signaled, passed, and swerved back into the right lane a few feet ahead of her. But rather than educate her, my close pass startled her, and she swerved and braked, almost losing control of her car. I realized she was just a preoccupied old lady with poor vision and low driving skill who probably had no idea she had triggered road rage. I suddenly felt very embarrassed.

One big reason for not trying to retaliate for transgressions or attempt any driver education on the road is the proliferation of hand guns in the United States. Before you ease up alongside a car door and give the hand signal switch to channel 1 or walk back for a cheesy chat, imagine the driver reaching under the seat for a hand gun. Getting your pride injured is nothing compared with bullet holes.

Get Over It

The most important reason for swallowing your pride and just getting out of the way is that cars and trucks are bigger than bikes. Given the relative weights between a

In a contest between a motorcycle and an LTV, we know who is going to come out second best.

bike and a car, or worse yet between a bike and a 4 x 4 crew cab dually pickup, we pretty well understand who's going to come out second best in a bump-a-thon. There isn't much you can do on a motorcycle to protect yourself against a driver who goes into a rage other than to get out of the way.

Sure, sure, you're thinking. *Stay calm when some idiot is trying to kill me.* Well, it isn't easy to just get over it, but that's what's needed. One calming tactic psychologists suggest is to imagine the other person as something really silly, say a human-size Daffy Duck, a cigar-smoking alligator, or Homer Simpson. It's harder to take a comic figure seriously. If you can just see a flicker of humor in the situation, you're on the right track. If you can't get over it, that's a message that you may have some psychological problems to work out.

If you can stay calm, you can use your wits plus the performance and maneuverability of your motorcycle to separate yourself from the other driver. In the serious situation in which a raging driver seems intent on running you over, take immediate action to get out of the way. Change lanes, drop back, accelerate, whatever. You might be able to position yourself on the opposite side of a big truck or tuck in behind a highway patrol car, for example. I have occasionally made a quick exit from the freeway and paused at the on-ramp for a few seconds to separate myself from an aggressive driver. On one occasion, I shook a tailgater on a narrow two-laner by accelerating to warp speed until he was out of view behind a hill, then braking hard and dodging off onto a side road and hiding behind a bush. The point is, don't just ride along hoping an aggressive driver will go away. Take charge of the situation.

You're Only Paranoid If They AREN'T Out to Get You

When I'm riding along in traffic, I have no way of knowing the attitude or intent of other drivers, but I can watch for actions I feel are suspicious. For instance, I am suspicious of another vehicle pacing me, especially if it's a carload of macho-looking young men with no signs of friendliness or a vehicle with dark tinted windows. These folks could be just curious about my bike, or it could just be coincidence that the other vehicle speeds up or slows down when I do, but I'd rather err on the side of being paranoid. I know of one situation in which a fellow rider had a sudden blowout while riding next to a carload of suspicious characters, and the shop later found a bullet inside the tire. I don't even acknowledge their existence; I simply change speed or lanes to put space or other vehicles between us and get on with the ride.

Other drivers are more likely to give you respect when you give them respect. You don't have to be a wimp to be polite. When you enter a busy highway, dial on some speed quickly to avoid holding up traffic behind you. Signal your lane changes and turns at least three seconds in advance. In city traffic, avoid the obnoxious habits of sudden or frequent lane changes, tailgating, or blipping the throttle. Keep your headlight on low beam in the daytime and adjust it properly for nighttime use. When another driver is trying to change lanes in busy traffic, back off and give him some room. When following or passing another vehicle, maintain at least two seconds separation. When passing, don't crowd the other vehicle. Move entirely over into the other lane. Once you have passed, keep rolling fast enough to avoid holding up the vehicle you have just passed, even if the driver responds by speeding up.

If you dress the part of a bad guy in a terrorist biker movie, wouldn't you think other motorists would treat you as road scum?

Would a Sharper Image Help?

Think about this for a moment: the motorcycle you ride and the gear you wear have an effect on others. Movie-makers and advertising agencies continue to portray motorcyclists as criminals or dangerous scum, like those bad guys in *Road Warriors*. And some riders seem to enjoy fulfilling that image. How do we know those bad guys are seriously bad? Well, they dress the part, don't they? Lots of black, scraggly, sinister clothing with prominent spikes, chains, floppy braid, and assorted nasty weapons.

Face it: if your image evokes distaste or loathing in other drivers, you are sending the message that you are not worthy of their respect—and therefore not worthy of your road space. To put this another way, if you look like one of the bad guys in a terrorist biker movie, you shouldn't be surprised that other drivers treat you as scum rather than as a fellow motorist.

You can help defuse aggressive situations just by maintaining the appearance of a skilled motorcyclist who is in charge of the situation but respectful of others. Part of that is what you wear, and part of that is what you do. Consider the implications of quality riding gear in a color other than black and a clean, quiet machine with no-nonsense luggage.

Loud Pipes

Some riders believe that a noisy bike decreases their risk of a collision. Others apparently think that loud pipes are somehow part of their rights, that noise isn't anybody's business but the rider's, or that it's justifiable to make noise if that's the only way to make more horsepower. Some riders know their slip-on muffler generates an aggressive bark, but they reason that their pipes aren't really that loud. Contrary to those pseudo-serious Loud Pipes Save Lives stickers, noise basically annoys people and demonstrates that you are impolite and self-centered.

But does noise affect your risks of riding? Obviously, the drivers and bystanders behind you at the moment may be more aware of your presence, but the drivers who are most likely to collide with you are in front of you, not behind you. What may affect risk is the attitude others form about motorcyclists, and that may not be positive. A noisy bike tends to generate aggressiveness toward motorcycles. And shouldn't we expect that the driver who is annoyed by one rider's loud pipes or loutish behavior will take out his frustration on the next motorcyclist to happen along?

If you've replaced your stock (and legal) exhaust with something louder, at least pay attention to what other people are doing and where the pipes are pointed. For example, it's really obnoxious to fire up your bike with the straight pipes pointed directly at the restaurant window. Yes, everyone inside will turn to look at you, but they will not be admiring you. Push it across the parking lot and turn it around before you start it, and then ride away as quietly as possible. If you must ride through a quiet residential neighborhood at 5 a.m., keep the revs down. And see if you can stop blipping the throttle while you're waiting for a red light in front of the church on Sunday morning.

Being polite, neat, proficient, and quiet won't guarantee that you will avoid all the aggressive crazies out there, but it will go a long way toward reducing the tensions that can trigger aggressive confrontations with other motorists. And when you are confronted by an aggressive driver, remember that your job is to get out of the way and get over it.

Evasive Action

On more than one occasion, I have suggested that if you understand what's likely to occur in traffic, continuously scan the situation twelve seconds ahead, and know what to look for, you can usually make a few small corrections early and just avoid riding into a problem. If you wait until the problem gets closer, you have less and less time to take any evasive action. Frankly, if you wait until the last couple of seconds prior to impact to do something, it's probably too late to make any difference.

But once in a while you just don't get much advance warning of a problem. When teaching rider training courses, I used to pull ridiculous situations out of the hat as examples of emergencies that might occur with little warning. *You're riding down the freeway when a portable toilet tips out of the truck ahead. Should you brake or should you swerve? You're cruising across town when suddenly an escaped zoo elephant charges out into the street. What evasive action would you take?*

What surprised me is that I would often have some student come up after class, saying, "You're not going to believe this, but I *did* have to swerve around a portable toilet that fell off a truck. And just last year an elephant *did* escape from the zoo and was crossing the street." I discovered that whatever strange hazards I could think of

You may believe that you have the right-of-way over that right-turning car, but your job is to get out of the way and get over your indignation.

had occurred to some rider somewhere. Sooner or later, most of us will encounter some problem we couldn't have predicted, and we'll either take some evasive action or bite the elephant, so to speak.

Battle Stations!

When you are faced with an impending collision, there are only three evasive actions you can take with a motorcycle: speed up, swerve, or slow down. The trouble is, evasive maneuvers all depend on traction, and traction is a limited commodity. If you attempt to swerve while also braking hard, the bike tends to swap ends, fall down, or flip into a highside barrel roll. Pulling off a successful evasive maneuver requires that you make a split-second decision on what to do and then have the skill for the maneuver you've selected. To help prepare for that split-second decision, let's think through the advantages and disadvantages of those three evasive maneuvers.

When you are faced with an impending collision, you have only three options to choose from: speed up, swerve, or slow down.

Accelerating

Let's say you observe a car approaching an intersection from the other direction, and you suspect the other driver is planning an aggressive left turn without slowing or signaling. If you predict what's happening sufficiently in advance, you could gas it and squirt around the front of the car. Then again, maybe a garbage truck will pull out of a side street and you'll just end up planting your chin into the back of the truck.

The big advantage of accelerating is that motorcycles typically have lots of power. It's very easy to accelerate—all you have to do is roll the throttle open and hang on. Accelerating would be a good choice for a situation such as a driver merging onto the freeway who doesn't appear to understand the concept of yield. The big disadvantage of accelerating is that speed increases forward energy. And kinetic energy increases much faster than speed. That means that if you do end up colliding with something at a faster speed, the impact forces will be much greater. For instance, the impact force at 60 mph is about 150 percent greater than the impact force at 50 mph.

Speeding up also makes it harder to change direction. You might be able to swerve around a car at 30 mph, but not at 40 mph. And even if you do manage to accelerate around the left-turner and then realize you've got to brake hard to avoid slamming into the back of that garbage truck, your chances go into the garbage, so to speak. Once you've accelerated, you've pretty well canceled out the other options. So accelerating is seldom a good evasive tactic for situations such as a left-turner at an intersection.

Swerving

Maybe you could swerve around the offending driver. Swerving doesn't increase forward energy, so it is possible to swerve and then straighten up and brake hard without increasing braking distance. Of course, swerving successfully depends on being able to predict which way the obstructing vehicle is going to move and being able to swerve the bike without dropping it. If you choose to swerve, it would be helpful to know whether the driver is going to continue or is going to panic and screech to a halt halfway across your lane. The behavior of other drivers is hard to predict.

Swerving isn't too clever for animals in the road, either. A loose dog may be homing in on your front wheel no matter which way you swerve. And a wild animal such as a deer or antelope will very likely try to evade you with sudden, unpredictable changes of direction. If you manage to swerve around an animal scampering around on the pavement, it's probably more luck than skill. Of course, there are times when swerving is the best maneuver. Let's say you don't realize that dark spot in the pavement is a deep pothole and you need to swerve around it. Or you need to swerve to position the bike to cross a hazard such as a slippery railroad crossing.

Be aware that swerving can eat up all of the available traction, even at modest street speeds. If you're trying to do a maximum effort swerve, you really can't afford to squander any traction on accelerating or braking. You could brake first to scrub off some energy, then get off the brakes and swerve. Or you could swerve first to

Swerving is a good choice to avoid or negotiate fixed surface hazards. For instance, you could swerve over to the left side of the lane and then swerve right to get lined up to cross these slippery wooden aprons surrounding the rails.

avoid the problem, then brake or accelerate. But swerving while either accelerating or braking is very likely to result in a slideout.

The big problem with swerving is that the normal survival reaction to an emergency is to snap off the throttle, and that eats rear-wheel traction as the engine tries to slow the rear wheel. A successful swerve requires that you maintain a steady throttle until the bike is straightened out again. Frankly, when faced with an obstruction such as a garbage truck in your path, you are very likely to panic and roll off the throttle before you can resist the urge. That's why few riders manage to pull off a maximum-effort swerve without dropping the bike.

There's a lot of evidence indicating that we revert to habits in emergencies. If that's true, then the best practice for swerving is probably just riding a really twisty road that requires lots of aggressive leaning, so that pushing forcefully on the grips becomes part of your habit patterns. If you are paranoid about leaning the bike over into sharp turns, it is unlikely that in an emergency you'll manage more than a gentle swerve. If you're used to leaning the bike over to steep lean angles in tight curves, you'll probably swerve when it's called for without having to think about it. In my opinion, practicing emergency swerves is a waste of time.

Braking

Hard braking is a reliable evasive maneuver and probably the best tactic for avoiding intersection collisions and wild animals. It's also a skill you can practice, both on a braking chute and in your daily riding. On today's motorcycles, the front brakes are typically more powerful than the engine, and today's tire compounds have excellent traction. With the correct technique, you can probably bring the bike to a stop in less distance than it took the engine to accelerate up to that speed.

Many motorcycles are available with exotic brake systems such as ABS, but brake systems can't save you from the mistake of attempting to swerve while braking or attempting to brake hard while leaned over in a curve. And lightweight sportbikes with double disk systems, multiple piston calipers, and sticky tire compounds add up to awesome braking power that can literally stand a motorcycle on its nose with a modest squeeze on the brake lever. But, regardless of your machinery, hard braking requires some skill. And the only way to gain skill is to practice the right techniques.

What If You Can't Stop in Time?

In spite of your best efforts, you might not be able to stop short of a collision. Some police academies still teach laying it down to motor officers, even though police motor pools these days are full of bikes with good rubber and ABS. Some riders have suggested crash jumping, a technique of standing up on the pegs at the last second and vaulting upward to clear the other vehicle. Other riders think it might be better to just slide off the bike to avoid getting caught between the two vehicles. Some manufacturers are working on motorcycle airbags to help cushion a rider against an impact.

It might sound a little macabre to think about crashing into things, but if you realize that you're going to crash into something, wouldn't the highest priority be to reduce the impact forces? None of the above tactics do much to reduce forward energy, and all of them assume you've got the time and the focus to do something other than hang on with wide eyes.

Even if you realize you can't stop short of a collision, you can reduce the injury forces by staying on the brakes right up to impact.

Yes, crash jumping might allow you to fly over the left-turner as your bike slams into the side of a car, but it's not very likely you could jump over a truck-based van or pickup. Sure, you could lay it down, but a bike doesn't stop just because it's grinding along on the foot pegs and axle nuts, and you could get seriously injured if it highsides. Sliding off the bike? Not for me. There might be an advantage to airbags on a motorcycle, but only if the systems can be made to work flawlessly. It would be terribly inconvenient if the airbag deployed due to an electrical malfunction while I was riding in rush-hour traffic.

From my perspective, if you've got time to do anything, you've got time to brake, and braking reduces the impact force. Rubber has a lot more traction than plastic or steel does. If I can't avoid a smasho, my theory is that it's a lot better to collide at 10 mph than at 30 mph. I'll keep it on the rubber, thank you, and brake hard right up to impact.

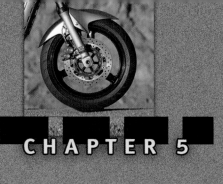

CHAPTER 5

Booby Traps

SURFACE HAZARDS

Here's Biker Bob, tooling along his favorite road, braking smoothly before each turn, scrutinizing the shape of the curve ahead to plot the right line, leaning the bike by pushing on the low grip, and rolling on the gas to maintain speed and ground clearance. The air is heating up, but it's not uncomfortable. Traffic is light, the pavement is dry, and there haven't been any deer migration signs. You can't see his expression inside his Shoei, but he's had a grin on his face for the last 100 miles. This, thinks Bob, is what motorcycling is all about.

Suddenly, as Bob rolls on around a left-hand sweeper, the rear tire steps sideways. Bob's heart leaps into his throat and his survival reactions take over: He snaps off the throttle. Before he can comprehend what's happening, the machine slams down on its side and squirts off into the trees in a trail of shattered plastic. Bob won't even remember coming off the low side. His next memory is of sliding and tumbling and how unforgiving the pavement feels hammering through his leathers.

As he painfully gets up, Bob reaches for his throbbing right elbow and recoils as he feels something slippery. In spite of the pain, he twists his elbow around to look for the source of the blood. His elbow is slippery, but it isn't blood. Rubbing his glove finger in the liquid, he smells it. Oil! Biker Bob has just gotten a lesson about surface hazards. He had been so engrossed in the curves and his cornering technique that he had failed to notice a trail of spilled diesel oil.

The very thing that makes motorcycles so much fun to corner is also their Achilles' heel: two-wheelers demand traction just to balance upright. If a car or sidecar rig loses traction on one or two tires, the driver can be pretty ho-hum about it. But if a two-wheeler loses traction on even one tire, the rider will be lucky to avoid a falldown.

Instinctively, we all know this. But you may not understand how to detect surface hazards or what to do about them. Even when you see changes in the road surface, you may not comprehend how different surfaces change the traction equation. And when a tire suddenly loses its grip on the road, your survival reactions tend to work against you. Let's think about some common surface hazards and then consider some techniques for keeping the rubber side down even through those slippery spots.

Remember that two-wheelers are balanced by constantly steering the front wheel from side to side. Front-end geometry helps balance the machine automatically by constantly steering itself into a balanced condition. To turn, you unbalance the machine until it falls over into a lean and then control the angle of lean by adjusting pressure on the grips. Balance is so automatic that you may not think about how traction is related to balance. But it is important to understand that balance depends on front-tire traction, whether it's the front-end geometry balancing itself or the rider making steering inputs. And, as Biker Bob discovered, a rear-wheel skid in a curve can cause a slideout.

Traction

That rolling grip between the rubber tire and road surface is really a matter of the rubber changing shape slightly to conform to the little dimples and bumps in the surface. So traction involves both the tire and the surface. Slide your hand over some carpet, and you'll feel resistance as your skin tries to conform to the lumps and bumps of thread. Slide your hand over a plastic countertop, and there is much less resistance, or traction, because there are fewer lumps or bumps into which your skin can squeeze. A rough concrete road has more traction than does a shiny steel plate. Dribble a little water on the smooth countertop, and you'll see that traction decreases even more when wet.

Hard rubber has less traction than soft rubber does because compliant rubber can more quickly squish into the surface irregularities to get a grip. That's also why too much pressure in a tire reduces traction. If a tire is overinflated, it can't as easily squeeze into conformity with the pavement. Lower pressure improves traction, which is an advantage for unpaved roads but would overheat the tire carcass at highway speeds. So tire pressure is a compromise between traction and reliability.

With correct pressure in your tires for highway speeds, how much surface area would you guess your tire contact patches have? Would you say that both tires together have about as much area as this page you're reading? Would it surprise you to know that the contact patch area of either of your tires is about the same size as one of the paragraphs on this page? Considering that tire traction is the connection between the bike and the road, you should never scrimp on tires, and you should check frequently to ensure that tire pressures are correct for the load you intend to carry.

Study the Surface Texture and Color

Biker Bob crashed because he was allowing his mind to wander just enough that he ignored the road surface. On public roads, creative thoughts, scenery, and even cornering lines must always be secondary to surface traction. What should Bob have been looking for?

One key to spotting surface hazards is recognizing that you have a pretty good idea of the available traction of the surface under your tires at the moment. So the technique for spotting potential traction changes is looking for changes in surface texture or color. If you see a change in the texture or color of the surface ahead, that indicates a possible change in traction. For example, if your tires are now on clean pavement, you know by the feel that traction is good. But if the color and texture of the surface ahead changes to something else, that's an indication that traction is different ahead. For instance, if the surface of the road ahead has a rougher texture, you

Is that new pavement ahead or loose gravel? The change in color and texture alerts you to the probability of a traction change. Actually, the surface ahead is loose gravel spread over a new coating of soft asphalt. When you see a change in the surface color or texture, you should reduce traction demands until you figure out what the change means.

might predict that it's loose gravel. Had Bob been observing the surface, he might have noticed the darker color and multicolored sheen of spilled oil on the surface and taken the hint that traction was getting scarce in the middle of the lane.

You know about traction under your tires at the moment because you can feel it. The surface ahead has a rougher texture, which is a clue that traction is different. In this situation, the rougher texture happens to be loose gravel covering a sewer installation. You can't depend upon official warning signs for such situations.

Slick Surfaces

Most of us understand that frost is slippery, and we know what frost looks like: you can see the white color or perhaps observe the twinkling crystals of frozen water. Shiny steel construction plates obviously have a smooth texture that hints at less traction. Railroad tracks get polished smooth by passing traffic, and many crossings have wooden or plastic aprons that can be very slippery when wet. Less obvious are the grease traps left in the center of left-turn lanes by idling vehicles, spilled fuel that blends with the color of the asphalt, and various contaminants that collect on the road surface during dry weather. Some white plastic lane markings are almost as slippery as frost, and they are just as obvious. As with that countertop experiment, slick surfaces get even slicker when wet. It takes about a half hour of downpour to wash off the accumulated drippings and droppings, especially if it hasn't rained for a while. Clever riders take a break during the first half hour of a fresh rain to allow time for the surface to regain traction.

It takes about a half hour of steady rain to wash away the various slippery contaminants that have collected on the pavement. That's the reason for taking a break when it first starts to rain after a dry spell.

Any soft paving material that wears away quickly can be slippery when wet. Bricks have reasonably good traction when dry, but the brick dust mixes with rainwater to make slippery clay. Wooden bridge decks or railroad crossings can be very slick when wet, as the wood particles mix with water to form a slimy paste. You won't get reliable texture or color clues about such hazards because the particles look the same as the rest of the surface. Just file away in your brain that when wet, brick and wooden surfaces get just as slippery as wet clay.

Some white arrows and lane markings are made of shiny plastic that can be very slippery when wet. Try to keep your tires off anything white.

Railroad crossings have aprons next to the rails that are often made of wood or plastic that can be just as slippery as the shiny steel when wet. The big hazard is when the tracks cross the road at an angle.

The brick surface of this old street has good traction when dry, but when it rains, brick dust mixes with rainwater to make slippery clay.

When it rains, wood particles mix with water to make a slippery lubricant.

Loose Stuff

We must also be aware of flat debris on the surface, such as a flattened soda can, a pizza box, or a crushed plastic oil bottle. If you put your tires over any such loose objects, they could lose traction with the road. For instance, if you happen to be braking when your front tire rolls up on top of a flattened cardboard box, the tire can grip the box, and the box can slide across the surface like a ski under your front wheel. If it isn't obvious, you'll lose steering, and if you don't quickly release the front brake to roll off the box, you'll lose balance.

This flattened cardboard box may not look dangerous, but if you are braking while crossing it, you could lose control or balance.

Gravel lifts the rubber off the pavement surface and acts like little ball bearings rolling around under the tire. In many parts of the country, highway crews seal coat the surface by spreading loose gravel over tacky oil and then letting traffic grind the gravel into a new layer. They don't always put up warning signs, or the signs may not follow the crew down the road. Loose gravel on the road has a rough texture and often a lighter or different shade of color. Companion clues for loose gravel on the pavement are the painted lines disappearing under the stones and dust thrown up by passing vehicles.

Sand, dirt, and mud are more insidious because such loose stuff may be the same color and texture as the hard surface underneath. Best clues for such hazards are how the pavement relates to the surrounding roadside. In farm country, be aware of field work adjacent to the road. Farm equipment can track a lot of fresh mud or dirt onto the road. Be wary of pavement downhill from a field that has been plowed, especially following a rainstorm or if it has being irrigated. Out in the country, roadside dirt and sand can drift onto the surface at any time of year, yet look just like the hard paving. Here, the relation of the road to the roadside is the best clue. Wherever there is a dirt bank uphill from the road, be wary of loose dirt or sand that may have drifted out onto the surface.

This seal coating operation is obvious here, but if there are no warning signs or cones, your only clue may be the different surface texture.

This may look like only a little water running across the road, but actually it's six inches of slippery mud washed out of that field on the right by last night's rainstorm.

Narrow canyon roads in the southwest United States typically don't have ditches. Such roads in dry climates are infamous for having loose sand blown out by strong winds or washed onto the surface during thundershowers. A rain shower can flush several inches of slippery silt over the surface wherever the road dips to a lower elevation than the surrounding landscape. You may catch a glimpse of dirty color, but your best clue is simply being aware of where mud could wash out. In the spring, in climates where temperatures drop below freezing in the winter, leftover sand from wintertime maintenance tends to gather near intersections, usually collecting as a berm toward the outside edge of the wheel tracks. When you see construction taking place ahead, whether a shopping center or a bungalow, be prepared for dirt and mud to be tracked out onto the surface by the tires of construction vehicles.

Conserving Traction

If the whole lane has a traction problem such as loose gravel, it is important to reduce lean angles in turns and to avoid any sudden throttle, steering, or braking inputs. On slippery or loose surfaces, it is just as important to avoid suddenly rolling off the throttle. In Biker Bob's situation, his panic survival reaction to roll off the gas transferred weight off the rear tire and applied engine braking that demanded more traction. The front tire wiggled on the slippery surface, but it was the rear tire that slid out and caused the crash. Maybe Bob couldn't have saved the day by smarter control, but perhaps holding a steady throttle would have conserved just enough traction to slither through without falling.

The tactic for slippery off-camber surfaces is to lean the bike to keep your wheels perpendicular to the road surface.

OK, let's assume that Bob knew what to look for and that he spotted the oil. What could he have done about shrinking traction? The trick is to conserve whatever traction you've got. On Bob's road, the oil was only in the center of the lane. Bob could simply have slowed down and kept his tires out of the oil streak. And even if the oil spill covered the whole road, Bob could have modified his line to get the bike vertical as he crossed the slippery section.

What about road camber? What if the road slants off to one side? The veteran tactic is to counterbalance the motorcycle to keep the tires perpendicular to the road surface. If the tires do slide, the bike can slide sideways with less risk of falling down. It's the same tactic that's used for riding across a patch of wet grass, glare ice, or loose gravel on a surface that isn't level.

Reducing speed for corners also reduces traction demands. The slower the speed, the less the side loads on the tires to push it around the corner. Let's imagine Bob approaching what appears to be a seal-coated section of road with deep, loose gravel. Bob could straighten the bike up and brake hard to scrub off speed before reaching the gravel, then ease off the brakes and roll back on just enough throttle to stabilize the bike.

Dirt riders use the throttle to steer through loose gravel. Of course, if you don't have those "big doggie" knobby tires, you won't be able to throw a gravel rooster tail, but it helps to follow the dirt-bike advice: when in doubt—gas it! Unless you've got knobby tires that provide better sliding control, it's best to keep your feet on the pegs and keep speed down.

Ah, but you never ride off pavement, right? What about detours? Faced with a detour on some highway construction project, you can either turn around and go home or ride the dirt. If you are faced with a muddy or gravelly detour, remember that a narrow motorcycle doesn't have to follow the truck tracks. Look for the best traction. Find a strip of road that hasn't been churned to a mess, put your tires over the best surface, and follow the slippery surface techniques, including leaning the bike to keep the wheels perpendicular to the surface.

When riding through a detour or construction area, put your tires over the most tractable surface, even if it's not the tire tracks of other vehicles.

If your motorcycle does get stuck in a muddy rut and threatens to fall down, don't be a hero. Get out of the way, and let it do what it wants without frying your calf or breaking your leg in the process. Plastic is cheaper than surgery.

Riding Practice

If the thought of riding on wet grass or slippery mud makes you nervous, you aren't alone. But sooner or later, you're going to have to ride on a slick or loose surface. The solution is to gain skill rather than just worry about trying to avoid surface hazards. Borrow someone's dirt bike, and practice with those knobby tires at first. Wait for the snow to melt, put on all your crash padding, and go find some slippery and loose surfaces to ride on your street machine. Ride slowly around the back lawn. Try that fire road or power line road. Find a nice gravel farm road, or go exploring those dirt roads up in the national forest. Watch for texture or color changes ahead. Remember the techniques:

- Reduce speed
- Weight on foot pegs
- Pick best surface; follow smooth lines
- Steady throttle hand
- Bike perpendicular to the road surface.

Once you've gotten in a few hours on some unpaved back roads, you'll lose a lot of paranoia about a few little patches of gravel or a slippery wooden bridge.

Curbs Ahead

Rider Ralph is cruising down a four-lane divided arterial on a warm summer evening, minding his own business and thinking about what he will do when he gets home. Then he notices some construction cones and a sign that says BUMP. When his front tire bounces down onto the gouged-away surface, he realizes that the old asphalt has been ground away in preparation for repaving. A novice rider might have been unnerved by the tires wiggling around in the grooves, but Ralph is a veteran rider, and he knows the bike will find its way through a little uneven pavement.

Traffic in the right lane is slowing, and Ralph realizes traffic is merging into the left lane. Ralph picks a space and eases the wiggling bike over toward what appears to be smoother pavement. But suddenly, just as his front wheel reaches the raised edge, the handlebars are yanked from his grasp. The bike seems intent on falling over on its left side, and even after pulling as hard as he can on the grips to countersteer the machine upright, Ralph can't maintain balance. The bike crashes over hard on its side, with Ralph's leg trapped between the

The rough road surface where the paving has been ground away may cause your tires to wiggle around, but the real hazard is that raised pavement edge on the left.

frame and the road. His motorcycle ride is over for the evening—and for the months it will take for his broken bones to knit.

What caused Rider Ralph's crash was the exposed edge of the old pavement that had been left in place, with the asphalt in the right lane ground away. The raised edge of the pavement formed what you can think of as a curb right out in the middle of the street. For an automobile driver, merging into a curb in the middle of the street might have resulted in a front end bent out of alignment or a dented wheel rim. For a motorcyclist, attempting to cross the edge of the pavement resulted in a spill and serious injuries to both bike and rider.

The raised edges at the sides of the ground-away pavement are like low curbs that can easily trap the front tire of a motorcycle and cause loss of balance.

Rider Ralph isn't the only motorcyclist who has been surprised by a hard pavement edge, and that includes veterans who you think would have learned everything. What appears to be just a bump or a crack in the pavement suddenly upsets the bike, and the hapless rider can't maintain balance. I call such pavement edges edge traps because of the way a motorcycle wheel gets trapped against the raised edge of the pavement, making it impossible to steer.

Two-wheelers are particularly vulnerable to pavement edges or grooves. Remember, a two-wheeler is balanced mostly by steering the front wheel, whether that's a result of front-end geometry or rider input at the grips. For example, if a motorcycle starts to fall over to the left, you can steer the front wheel more to the left to rebalance. The term for this balancing act is *countersteering* because we initially steer opposite—counter to—the direction of lean. It's also how we control direction. To turn right, push on the right grip. To straighten up from a right turn, push on the left grip.

Countersteering explains why edge traps are so hazardous to two-wheelers while only a jarring, wheel-bending inconvenience to other vehicles. A car or a sidecar rig can slide sideways without losing balance, but if the rider of a two-wheeler loses steering for more than a couple of seconds, it becomes very difficult to maintain balance. Easing up to a curb, you can maintain balance right up to the point where the front wheel contacts the edge. After that, with the tire scrubbing along the edge of the curb, you can't countersteer to maintain balance.

When you find yourself in a lane where the pavement has been gouged away, the feeling of the rough surface prompts you to start looking for a smoother place to ride. There's that smooth shoulder beckoning you to ease on over or that nice new pavement on the other lane. But if you try to ease over the edge, your front tire is likely to get trapped, and you'll lose balance. It's important to recognize that even a modest pavement edge can cause a spill if you attempt to ease over it at a narrow angle. In effect, a raised pavement edge is just like a curb at the side of a street.

How do you get across a curb without falling? The trick is to cross it aggressively at a maximum angle rather than attempting to ease over, and to use a little power to bounce the front wheel up. Imagine trying to ride your motorcycle over a curb, up onto the sidewalk. First, you'd want to slow down to avoid bending a rim. Then you would want to get the bike pointed straight at the curb, or at least at a 45-degree angle, and roll on some throttle to bounce the tire up over the edge.

In tests conducted years ago by the Motorcycle Safety Foundation, professional riders attempting to swerve around an obstruction from pavement to a gravel shoulder and back onto the pavement again were amazed when several crashes occurred.

To climb over a hard pavement edge, first swing away, then steer back at a wider angle, get a good grip on the bars, and roll on some throttle to drive the front tire up onto the higher surface. The minimum approach angle is 45 degrees.

Looking a little more closely, the experts discovered that a spill was more likely if the rider swerved back toward the pavement edge at an angle of less than 45 degrees.

Edge traps come in a variety of disguises. You'll have to spot them for yourself, because you're probably never going to get a warning sign that says Motorcycle Edge Traps. Newer asphalt often sinks under the pounding of traffic, exposing the sharp edge of adjacent concrete pavement—a common situation in which an older road has been widened or lanes repositioned. Old paving several layers down may shift or sink, allowing a groove to form at the surface. When a road is repaved, there will be a steep raised edge above the shoulder until it is filled and graded. And even when the shoulder is graded level with the pavement, your front tire can sink in the soft gravel and be trapped on the edge. Any location where you must cross a raised pavement edge is a serious hazard.

Heads up! This temporary lane crosses an edge trap. To cross this raised edge, swing over to the right, then swerve back to the left to drive your front tire up onto the raised concrete surface.

Whenever you approach a work zone or observe a change in pavement ahead, start looking for edge traps. As with all surface hazards, the trick is to look for changes in surface color or texture, especially any ground-away pavement or shadows that indicate grooves or raised edges. You already have some idea of the surface you're riding on. When you see a different surface ahead, you should be prepared for the transition from this surface to the next. Even at night, you should be able to distinguish between asphalt and the smoother, lighter appearance of concrete or the shinier appearance of a polished steel construction plate or streetcar rail.

If you don't have to change lanes, just stay away from those edge traps, especially those curbs at the sides of a lane where pavement has been ground away. Even if there is a pavement edge sauntering into your lane, you can usually sneak by a few inches away. The key is to avoid letting your front tire get close to a raised edge or to a groove.

White Curbs

One very insidious type of edge trap is the white line between two merging traffic lanes. For instance, the on-ramp to a freeway may be separated from the freeway lane by a long white line to provide an acceleration lane. But sometimes the white line is painted on a curb-shaped lane divider. Such curbs form serious edge traps, and they are particularly difficult to see at night. Since you can't always predict whether a solid white line is painted on a level surface or on a divider curb, the smart tip is to avoid crossing solid white lines at merging locations. Where it is safe to change lanes, the solid white line will change to white dashes. In some states it is illegal to merge over a solid white line.

You may be tempted to change lanes over that white line, but don't do it. The white line in this situation is painted on a narrow island that could knock the wheels out from under you.

Slick Edges

Railroad and streetcar tracks can form great booby traps for motorcyclists, even when the rails are level with the surface. Remember, if the front tire starts to slide sideways or gets captured by a groove, it instantly gets harder to keep the motorcycle balanced upright. Railroad crossings are especially hazardous when the tracks cross the street at a narrow angle, at a curve in the road, or parallel to your path of travel. Streetcar tracks are especially dangerous because the rails often run down the middle of a lane or wander from lane to lane. Cable car tracks such as those in San Francisco are a special challenge, with two streetcar rails plus a steel-lined cable slot.

Cable car tracks, such as these in San Francisco, are a special challenge, with two rails plus a steel-lined cable slot.

Working your way through old railroad sidings without dropping the bike can be a real challenge. It's important to cross each rail at maximum angle, preferably 45 degrees or more.

Try to avoid X and V traps like this, where your tire could drop into a slot and wedge tight. In this situation, you could sneak by on the narrow patch of pavement. If you must cross an X or V, cross at maximum angle, not parallel to the rails.

The important tactic for negotiating rails is to keep your tires out of the grooves, and when you must cross a rail, treat it as an edge trap. Swing away from it, then steer back across at an angle. Try to get the motorcycle vertical and stable as you cross the rail, even if you have just completed a swerve. The wood, plastic, or steel covers adjacent to the rails at street crossings should be assumed to be slippery even when dry and treacherous when wet. In industrial areas, some railroad spurs are used only occasionally, so you shouldn't be surprised at gaping holes and deep grooves near the rails that never seem to get fixed.

X and V Traps

Sometimes you will encounter two tracks that cross each other or come together in the middle of the street. Such connections form serious X and V traps where a motorcycle tire will slide into the V or even drop into a narrow slot and wedge tight, with obvious consequences. When you observe such X or V traps in the street or grooves in the planks, the trick is to pick a path of travel that gets around the Xs or Vs or at least crosses them at the maximum angle you can achieve in the maneuvering room you have available.

Construction Plates

Those giant steel plates construction crews use to cover holes in the street may get polished to a shine, but the edges are just as hazardous as the slick surface. The plates are thick enough to form edge traps at the sides. There is an additional reason to stay away from the edges: the plate may be a few inches narrower than the hole in the street or may have shifted under the pounding of truck traffic. Where a normal automobile tire would bridge a 4-inch slot at the edge of the plate, a motorcycle tire might be just narrow enough to drop in for a serious visit.

Steel construction plates are usually polished slick by the tires of passing vehicles, but the edges of the plates are often thick enough to form serious edge traps.

Although you must be paying primary attention to other vehicles while riding in traffic, a veteran rider learns to maintain awareness of surface hazards as well as traffic and chooses a path of travel that puts the tires on the most tractable pavement. When you do spot an obvious edge trap ahead that you know you'll have to cross, you can simply maneuver your motorcycle to cross it correctly and continue to focus on traffic.

The Hurt Report indicated that only 4 percent of motorcycle accidents were triggered by surface hazards. That's why rider training courses don't waste any time on loose gravel or edge traps. But remember that the Hurt Report was based on crashes in the Los Angeles area. Other cities, such as Seattle, St. Louis, or Washington DC have different surface hazards than Los Angeles does.

Wherever you ride, if you drop your machine trying to ease over an edge trap, the statistics for you will be 100 percent. So you might want to practice some edge-crossing exercises on your own before you get the big test out on the streets, and keep edge traps in mind when you are riding in an unfamiliar area.

Trouble Ahead

One of the reasons riders get snagged by edge traps is that we don't usually get fair warning of the problem. Road contractors must use specific signs for specific construction situations. For example, the suggested warning sign for a change in pavement elevation might be Bump. The construction contractor may get reports that a surprising number of motorcyclists have crashed in a work zone, but it isn't clear why the crashes occurred. Road maintenance departments aren't trained about the dynamics of two-wheelers, so they can't be expected to understand why a bike might crash. The common misconception is that it's just a matter of an inexperienced rider, excessive speed, or inattention. Various warning signs have been tried, including

OK, this is a fictional sign, but maybe if they put up signs like this for edge traps, the problem would be more obvious.

Whenever you see construction zone signs like this, you should be prepared for an edge trap such as a raised pavement edge. A bump can angle across the lane, creating a serious edge trap.

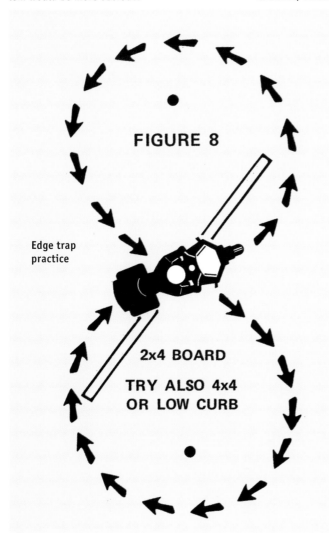

FIGURE 8

Edge trap practice

2x4 BOARD

TRY ALSO 4x4 OR LOW CURB

Bump, Abrupt Lane Edge, Motorcycles Use Extreme Caution, and Motorcycles Do Not Change Lanes. If Ralph had seen a sign that said Curbs in Road, he might have understood the problem. When you see orange construction zone signs, you should be prepared for surface hazards such as loose gravel and raised pavement edges.

Riding Practice

Here's an exercise you can practice to gain some experience crossing edge traps. Be sure to wear your crash padding just in case you haven't quite absorbed the correct techniques yet. Ride a figure-8 path over different edges, concentrating on positioning your motorcycle to cross as close to a right angle as possible and using a bit of throttle to drive the front tire up and over. Yeah, it gets harder as you move down the list.

- A wood 2 x 4 or 2 x 6 that's at least 6 feet long
- A low curb
- A stiff garden hose
- A large-diameter rope that's at least 10 feet long

The unfortunate reality is that the pavement doesn't go on forever.

Running Out of Pavement

It had been a long day in the saddle. I was homeward bound from Denver to Seattle, trying to make time on the superslab. The afternoon had been baking hot with gusting crosswinds across eastern Utah, so when night fell, I kept riding to take advantage of the cooler evening temperatures. The pavement was smooth and so new it was still black. They hadn't even painted any lines yet. All I could see of the dark pavement was the next hundred feet or so that would momentarily be illuminated by the headlight beam and then quickly pass under my tires. I began to notice road signs lying face down on the shoulder, apparently leftovers from the repaving work. But then something odd attracted my attention: the lights of cars ahead seemed to be wiggling sideways. I blinked my eyes. Maybe I had been too many hours in the saddle.

And then my headlight beam flickered off the end of the pavement into deeply rutted dirt. The paving just ended. With my brain struggling to comprehend what was happening, the loaded bike dropped off the edge at 60 mph and plowed into the soft earth, the front tire dodging one way and then the other. Fighting for control, I rolled on the throttle to roost the bike forward. Several hundred feet of black terror later, the front tire bounced up onto smooth pavement and I was again cruising through the black night as if nothing had happened.

Apparently, all four lanes of the freeway had been torn up for repaving, and the construction signs had blown down in the afternoon wind. The wiggling taillights were from drivers ahead plowing through the ruts.

It's easy to think of yourself as either a street or a dirt rider, as if your machine rather than your skills defined you. But I've seen some touring machines sporting proof they have experienced off-pavement missions to Prudhoe Bay or Tierra del Fuego. I've also seen more than a few dual sportbikes dressed with big fuel tanks and shiny aluminum adventure-touring cases but nary a dent, scratch, or speck of dust in the crevices. Obviously, some riders are more concerned about the adventure-touring image than in getting off the pavement. Back in the good old days before manufacturers and magazines started labeling bikes by type, we rode whatever we owned and went wherever we felt like going.

Now, obviously, street motorcycles are designed with a bias toward hard surfaces. But the pavement doesn't go on forever. There are times when we must ride off pavement, if only through a short detour or across the grass into the rally campground. And if you're a serious motorcycling traveler, you should possess sufficient off-pavement skills to handle a few miles of dirt without freaking out.

Dirt

For talking purposes, let's refer to all unpaved surfaces (sand, gravel, clay, grass, dirt, and so on) as dirt. Dirt does provide traction, although in ways different from what we expect of clean, dry pavement. Pavement just sits there. Dirt moves around dynamically. On pavement, the predictable traction gives you confidence to make precise steering corrections to control balance and direction. On dirt, traction is predictable, but it's not that firm connection you're used to on clean pavement. When you feel the tires dance around on pavement, that's a street feedback that you're about to get down and personal with the ground. On dirt, you not only need to avoid panic when the tires don't go exactly where you're thinking but also need to master some different control skills.

Riding on dirt requires some different control skills.

If you do suddenly find yourself facing a dirt road on your touring machine with street tires, you can increase traction by lowering tire pressures. Lower pressure means a larger footprint and better conformity to the surface. Dirt bikers sometimes run pressures as low as 8 or 10 psi. But remember that lower tire pressure also increases tire flex, which dramatically increases temperature. So if you do drop the pressure to do a little off-pavement exploring in Utah or to get through an unexpected sand dune on an Arizona highway, be sure to pump the tires up again before you roll back up to highway speed.

Balancing and Steering on Dirt

Even though there are tremendous differences in traction between different unpaved surfaces, the same basic techniques apply. On pavement, we balance mostly by steering the front wheel to control balance and direction. If the machine starts to fall over toward the left, we can countersteer the contact patch more toward the left to get the bike balanced again. On dirt, countersteering still works but not as predictably or as quickly as on good pavement. In loose or soft stuff, the front tire tends to plow sideways for a while instead of causing an immediate adjustment of balance. Two tactics that are essential to riding off-pavement are shifting body weight on the machine and steering more with the throttle than with the handlebars.

Load the Foot Pegs

You'll often see novice riders trying to negotiate loose gravel or wet grass by sitting bolt upright in the saddle and skidding their boots across the ground. Dragging your bootskids is a survival reaction to the panicky feel of steering being less responsive, but it doesn't do what you might expect.

Allowing your feet to waggle around upsets balance. The more novices drag their feet, the wobblier the bike gets. Next time you're in a position to observe riders negotiating a bit of dirt, you'll notice that the experts stand on the pegs and let the bike work around under them. Notice that with weight on the pegs, the expert rider braces against the handlebars and saddle and shifts weight to lean the bike.

The rider of a lightweight dirt bike may use a planted boot to help control the machine in a slide, but on a heavyweight touring machine with street tires, it's smarter to stand on the pegs. If your rubber tires don't have enough traction to keep a loaded touring bike upright, your leather boots probably won't do any better. What's more, dragging your feet on the ground is an invitation to broken ankles and barbecued shins. If your toe happens to catch on something solid, your foot could be bent back under the foot peg quicker than you can say "orthopedic surgeon."

High or Low Center of Mass?

When a rider is planted firmly in the saddle, with feet on the pegs and knees against the tank, the rider and bike move more as a combined mass, with a combined center about halfway between the rider's knees. Now, if the rider stands up on the pegs, doesn't that raise the combined CoM? Yes, by standing on the pegs, the rider's CoM will be higher. But be aware that a low CoM on a two-wheeler doesn't necessarily contribute to easier balance. Those skyscraper dual sport machines with big fuel tanks up high can be as controllable in loose gravel as a low-slung cruiser, and even more controllable with the rider's weight loaded down at the foot peg level.

Standing on the pegs allows the rider to more or less disconnect from the bike's mass, which allows the rider to lean the bike more quickly. Dirt riders typically stand on the pegs most of the time, leaning the bike separately from their body position for different conditions. The same tactic works for street bikes on dirt, although with more sluggish results.

Standing on the pegs raises the combined center of mass, which should make the bike more top heavy, but that's not so.

Standing on the pegs, the rider can more quickly lean the bike independently of the rider's mass.

The motorcycle is carrying the same weight, but separating the motorcycle's mass from the rider's provides more flexibility in controlling balance and lean angles. It is also a lot easier on your spine and kidneys to cushion bumps and dips with bent legs. It isn't necessary to stand on the pegs for miles and miles of hard-packed dirt or firm gravel, but when you are picking your way through a rutted detour or across a bumpy field, standing on the pegs will give you both better control and fewer spine-jolting body slams.

On some machines, style gets in the way of ergonomics. For example, the stylish forward-mounted footboards typical of cruisers make it very difficult and cumbersome to stand up and unload the saddle. Likewise, the forward-mounted handlebars of some sportbikes make it awkward because you just can't reach the bars while standing on the pegs.

Steering in the Dirt

With reduced traction in the dirt, countersteering doesn't produce the quick changes of direction the street rider expects. Besides, the front tire is giving lots of nervous feedback that it's on the verge of washing out, and it probably is. The street instinct is to strangle the handlebars with a death grip, look down at the gravel just ahead of the front tire, keep the bike absolutely vertical, and let it go wherever it seems to want to go, even if that's off the edge of the road.

The reasons for the falldown feeling while trying to countersteer in soft sand or loose gravel is that the contact patch of the tire expands forward and backward, dramatically increasing steering effort. The quick street-style countersteering inputs don't seem to result in the bike rebalancing or changing direction. Since countersteering is a lot more sluggish in the dirt, the trick is to use more body English, keep the machine vertical, and steer more with the throttle.

After all, sliding the rear end sideways is another way of pointing the front end in a different direction. You can make the rear tire slide by rolling on the throttle, by snapping it closed, or by dabbing the rear brake. Consider that when a tire starts to

The rear tire tends to slide away from the direction of lean, so sliding the rear end helps steer the bike.

slide, that end of the bike heads off on a tangent, or downhill if on a sloping surface. For example, if the bike is in a left turn, sliding the rear wheel will point the bike more to the left.

Cruising Speed

If you've narrowly escaped a crash while slip-sliding through loose gravel spilled on the pavement, you can be excused for thinking that gravel or sand has no traction at all. But the truth is that gravel, sand, and other loose surfaces provide different traction at different speeds because even small stones have a resistance to being pushed aside, and the resistance increases with velocity. A gravel road can provide more predictable traction at 40 mph than at 4 mph.

Experienced riders may cruise unpaved roads at considerably higher speeds than novices do, not because they are fearless big dogs but because the correct speed results in better control. Riding too slowly through deep sand or gravel will allow the front tire to sink and plow so badly that you lose balance. At a faster speed, the tire floats on top. And don't forget that faster-spinning wheels provide increased gyroscopic stability. But, as Chris Scott points out in his book *Desert Biking*, you don't want to get carried away on narrow roads with a limited view. At speeds in excess of 50 mph, it's difficult to react quickly enough to the ever-changing terrain.

Skilled riders cruise unpaved roads at higher speeds because the correct speed results in better control.

Inertia

On slick or loose surfaces, it is important to be more aware of inertial energy and use it to your advantage. Increasing speed increases forward energy, which can work either for or against you. Let's say you are on a wet clay detour that descends into a deep gully with a steep uphill climb on the other side. Slowing at the top allows you to let the bike increase speed as you descend without wasting traction on braking. The faster speed at the bottom means increased forward energy to help carry the bike up the hill without the need for more engine power, which would result in wheel spin. If you need to control downhill speed, select a lower gear and use engine compression on the descent, but stay away from that front brake.

Approaching a short section of loose sand or deep gravel, a short burst on the throttle in third gear may be much better than slowing down and attempting it in first gear. When traction is limited, shifting up a gear helps prevent sudden wheel spins.

Braking

On tractable pavement, it's a good habit to use lots of front brake and very little rear brake. But as traction goes away, you need to favor the rear brake more and use the front brake less. The trick is to apply just enough braking to slow the bike, but not so much that you skid the tires. With today's powerful front disc brakes, even a little squeeze may be too much. If you aren't familiar enough with braking to be able to feel when your front wheel is beginning to slide, you're probably better off avoiding the front brake entirely until you get back on pavement.

ABS brakes are great for avoiding falldowns during maximum-effort stops, providing you're stopping in a straight line. Most ABS systems use wheel rotation sensors to determine when the wheel is losing traction. The ABS computer may not respond to a sideways slideout as long as the wheel is still turning. And, of course, ABS won't save you from a slideout caused by over-enthusiastic countersteering or suddenly snapping off the throttle. Where you might want to skid the tires to get the bike stopped, ABS won't allow that, with the disconcerting feeling that the brakes have failed. Most riders switch off the ABS for riding on dirt if the system allows.

Riding Practice

Skills improve only through practice. The bottom line is that whatever skills we find difficult are the ones we need to practice. If the thought of riding on loose gravel makes you break out in a cold sweat, the message should be obvious: you need some dirt time. The only way to improve off-pavement skills is to spend some time riding off the pavement. It's not a bad idea to spend at least one day each year riding some unpaved back road such as an all-weather forest service road or a country farm road. Remember, when you encounter one of those End of Pavement signs, you'll be plowing off into the soft stuff on whatever bike you normally ride. Sooner or later, you should do some dirt time on your favorite traveling motorcycle. But if your only machine is a heavyweight, you probably don't want to attempt any serious off-road excursions, even with knobbies. A big bike can be impossible to extract from a bottomless sand pit without some heavy-duty assistance. If you are concerned about dropping your expensive roadburner on some lonesome back road, one very acceptable option for off-pavement practice is to borrow a dirt bike or dual sport machine for the learning phase, and then take the heavyweight out later after riding the dirt has become more familiar.

One reason for the increased sales of machines in the 350cc to 650cc range (such as the Kawasaki KLR 650) is that exploring back roads is easier and more fun on a smaller, lighter bike. Riders are learning the advantage of owning both a big-bore road bike and a midsize dual sport or off-road machine. You don't really need a BMW 1200cc roboboxer to explore a forest service road. A 650cc bike with dual sport or dirt knobbies will have adequate traction, ground clearance, and power for some real adventure touring.

Here are some techniques to remember while practicing off-pavement skills, especially on a motorcycle with street tires:

- Plan a path of travel that puts your tires over the best surface.
- Shift body weight and lean the motorcycle to keep the wheels perpendicular to the road surface.
- Stand on the pegs in difficult situations.
- Steer more with the throttle. Use controlled bursts of power to slide the rear end toward the outside in gravelly corners.
- Use inertia rather than engine power to carry the machine uphill or through tough sections.
- Start a downhill section very slowly. Use engine braking to keep speed in check.
- Stay off the front brake.

Improving off-pavement skills will do more than help avoid embarrassment when there is a muddy detour or a little wet grass at the campground. Some of us will actually admit that we enjoy exploring roads that are less traveled—even if not hard surfaced. After all, there are more unpaved roads out there than paved ones. A skilled motorcyclist should be able to choose a road without being hampered by a self-imposed limitation of riding only on pavement.

Deer strikes are a big hazard in many parts of the country. Even a small deer can do major damage to a vehicle, especially to a motorcycle. Where there are signs, we really need to ride conservatively, even if we don't see any deer.

Deer, Oh Dear!

The rally is over and riders are heading home on a quiet Sunday morning. The rally site in a small farm town far from any big city is attractive to motorcyclists, but the green pastures in the valley are also attractive to deer. There are warning signs, of course, but when you have many miles to cover and the bike you're riding is fast and stable, it just doesn't seem appropriate to poke along. What's more, deer are most active in the hours near sunrise and sunset, and it's well past dawn as Beemer Bill heads out with his riding buddy. The sun is beginning to warm up the day, the road is dry, the curves are nicely banked, and there are few other drivers up and about on the road.

Suddenly, out of the roadside bushes, a deer attempts to leap across the road at the very instant that Beemer Bill is cruising by. Deer and bike collide with a sickening thud. Bill is tossed off the bike and tumbles down the road, unconscious; the deer is thrown into the ditch, its neck broken. The crash is over in an instant. A cell phone call from Bill's buddy initiates a rescue effort. Within the hour the unconscious rider is transported to the hospital. He survives, but his riding season is over, and he may never get back on a bike.

There are a lot of booby traps that the unwary motorcyclist can ride into in the city, including innocuous-looking alleyways, white plastic arrows glued to the pavement, missing manhole covers, raised pavement edges, railroad tracks, steel plates, and loose sand. Out in the country on those twisty back roads we love to ride, one major booby trap is a wild animal, especially wild deer. Deer are so delicate and demure that it's hard to think of them as a hazard. But when you come upon the sickening sight of a dead deer along the highway, it's another reminder of the danger, both to the animal and to yourself. It's a double tragedy when we hear of a motorcyclist involved in an animal strike.

When a motorcycle collides with a deer, it's very likely the rider will be seriously injured.

The late Larry Grodsky, motorcycle safety guru, *Rider* magazine contributor, and Stayin' Safe riding instructor, was killed in a deer strike in Texas in 2006, much to the shock of motorcyclists who looked to Larry for safe riding tactics. If anyone should have known how to manage the risks of riding, it would have been Larry. And he certainly should have known how to avoid deer, since he lived in Pennsylvania, the state with the highest number of deer strikes in the nation. Shocked motorcyclists pondered the meaning of Larry's death. If Grodsky couldn't outwit deer, what chance did the rest of us have? The sobering answer is that deer are a significant hazard for motorcyclists, and we all need to get much smarter about dealing with them.

Statistically speaking, vehicle collisions are the major motorcycling hazard, and as motorcycling experience builds and we get a little smarter, our risks of car-bike collisions should decrease. But the risk of animal strikes remains high because animals are so difficult to predict and their numbers are rapidly increasing. Wild deer are found all over North America in large numbers, and they have habits and instincts that put them on collision courses with motor vehicles. Wild animals displaced by urban sprawl are left wandering in search of mates, which often leads them to busy roads. NHTSA reports that vehicle-animal collisions increased by 24 percent between 1993 and 2001. The Insurance Information Institute describes the current situation as "an explosion in the deer population . . . leading to a continuing increase in deer-car collisions." State Farm Insurance estimated that for a recent year there were 1.5 million vehicle-deer collisions in the United States, with 150 motorists killed and $1.1 billion in vehicle damage. Of course, those statistics are primarily from animal-automobile collisions. We don't know how many of those deer strikes happened to motorcyclists. We do know that when a motorcyclist hits a wild animal, the chances of injury or death is much greater than for the average motorist.

The typical deer strike occurs when the animal suddenly leaps in front of the vehicle, often at night or around dawn. The vehicle slams into the deer with sickening consequences. What's startling is the amount of damage even a small deer can do to a speeding vehicle. What's so insidious about motorcycle-deer collisions is the unpredictability. You may have ridden for hundreds of thousands of miles, proficiently avoiding thousands of left-turners, alley jumpers, edge traps, graveled corners, and decreasing-radius turns. Then, on some easy country ride after breakfast, a deer suddenly leaps out of the bushes into your path, and thud!

Some areas seem to be more heavily populated with deer, so if you're traveling from state to state, you should pay special attention in those states with a high frequency of deer strikes. State Farm Insurance lists the states with the highest number of accidents involving deer between July 1, 2004 and June 30, 2005:

1. Pennsylvania
2. Michigan
3. Illinois
4. Ohio
5. Georgia
6. Minnesota
7. Virginia
8. Indiana
9. Texas
10. Wisconsin

Deer Instincts

To understand what to look for and what to do about deer, let's consider their instincts and habits. Deer are cautious and prefer to hide in the bushes and trees. They like munching on tender foliage. So in the summer, expect wild deer in forested areas or riverbeds where the trees and underbrush provide lots of cover and fresh salad. That lush roadside grass the highway department keeps mowed is a dinnertime favorite. In deer areas, you should expect deer feeding along the shoulder of the road in shady areas. In the daytime, a deer feeding on the road shoulder will have its head down, so it may look like a log in the ditch, or a mossy boulder, or a crumpled cardboard box. When the head comes up, you'll immediately see those large ears and perhaps a rack of antlers. Any time you see what you think is a deer, it's best to brake hard immediately. If it's not a deer, you'll have practiced the correct skill to avoid a deer strike.

Farm valleys are prime deer areas because of the availability of water and grass, and many valleys are also historic deer migration routes. Wild grazers such as deer tend to migrate in herds, moving toward higher elevations in the spring and returning to lower elevations in the fall. They follow age-old migration routes that predate the highway by thousands of years. The importance of that to the touring rider is that risks are greatest where the highway intersects the migration route.

Why do you think those yellow Deer Crossing signs get put up along certain sections of farmland or scenic forest roads? Would you believe the highway department or the for-

Deer migration signs should set off warning alarms in your head, especially at dawn and dusk during the spring and fall migration seasons. You would be wise to slow down and cover your brake lever.

est service hires game wardens to count deer migrations that cross the road? Wrongo, Big Dog. What really happens is that the road crews count dead deer, and when too many carcasses and shattered grills have been found on one particular section of road morning after morning, they put up a sign. The same holds true for antelope crossings in the grasslands of Wyoming and Colorado and for moose crossings in Alaska, British Columbia, Northern Idaho, Montana, and New Hampshire.

Those deer signs are a big advantage to motorcyclists if the situation registers between your ears. One good step is simply to slow down. Decreasing speed gives you more time to spot an animal, more time to react, and a greater ability to maneuver. *OK,* you may think, *but how about that pickup truck on my tail?* Well, if you're riding into a deer zone, why not be polite and let the pickup driver go first? By now, you should be able to figure out how to shake a tailgater using some clever tactic other than just screwing on more throttle.

When you spot deer along the road, it's smart to brake to a stop and wait for them to do whatever they are going to do. The Insurance Information Institute recommends a long blast on your horn.

Motorcyclist Instincts

Why aren't motorcyclists more proactive about avoiding deer? We typically become aware of traffic hazards such as left-turning SUVs, but wild animals are different. We see the warning signs, but it just doesn't seem appropriate to slow down in deer areas when other drivers are continuing at speed. Besides, there are so many deer zones that it would really slow down a trip to creep along through every one. At least, that seems to be the prevailing thought. This failure to comprehend the risk turns deer strikes into a gamble that's out of the rider's control. Avoiding deer strikes requires a slightly different attitude. Once the deer leaps into action, there isn't much time left for braking, so smart riders are already prepared to brake when riding into a suspicious area and prepared to brake aggressively when a deer is spotted. Since braking is your primary evasive tactic for deer, you'll want to shake tailgaters and keep some right-hand fingers curled over the brake lever in a deer zone or anywhere there are wild animals.

Let's say you've spotted the Deer sign, reduced speed, covered the brake lever, and momentarily pulled on to the shoulder to let a tailgater on by. Can you really spot a deer ahead in time to react? And what should you do if a deer does leap out? Should you just keep riding along at the same speed, or should you attempt some avoidance maneuver?

Evasive Tactics

Suddenly, you spot a pair of ears rising up from the roadside ditch. Should you slow down and then accelerate by as you would for an aggressive dog? Should you prepare to swerve as you would for a car emerging from an alley? Or should you prepare for a quick stop as you would for a left-turner? Unlike an aggressive dog, a deer may not show much interest in you until you get close. The deer may glance up at you and then nonchalantly go back to munching again. But when you get within 60 feet or so, the deer suddenly springs to action, jumping first straight ahead, then in a random zigzag wolf-evasion pattern. If it isn't obvious, the deer's first leap is in whatever direction it is facing. That's why hard braking is a smart evasive tactic.

When you suddenly realize that the log in the ditch has grown ears and antlers, or one of those white reflectors along the edge of the road starts winking at you at

Quick! Is that a deer feeding alongside the road or just a log? Don't feel embarrassed if you brake for a deer and find out it's just roadside debris.

night, or a Bambi tippy-toes out of the roadside underbrush, my advice is to do a quick stop. If the deer doesn't leap out in front of you at the last second, great. But when a deer does jump up out of the ditch and clatter around on the tarmac in your path, you'll be glad you got on the brakes early. If you're in the habit of making quick stops, you'll make a power stop automatically and think about it afterward.

What about swerving? It's tempting to think that you might be able to maintain speed and slip on by or swerve around the deer if it should leap out in front of you. But swerving assumes you can predict which way the deer will leap. The deer's typical zigzag wolf-avoidance pattern is random.

What about speeding up? After all, the greater your forward energy, the greater your impact force. You may have heard the folk tale of a motorcyclist riding at warp speed through the forest at night and slicing right through a deer without dropping the bike. Even if that folk tale was true for one lucky biker, I don't think it's a realistic approach. For every folk tale of slamming into a wild animal without getting hurt, there are several other reports of riders being seriously injured and motorcycles destroyed. And if the winking reflectors you expected to punch through happen to be the eyes of an elk, moose, or bear, the odds lean strongly in favor of the animal. A bull elk weighs about three-quarters of a ton, and a moose is even more massive. Elk and moose are common out west in northern Idaho, Montana, and British Columbia, and moose are plentiful back east in New Hampshire and Maine. Elk and moose may look stately and reserved, but they are big enough and feisty enough to attack people and motor vehicles if challenged. Along the AlCan Highway in Canada and Alaska, locals know better than to zoom up behind a moose on the road, blast the horn, and expect the critter to move over. If you observe a moose trotting down the road ahead, or even alongside the road, remember this: an adult moose is tall enough that the windshield on your bike would barely tickle his stomach, and he is strong enough to flick a fully loaded touring bike into the swamp with an easy toss of his rack. The moral is: give large animals lots of space and lots of respect.

Trust me, you don't want to butt heads with a 1,500-pound bull elk. The flashing light here means the elk with the radio collar is within a half mile.

When you see a moose sign in your travels, pay attention. An adult moose can weigh 2,500 pounds, and it will turn and charge you if it is angered.

On the Olympic Peninsula of Washington state in 1997, a rider managed to center-punch a wandering brown bear. The bruised bear muttered something about stupid bikers and meandered back into the woods looking for salmonberries. The motorcyclist was carted off to Olympic Memorial Hospital, where he spent the rest of his vacation time getting sewn and screwed back together. The message is: don't rush through forested areas.

In the Rockies, you will see raccoon, porcupine, skunk, and various other critters you might enjoy watching from a distance. Even a raccoon or porcupine is large enough to upset a bike if you hit it with the front wheel, so you probably don't want to try bouncing over any animal if you can avoid it. In Texas, it's armadillo. In Louisiana and Florida, you may encounter an alligator slithering across the road or a low-flying bird. Great Blue Heron are common near water all across the country. Great Blues are nothing to sneeze at; they have a wing span of about six feet. Wild turkeys are common along the east coast, and a turkey is heavy enough to knock you off your bike.

If you see what appears to be a roadside reflector winking at you at night, it is probably a deer facing in your direction.

Danger at Night

While antelope, elk, and moose munch away in plain view in the broad daylight, deer are more cautious. Deer seem to prefer hiding in the shadows in the daytime and feeding at night. That means the risk of deer strikes increases as the sun goes down. It's definitely something to think about when you are considering a nighttime transit on a highway passing through one of those scenic national forests. The high-risk times for deer strikes are between sunset and midnight and in the hour spanning sunrise.

At night, brown deer hide doesn't reflect much light, but deer eyes will reflect a brilliant white from your headlight, similar to a reflector on a roadside post. How do you tell if the reflector you see is on a post or on a deer? Easy: the deer eye blinks. If you see a reflector winking back at you, odds are it is a deer and it's facing in your direction.

Other Wild Ones

Of course, wild animals aren't the only four-legged road hazards you'll encounter. Farm animals loose on the road can present a mighty big target. Cows seem to be too relaxed to be concerned about vehicles, so they generally just keep doing whatever they were doing. Horses are a lot more skittish and excitable and are more likely to bolt in front of a vehicle or kick out at anyone who gets too close. If you come upon a herd of cattle or a flock of sheep being driven across the highway (or even down the highway), don't be too eager to elbow your way through the herd. It's one thing to have a longhorn steer rub up against a fence post—it's a little more exciting to have a steer scrape his horn down the side of your bike. The drovers will get them off the road as soon as they can.

Livestock on the loose. It's neighborly to notify the owners.

In the West, it's considered neighborly to report escaped beasts. If you see a herd of cattle making a quick getaway over a trampled fence, it's appropriate to find the nearest farm house and report it. Don't expect the farm hands to get excited. Loose animals are on a par with the tractor getting another flat tire. You may get a chat about the weather (or even a discussion of the relative merits of cruisers versus dual sports) and a cup of coffee before they head out to round 'em up. But they will appreciate the report.

Open Range

An Open Range sign is more than a warning that there aren't any fences to keep cattle off the road. Open Range means the animals have the right-of-way over traffic. Think of it this way: The farm isn't occupying land near the road; the road happens to trespass through the rancher's farm. The cattle belong there. You're a guest. It's up to you to get through the farm without injuring any of the rancher's livestock. Hit a steer, and you may get to purchase a locker full of beef in addition to some new bodywork for your bike.

The deal here is, the cattle belong; you're a guest.

What About Deer Whistles?

There are many different versions of ultrasonic animal alert whistles available. The theory is that the whistles moving through the air make a high-pitched ultrasonic noise that alerts animals to your approach and warns them to get out of your way. Given the potential for animal strikes, a passive animal warning device sounds like a great idea. But there are a couple of niggling questions. First, the whistles make noise in frequencies above human hearing. So how do you know if your deer whistles are actually working? Let's say a big South Dakota juicybug lodges in the orifice, silencing the whistle. How would you know? Even if your whistles are whistling as intended, is the volume really loud enough to reach an animal several hundred feet away? More to the point, I've been told that the hearing frequency range of deer is about the same as that of humans, so if you can't hear the whistle, deer probably can't hear it either.

You can find glowing testimonials about reductions in deer strikes after whistles were installed. Just read the deer whistle sales brochures. You'll have to make up your own mind about whether sales brochures are hype or fact. State Farm Insurance suggests that studies have not shown deer whistles to be an effective deer-avoidance method. Nor does the Insurance Information Institute recommend deer whistles as a tactic for avoiding deer strikes.

In my opinion, any device that depends on making the other guy get out of your way is probably not the smart approach. My survival theory about motorcycle hazards is that you should always be prepared to get out of the way of the other guy, whether the other guy is a left-turning Accord or a left-turning alligator. Feel free to bolt on whatever magic talismans you want, including a Back Off mud flap, a pulsating headlight, a string of garlic, a rabbit's foot, or a pair of deer whistles, if it makes you feel better. But the only reliable way to avoid an animal collision is to be attentive and get out of the way. On that, the insurance industry agrees.

Ferocious Fidos

I stopped to talk with the owner of a large dog the other day. I'd been riding along a quiet wooded back road on the way home, when I observed a large yellow Labrador sprinting through the trees on an intercept course with my motorcycle. He'd done this before, jumping off the bank next to the road and trying to make a carrier landing on the deck of the bike. So far, he hadn't managed to hit the bike, but he'd been rapidly improving his technique and was bound to get it right some day. This time, I squeezed on a little front brake to heat up the disk and then did a quick stop just short of where I figured Fido would make his landing. Sure enough, Fido vaulted off a roadside stump, flew through the air at about handlebar height looking for the bike, and made a four-paw touchdown on the pavement in front of me, right where he had calculated I should have been.

Dogs are allowed to run loose in some parts of the country.

This particular Fido wasn't really aggressive, he was just bored and looking for some fun. I figured I could make it up to the owner's door without losing any flesh. Knock, knock.

"Hello, is that big yellow Lab your dog? Well, he just about knocked me off my motorcycle, and this has happened before. I'd like to encourage you to either train him to not chase people or tie him up before he causes an accident that results in me being injured."

"Well, he's a pretty good dog. He doesn't chase cars. He only chases UPS trucks and motorcycles. We just don't have the heart to tie him up."

"Would you mind giving me the name of your insurance agent? I want to make sure you've got enough coverage to pay for hospitalization, motorcycle repairs, and lost time from my job if your dog manages to knock me down next time."

That particular community was rural, and letting dogs roam free was part of the lifestyle. There were even reports of dogs forming packs and attacking sheep herds while the owners were at work. The pet owners didn't seem to realize that Fido and his pals were playing wolf during the day and returning to their porches at dinnertime to greet the bosses. If you don't ever encounter loose dogs in your neighborhood, you can count yourself lucky. But if you happen to stumble onto a loose-dog community in your travels, you should be prepared to avoid injury to either yourself or the animal.

Over the years, I've had a considerable number of encounters with canines and their masters. I've noticed that dogs tend to take on the personalities of their owners. A well-behaved dog usually means a responsible owner. An untrained dog has trained the owner to obey. An aggressive dog is usually the result of a mean owner. Some dogs chase motorcycles, some prefer fire trucks. Others get a kick out of chasing joggers or snarling at the postman. Whatever the target, most dogs seem to enjoy chasing something. It works, too. If the dog chases a motorcycle, it soon goes away.

If you happen to have a snarling pit bull closing fast on your shin, it may seem that your biggest problem is becoming lunch. But the bigger problem is dropping the bike. Even a small dog can upset a motorcycle. If you've had any dog encounters, you may have noticed that dogs seem to head for the front wheel. This might be just a misguided attempt at rounding up the motorcycle for the kill. Fido may not understand the future consequences of diving under a half-ton bike, but his instincts say it will work. The fact is, a dog can bring a bike crashing to earth.

Veteran motorcyclists understand the importance of never allowing a dog to get close to the front wheel. Most of the time, that simply means being a little smarter than Fido. We may not know what dogs are thinking, but we can observe their behavior and take advantage of it.

Confrontations

Just as with motorcyclists, there are vast differences between dogs. Some dogs are merely playful, others are defending a territory that happens to include the street, and some mistreated or untrained dogs are aggressive enough to be a serious threat to anyone passing by. A vicious dog can be a serious adversary if you happen to find yourself in a confrontation. Those snarling teeth and belly growls are the real thing, and a vicious canine can inflict serious wounds very quickly. Let's ramble through some ideas about dog behavior and then consider some tactics for not getting bit or knocked off the bike.

Some dogs are merely playful, others are defending a territory that happens to include the street.

First of all, dogs seem to have a very sensitive attitude about their territorial boundaries but very little ability to reason. They often act out of instinct. An unrestrained dog can have a general turf as large as it wants to defend, a threat territorial zone of about twenty feet, and a critical territorial zone of about eight feet.

Second, dogs have developed behavior patterns to communicate dominance, aggression, fear, and submission. Fortunately, we can read some of this body language to help predict what a dog might do next. If a dog barks a lot with his tongue out and his tail wagging, he probably just wants to play. And, if he drops his head low to the ground with his mouth closed and his tail wagging, he is being submissive. But, if he pulls his ears back, raises his hackles (the hair on the back of his neck and shoulders), and stiffens his tail, he is getting apprehensive and could snap at you out of fear.

A dominant dog intent on defending turf will raise his upper body high, with ears erect, nose forward, and perhaps a paw raised. If he thinks there is a challenge, an aggressive dog plants his feet on the ground, pulls back his upper lip to reveal teeth, points his ears and nose farther forward, stiffens, and raises his hackles. He will caution you of his authority by staring you down with unblinking eyes and warn you of his seriousness with a deep chest growl.

If you understand that an aggressive dog is just defending turf and you don't need to be there, consider backing off. If you encounter a large, aggressive dog on

A dog's body language can help you understand what mood he's in.

the street, you are advised to avoid eye contact, remain quiet, and slink away with your head lowered, if possible. Sure, you're a Big Dog rider and Fido is just a dumb animal, but don't escalate a confrontation if you aren't prepared to lick your wounds.

If you encounter a problem dog more than once, you'll have to decide whether to slink away submissively and never come back, try to reason with the owner, or forget the owner and talk animal control into getting the dog locked up.

Apparently, for fun-seeking dogs, there isn't much sport in chasing something that is too easy to catch. The game is to calculate the speed of the approaching vehicle and dash out just in time to intercept it. Dogs typically have very good eyesight and hearing, so Fido often waits in the yard behind a bush or parked car, calculating a perfect intercept that he can reach if he sprints at top speed.

When Fido catches you at the intercept point, you might be able to get in a lucky kick with your boot, but the odds are that the dog has better reflexes than you do. And if this dog happens to be aggressively defending his territory, it's best to avoid holding out any fresh meat, even if you think your leathers could protect you against snarling fangs. Besides, attempting to injure the dog makes you the aggressor in the eyes of some owners. The clever approach is to outsmart the dog.

One good tactic for outsmarting Fido is to change speed unexpectedly. Most dogs have a maximum speed of only about 30 mph, so it is easy to outrun them on a motorcycle. If you slow down before entering Fido's turf, he predicts that he can wait a little longer before trotting off. Then, just as Fido gets up and starts racing toward the intercept point, screw on some throttle and accelerate out of range. Poor Fido gets left in the dust.

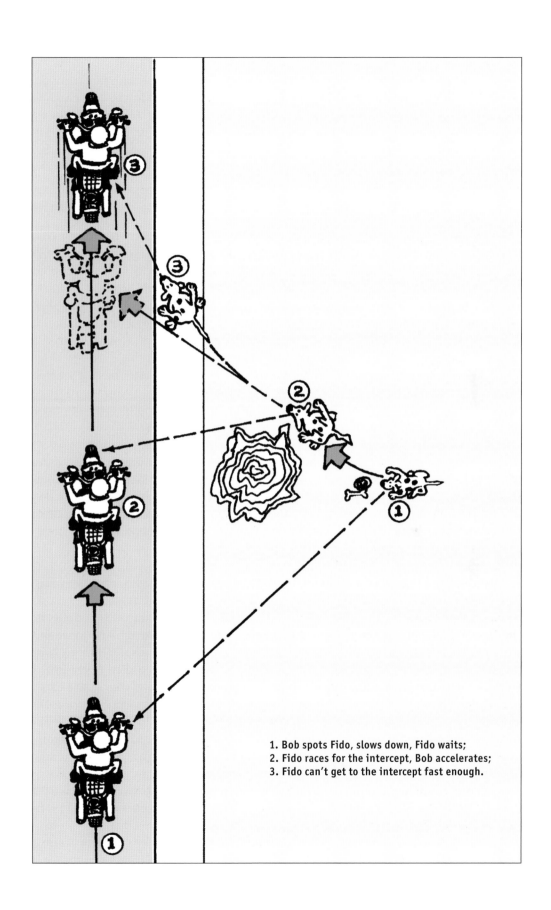

1. Bob spots Fido, slows down, Fido waits;
2. Fido races for the intercept, Bob accelerates;
3. Fido can't get to the intercept fast enough.

This is an acceptable tactic for keeping dogs away from the front wheel, with a few caveats: First, you have to spot the dog, which means being aware that there are loose dogs in that community, and watch carefully for dogs lurking in the shadows. Second, if you are one of the following riders in a group, this slow-fast technique will make you the prime target. The lead rider will outdistance Fido, but the dog will probably catch the second or third rider. Third, if you pull this same trick day after day to outrun a dog in your neighborhood, it won't be long before Fido cracks the code and learns to start the intercept sooner.

Repellents

If you continue to have too many dog confrontations in your community or on your travels, take a tip from the postal worker: carry some dog repellent with you. There are dog repellents available in small pressurized spray canisters as well as electronic repellers that emit a high-pitch scream that dogs prefer to avoid. To find a source, check with your mail person, local utility company, or a kennel equipment supplier.

Some motorcyclists report success in keeping aggressive dogs at bay using ordinary household ammonia. They carry a plastic squeeze bottle of a water-ammonia solution and squirt a trail of the smelly stuff on the pavement as they pass by. Dogs mark their territory by urinating, and urine contains ammonia, so to the dog you are marking the street as your turf. A submissive dog may agree to comply with your demand. But a really aggressive dog will just urinate over the top of your ammonia as a threat for you to back off, and you'll have to decide how far to retreat.

Dogs are not a universal problem for motorcyclists. Different communities vary in their tolerance for pets running loose, and local laws reflect this. In those areas where pets are allowed to roam, it is assumed the pet is harmless, at least until after the first bite. This means that Animal Control is probably not going to pick up a dog just because it snarled at you or ran into the street. But, we can do each other a favor by working to get problem dogs under control in our own neighborhoods.

Dealing with the Owner

It's worth a try to confront a problem dog's owner, but remember that by approaching the house, you are invading the dog's territory, which he is defending. If you do feel you can get up to the door without being devoured, consider discussing the problem with the pet owner. It helps if you have done a little research into local animal control laws so that you know what the rules are. And it is also helpful to keep your temper in control. You might try something like this: "Hello, I'm Biker Bob. I live just down the street a few blocks, so I ride my motorcycle past your house every day. Is that big pit bull your dog? What's his name? The reason I stopped is because I thought you would want to know that your dog chases vehicles. He's a nice looking dog, and I'd certainly hate to injure him if he runs out to chase me. I'd really appreciate it if you could do something to restrain him on your own property, so that we don't have to get Animal Control involved. Thanks for your time."

Keep in mind that the owner of a problem dog might be even meaner than the dog. If the owner is a reasonable person who just doesn't realize his dog is a problem, that conversation may trigger some action. But if the owner responds as aggressively as his snarling dog, the other option is to register a complaint with Animal Control or with the local police department or sheriff's office. Be aware that the legal eagles will want your name and address and will provide that to the dog owner if requested.

Aggressive dogs are sometimes rabid, and a bite can infect you with rabies. Trust me here, you want to avoid getting bitten by any dog. The treatment for rabies is no joke. If you should happen to get bitten by an animal, don't waste any time. Immediately get emergency medical attention and report the incident to the police, who may quarantine the dog until rabies tests are completed. Remember, that first bite also proves to authorities that the dog is aggressive, and Animal Control can then take steps to either have the dog restrained or put down.

The vast majority of pet owners care for their animals responsibly and keep them out of the street. But during your travels, be prepared for the occasional dog that is undisciplined or areas of the country where dogs are allowed to roam free. If you can be just a little smarter than the average Fido, you should be able to handle any dangerous confrontations without any pain or expense.

Just be glad they haven't figured out how to start the truck.

CHAPTER 6

Special
Situations

WHEN IT RAINS

I should have known better than to head up into the Cascade Mountains in early April without putting on my serious rain gear. I was zooming around sloppy-wet logging roads trying to find checkpoints on the Vintage Motorcycle Enthusiasts Bonehead Enduro, a not-too-serious ride with an emphasis on old guys and old bikes. And bones. All the checkpoints have bone connotations, such as the snow bone and the mud bone. Anyway, as the day wore on, the northwest drizzle was turning into a steady downpour and the logging roads were turning to a sloppy quagmire.

It was beginning to remind me of that scene from *Paint Your Wagon* where the guys are moping around the leaky saloon tent. That scene kept flashing into my mind as I tried to find the road through a steamy, muddy face shield. And instead of Lee Marvin splashing a stagecoach load of painted ladies down the creek, it was me on my BMW Enduro sidecar outfit, splashing up the muddy roads in a northwest deluge wearing my fabric riding suit without rain gear.

As I said, I should have known better. I had been commuting to work daily by motorcycle in Seattle weather for many years, and I've traveled enough in wet places to have figured out some serious rain-riding tactics. But the Bonehead Enduro reminded me of how easy it is to be overly optimistic about the weather. When I had started out that morning, I just hadn't believed how wet it was going to get. So I just put on my two-piece suit, which has a bonded Gore Tex seam-sealed inner lining.

The truth is, even in Seattle, most of the time it's not raining. When I head out for a ride, I wear riding gear that's comfortable for the day's general conditions based on what it looks like when I fire up the bike. Then, if the weather turns miserable later in the day, it's a long, cold, soggy ride home.

Even if you live in sunny Arizona, you'll occasionally get caught in some rain. And if you're from Arizona but traveling to the Oregon coast or western Canada, you'd better plan for some wet days. If you intend to ride cross-country or you live in a part of the world where rain is a regular feature, you'd be smart to carry rain gear always.

Riding in soggy gear is a bigger deal than just feeling miserable. Riding soggy is an invitation to hypothermia. It's cold enough snorting around mountainside logging roads in the rain at 40 or 50 degrees Fahrenheit, but at highway speeds the evaporative cooling of wet riding gear can chill you to the core within a few miles. And if you are becoming hypothermic, your thinking and muscle control are going to suffer. A couple of extra seconds of reaction time can easily mean the difference between a close call and a trip to the ER.

So let's think about being prepared for when it rains. First, let's consider some of the mechanics of both traction control and keeping dry, and then we'll offer some commonsense rain-riding tactics.

Traction Control

Once you've had your two-wheeler do the moon-walk on a rain-slick off-ramp, you can be pretty paranoid about a falldown every time you see the slightest pitter-patter of rain. It's important to realize that even wet pavement has areas of relatively good traction and a few really slippery areas. That's a clue that the slipperiness is caused by something more than just rainwater. The truth is, clean wet pavement has something like 80 percent of the friction of clean dry pavement.

Wet pavement can have surprisingly good traction, but there will be some areas that can be very slippery, such as the center of the lane near intersections or those painted stripes in the crosswalk.

Of course, the critical word is *clean*, and pavement rarely is. Passing vehicles drip all sorts of lubricants on the surface, including diesel oil, antifreeze, chassis grease, brake dust, and rubber particles. Note that antifreeze is so slippery that liquid-cooled race bikes must use only water in the radiator.

In addition to those slippery vehicle droppings, people toss, dribble, and spit a variety of lubricants out the window, including cigarette butts, hamburger wrappers, French fries, ice cream, pizza, soda pop, and used diapers, to name just a few. That road debris doesn't simply evaporate. Most of it gets squished into particles and mashed into the pavement. A little moisture mixed with those particles can create a slippery goo that really reduces traction. That's why the road seems so treacherous after just a little mist or morning dew: it's the slippery goo, not just the water.

When it first starts to rain, you can actually see the slippery goo floating away.

The only really good pavement cleaner is a steady downpour that lasts long enough to float that accumulated slimy stuff into the gutters. That offers us two lessons: First, the longer it has been since a good rainstorm, the more slippery the pavement is likely to be when it finally does rain. If it has been dry for a while, you can actually see the slime floating away. Second, the pavement is slickest when it first starts to rain, before enough water has fallen to flush away the slippery stuff. Just a little sprinkle or some morning mist may leave the road slippery hours later. Those lessons are especially important for riders who live in dry climates.

Once the road gets washed clean, both asphalt and concrete paving can have decent traction in the rain, with some obvious slick exceptions. Shiny spots such as plastic arrows, crosswalks, steel plates, grated bridge decks, or railroad tracks are treacherous when wet. Loose objects such as leaves or flattened cardboard are even more hazardous when damp. Use more caution when following commercial trucks or transit busses, both of which are notorious for oil leaks. A vehicle with leaking seals will continue to dribble a fresh coating of oil on top of the rainwater. That's a good reason to ride in the wheel tracks of other vehicles, rather than right in the center of the lane.

Hydroplaning

Water escapes from under a tire by squishing out sideways along lateral grooves in the tread. A good rain tire will have deep angled grooves that point out toward the sides of the tread. The good news is that motorcycle tires have a relatively long, narrow contact patch compared with auto tires, and a narrow contact patch can more easily push the water aside. The bad news is that today's wide-profile motorcycle tires (which handle so much better in the dry) are more likely to hydroplane over standing water.

Roughly speaking, the typical low-profile radial car tire will start to hydroplane (lift up on top of the water) in one-half inch of standing water at about 60 mph. The wider your tires or the deeper the water, the more likely they are to hydroplane at the same speed. That's something to consider when you're thinking, *Hey, maybe I could fit a 170/50-17 on the back instead of that old-fashioned 140/80-17.*

And while we're talking tires, remember that a worn tire with shallow tread grooves won't eject as much water from the contact patch. One of the advantages of a new tire is deeper grooves and therefore a higher hydroplaning threshold. Different rubber compounds also have different traction characteristics, but that won't make any difference if the tire is hydroplaning.

It's also important to keep your tires pumped up to correct pressures. Tires actually flex a lot more than you might think and form ripples or waves as the tires rotate against the ground. An underinflated tire can form a big ripple ahead of the contact patch that traps water and increases the risk of hydroplaning. An overinflated tire is less likely to trap water, but the tread isn't as resilient so the tire has less traction. A properly inflated tire has a better chance of pushing down through the water and maintaining a grip.

Water Ingestion

Don't worry about your engine drowning from too much water being thrown around in the airstream. Water is vaporized during intake and turns to steam during the heat of combustion, and steam can actually help increase horsepower. But solid water doesn't compress, and if the engine swallows enough water while running, it will lift the cylinders right off the block or collapse the pistons. So don't ever try to splash through a puddle that is deeper than your air intakes.

Water is more likely to affect electrical and ignition systems. Corroded connectors or cracked coil insulation are more likely to cause electrical failures when wet. It helps to have all those little rubber boots intact and snug around spark plug wires, for example.

Keeping Dry

When it rains, one big priority is to keep warm, which starts with keeping your body dry. The traditional way to keep dry is to add a layer of waterproof rain gear over your normal riding gear. That's still a reliable approach to rain riding, especially if what appeared to be a little mist this morning turns into an all-day gully washer. We've got a lot of different styles, features, and qualities of motorcycling rain gear from which to choose.

What I should have been wearing on that Bonehead run is the Norwegian fisherman-style bib pants and hooded jacket that I used for commuting through Seattle winters, plus boot and glove covers.

This heavy two-piece rain suit made for commercial fisher-men is bulky to carry but easy to get into. That makes it a good choice for commuting but not for travel. The bib pants don't leak in the crotch, and the tall jacket collar extends up inside the helmet.

A lightweight one-piece rain suit packs small, which makes it good for travel. But a one-piece suit can be a struggle to get into while standing alongside the highway in a downpour.

One-Piece Versus Two-Piece Rain Gear

For traveling, you'll want rain gear that packs small and light. In general, you'll find that a one-piece rain suit packs up into a smaller package than a two-piecer does. But unless you have double-jointed shoulders, you'll also discover that a one-piece rain suit is more of a struggle to get into while standing under a freeway overpass with trucks blasting by. It's a lot easier to slip your boots through the bulbous legs of over-size fisherman-style bib rain pants and then put on a separate jacket.

There are now many fabric riding suits that are reasonably water resistant that will work for either travel or commuting, available in both one-piece and two-piece designs. For travel, you may find it more practical to have a two-piece suit with multiple layers that you can add or remove. For commuting, you'll probably be happier with a one-piece step-into style because you'll be putting it on or taking it off inside a building rather than alongside the road.

When I got my first water-resistant fabric adventure touring suit, I wondered whether a breathable membrane would keep me dry without added rain gear. The question got answered on a trip to Great Britain when the sky opened up and I was caught on the M25 Motorway without any opportunity to stop and add the rain gear. By the time I got to the next rest area twenty miles farther on, I'd given the suit a good rain test. I stayed reasonably dry inside, although the front jacket pockets filled up with water through the unsealed zippers.

The point is today's adventure touring fabric riding gear is water-resistant enough to weather a few wet days without adding an additional layer of waterproof rain gear over the outside. And for those clever enough to stuff their maps into a clear plastic bag, even leaky pocket zippers aren't a serious problem.

Evaporative Cooling

There are two schools of thought on making fabric suits comfortable but water resistant. One is to use fabric with a bonded layer of breathable water-resistant material on the inside, such as Gore Tex. The other concept is to use an outer fabric with a loose weave and provide a separate water-resistant liner. Jackets and pants with bonded layers tend to be less breathable, but you don't have to change anything if it starts to rain. Gear with separate waterproof liners are more comfortable in the dry, but the disadvantage is that you have to remove your outer gear to put on the waterproof liners. The additional disadvantage of garments with a loose weave is that on rainy days the outer material soaks up water all the way through, which contributes to evaporative cooling. My personal preference is for fabric riding gear with the water-resistant layer bonded to the inside, rather than a removable liner.

Of course, you can add a layer of rain gear over the top of a fabric suit, but it needs to be much larger to fit over the bulk of your riding gear, especially if there are impact pads inside. You can also add various covers to seal off the areas where rain and cold air

There is a wide choice in fabric riding suits that are water resistant enough for serious travel in normal conditions without additional rain gear. The outer garments may have a breathable layer bonded to the inside of the fabric, or the shell may be breathable, with separate waterproof insulated liners.

Keeping your neck warm and dry is a high priority in wet conditions. This wind triangle secures around my neck inside my jacket collar, sealing the area between helmet and jacket.

air tend to get past the openings. For cold or wet weather, I wear a windproof, waterproof neck triangle that seals off the opening between my jacket collar and helmet. There are glove covers that keep your leather gloves dry and seal off your jacket sleeves. Although some leather gloves include rain covers and others have water-resistant linings, the only way to really keep your hands dry is to add a waterproof layer over the outside. One tactic that works is to buy some XXL-size unlined rubber work gloves, which you can wear over your leather gloves when it rains.

There are also boot covers that tuck inside your pants legs. Rubber boot covers will keep your boots dry once you figure out how to slip them on over your soggy leather boots. The trick is to pull a plastic baggie over your boots first; then the rubber will slip right on. The alternative I prefer is fabric boot covers that wrap around my boots and secure with hook and loop strips.

Rain Riding Tactics

At the first patter of raindrops, the temptation is to crank up the gas and beat it out the other side of the cloud. That's a standard practice to get through desert thundershowers but not wise for riding around cities. Remember, the road is most slippery when it first starts to rain after a dry spell, especially in and around big cities where traffic is ever-present. So the smarter tactic in heavy traffic areas is to take a break for a few minutes and let those bumper-car drivers slip, slide, and bash into each other while the accumulated goo gradually washes away. A half-hour break is a wise precaution and also gives you a good reason to get warmed up and put on the serious rain gear if it looks as if it's going to be more than a shower.

When it first starts to rain, clever riders take a half-hour break to allow the slippery goo to wash off the surface.

Scrutinize the Surface

Remember about those commercial vehicles leaking fresh oil? It's most likely that any oil will be dribbled down the center of the lane, but it also spreads downhill on cambered curves. Watch for any beading up or rainbow sheens that indicate oily areas, and keep your tires out of the slippery spots, especially when approaching intersections and in turn lanes.

While rounding a curve or a cambered freeway ramp, try to stay in the uphill wheel track, and reduce speed to reduce lean angle. Adjust your line to cross railroad or streetcar tracks as close to 90 degrees as practical, and maintain a steady speed and direction when crossing any such slippery areas. The aprons laid next to railroad tracks can be as slippery as the shiny rails. The old style aprons were just wood planks. Today you'll see more plastic aprons. In the rain, both wood and plastic can be extremely slick. Expect that brick streets and wooden bridge decks will be especially slippery when wet. Try to keep your tires away from painted lines, plastic arrows, manhole covers, and loose objects such as leaves.

Negotiating these streetcar tracks is a challenge even when dry. But it's even more challenging in the rain when the brick dust mixes with water to make a very slippery lubricant.

Those plastic aprons laid next to railroad tracks at grade crossings can be really slippery when wet.

Smooth Is Good

When riding on slick surfaces, you probably won't need any reminders to reduce speed to make up for the reduced traction. What's really important is to avoid any sudden changes of speed or direction that demand more traction. Even if you feel your tires let go for a moment, it's important to avoid that sudden disastrous instinct to snap off the throttle or jam on the brakes. If the bike can recover, it will. Don't do anything to make the situation worse. To avoid having to make any sudden evasive maneuvers, drop back farther behind other vehicles. Minimum following distance in the rain should be four seconds.

Keep the Wheels Perpendicular

For really slippery areas such as steel plates, place more of your weight on the pegs, and try to keep the bike leaned so that the tires are perpendicular to the road surface. That way, if the tires do lose traction momentarily, the bike can slide sideways a bit without immediately falling down. When you have to cross slippery railroad tracks, try to get the bike lined up to cross at a maximum angle, at least 45 degrees.

Use Both Brakes

On rain-slick pavement, your braking technique must be modified for machines with independent front-rear brake systems. You can use more rear brake than on dry pavement for the same bike loading. That's because there will be less weight transfer to the front and therefore less traction for braking on the front. In the rain, you have less total traction available for braking, but you can share braking almost equally between front and rear.

When you are crossing a slippery area such as surface markings made of shiny plastic, ease off the brakes when crossing, then apply the brakes on the other side.

Brake in a Straight Line

When slowing or stopping on wet pavement, try to brake in a straight line. For example, when approaching a sharp turn, use both brakes to decelerate with the bike vertical, then get off the brakes before you lean. If you realize you are going to cross a slippery area such as a plastic arrow while braking, momentarily ease off the brakes as your tires cross the plastic.

Get on the Brakes Early

When approaching an intersection where you may have to stop, apply both brakes lightly to get the friction surfaces dried off and warmed up. The stainless steel alloys used in most disk brake systems are beautiful in the dry, but some have embarrassingly low friction when wet.

In the rain, ride the brakes lightly to keep the friction surfaces warmed up. When you see an intersection ahead, brake early to give yourself lots of stopping distance.

If the disks or pads are wet, it may take a revolution or two to squeegee enough water off the disk to get full braking effort. If you panic at the delayed braking reaction, the tendency is to squeeze the lever harder, which then results in the wheel locking up as the disk suddenly dries off and grabs. If you should overbrake on the front, release the lever and squeeze more gently. If the rear tire starts to slide during a straight-line stop, just stand on the pedal and slide it to a halt to avoid a possible highside crash. The solution to such problems is to ease on the brakes earlier and smoother and to put your tires over the most tractable surface. For instance, traction is usually better in the wheel tracks of other vehicles than in the center of the lane where oil tends to collect.

Don't Get Zapped

An average of 60 people are killed and 300 are injured each year by lightning in the United States, according to the National Weather Service. All thunderstorms produce lightning. In the Southwest, rain can evaporate before reaching the ground, but the storm can still produce lightning strikes, sometimes as far as ten miles from any rainfall. Your average chance of being struck by lightning in the United States is only about 1 in 280,000, but if you are riding a motorcycle into a Florida or Louisiana thunderstorm, your odds of a hit go way up. The highest density of lightning strikes in the United States is in the Southeast, especially the Gulf Coast and Florida. In 1991, there were 16.9 million lightning flashes in central Florida. If you weight lightning fatalities by population, the top states are Wyoming, Utah, Colorado, and Florida, according to the National Lightning Safety Institute. No, riding on rubber tires won't insulate you from a lightning bolt.

If you feel a tingling on your skin or your hair stands up or the time between flash and boom is less than ten seconds, lightning could strike in your vicinity at any moment. When you see a lightning bolt, start counting. If you hear the thunderclap before you have counted to thirty, you are close enough to get hit. Your best chance of not getting struck is to get away from metal objects, get away from tall structures such as trees or power poles, and get inside some sturdy building or inside an enclosed vehicle. Avoid hilltops or continuing uphill into a thundershower. If you have no other choice, get off the bike and go into a low ravine. Do not sit on the ground, but squat low on the balls of your feet to minimize ground contact.

Out in the desert, it doesn't have to be raining for a sudden wall of water to come roaring across the road, the result of a thundershower miles away.

Out in the Desert

Out in the desert, away from civilization, you have a bigger problem with thunderstorms—flash floods. On average, floods kill more Americans than do lightning, tornadoes, or hurricanes. In Utah, Nevada, Arizona, and New Mexico, you'll see monstrous steep-sided ditches carved across the landscape, sometimes twenty feet deep and eighty feet across. These are washes created by sudden thundershowers, often many miles upstream of the wash. The sun-baked desert soil can't soak up the water fast enough, and large torrents of muddy water will race across the landscape for miles at speeds of 10 mph to 20 mph, tearing out soil and roads in its path. A flash flood in Colorado was clocked at 50 mph!

A touring rider from Iowa or New Jersey may not appreciate while riding under a blue Arizona sky that a thundershower way off in the distance has created a flash flood that is now roaring across the desert at urban traffic speed. Rather than attempt to build bridges across washes, the expedient fix is just to build the road down into the wash and across to the other side. It's a lot easier and cheaper to replace the road than to replace a bridge that has been washed away.

Experienced desert riders understand the importance of not zipping over a hill until they can see what's on the other side, especially if there's a warning sign. They want to know that a dry wash really is dry. And if you do encounter a flooded wash some day, don't be foolish enough to attempt to ride through the water. At just 12 mph, a foot of water will knock your bike off its tires. And even if you don't get swept away by the current, there may be a big hole carved where the pavement used to be. Park the bike up at the top, break out the refreshments, and appreciate the show until the flood has passed by.

When You're Hot, You're HOT

I had started the day at a campground in Wyoming and intended to make a fast transit across Nebraska on my way to Wisconsin. Thunderclouds over the Black Hills of South Dakota kept the temperature pleasant most of the morning. But as I dropped south into Nebraska, the temperature soared, and a strong southwest wind howled across the prairie, blasting me with hot, dry air. I stopped for coffee about 10 a.m. By noon, I started to get a headache, then my legs began to cramp, and a few miles later my stomach was tying itself in knots.

If you want to survive those long, hot transits across a dry landscape, you need to develop some serious hydration and cooling tactics.

Late for lunch and low on fuel, I looked for a restaurant and a gas station, but there was only a convenience station at the junction where I needed to turn off. So I filled the tank, bought two cans of ice-cold soda, and planned to find a nearby park where I could make my own sandwich. I was thirsty enough to down both sodas on the spot, but the station was dirty and congested, so I went looking for a wayside where I could get out of traffic and into some shade.

A few miles down the road, I found a state park. I felt exhausted, my head was throbbing, and it was all I could do to park the bike and drag myself to a picnic table. As I unzipped my jacket and started to gulp down the first can of cold pop, my stomach cramped so badly I almost blacked out. I doubled over with my head down on the picnic table, feeling as though some invisible ghoul were plunging a knife into my belly, but I had no energy to fight back.

I managed a few sips of the soda, then some water, and as I slowly recovered, I mentally kicked myself for not listening to the signals my body had been sending for the last hundred miles. Those leg cramps were a message: *We're running low on water down here, Bunkie!* Thinking back, I hadn't had anything to drink since that coffee at midmorning. The leg cramps, the headache, the nausea—yep, all the classic symptoms of heat exhaustion. I'd been too focused on covering the miles and not focused enough on hot-weather riding tactics. Heat exhaustion had snuck up on me because the temperature was up, but not like one of those triple digit scorchers that really gets my attention.

I remembered a ride I had taken south over the Siskiyou Mountains from Oregon to California that turned into a scorcher. Up at 4,000 feet, it was cool enough. But 100 miles later, descending into the

A water-soaked cooling vest under your jacket really helps in hot weather.

Sacramento Valley was like riding into a broiler oven. By the time I reached Oroville, the temperature signs were flashing 118 degrees Fahrenheit, and I had another 150 miles to the rally site at Mariposa. To continue that ride, I needed to go into desert survival mode.

On that trip, I kept the full riding gear on, including pants, jacket, insulated leather boots, gloves, and a knit-neck cooler that I saturated with water from a squeeze bottle. As quickly as the fabric dried out in the blast-furnace wind, I would flip the face shield open, squeeze a gusher of water down my chin, and slam the face shield shut again. Whether riding or stopping for more ice water, other people stared at me in disbelief. Peering out of their air-conditioned cars or sitting in an air-conditioned fast-food joint, they just couldn't grasp the concept of someone being outside in 118-degree weather, bundled up in heavy clothing.

While I was recovering at the park in Nebraska, I reminded myself about how the human body reacts to even tiny changes in temperature of the core organs. The human body won't tolerate much of a drop in core temperature (hypothermia) or more than a couple degrees rise in temperature (hyperthermia) without taking drastic action. When you're hot, you're HOT. The tactics the body uses to deal with heat stress include sweating, vasodilatation, increase in heart rate, and reduction of blood pressure.

Sweating

Sweat (perspiration) evaporates on the surface of the skin and clothing. The process of evaporation actually cools the surface of the skin, transferring heat from the skin to the air. While sweat contains a few chemicals, it's mostly water. Run low on water, and your body will start complaining. I hadn't been replenishing the water I'd lost through sweating. I should have been drinking about a pint of water every hour, not just two cups of coffee all morning. And that carbonated soda wasn't a good idea either. I should have been carrying water and drinking it frequently. Serious endurance riders wear a water bladder with a drinking tube so they can stay hydrated while riding.

Vasodilatation

If the core starts to heat up, blood vessels enlarge to circulate more blood (and therefore transfer more body heat) toward the skin. If air temperature isn't much higher than body temperature, evaporating sweat helps transfer the extra heat to the air. Of course, if the sweat evaporates too quickly, or if the body runs out of water, the skin dries off and begins to absorb heat from the air. The increased blood flow from vasodilatation just pumps more heat back to the core.

Heart Rate and Blood Pressure

The heart responds to rising core temperature and vasodilatation by increasing the heart rate to keep filling those enlarged blood vessels. The heartbeat can be 50 percent to 70 percent faster than the resting rate. If the core continues to heat up, blood flow is shunted away from muscles and the brain in an attempt to carry heat to the skin, and blood pressure drops.

With my core struggling to get rid of excess heat, it's no wonder my head was pounding and my stomach was churning. My arms were tired. My legs were cramping. I was starting to feel woozy. It's lucky I found that rest area before I blacked out and crashed.

Heat Cramps

Muscle cramps caused by heat usually affect the legs and lower abdomen first but can also affect the arms and shoulders. Heat cramps are a symptom that the body's water supply (electrolytes) are running low, just as when the water evaporates out of your bike's battery until there isn't enough power to crank the engine anymore.

You don't want to ignore heat cramps because you're not going to feel better until you replenish the water. Take a break, find some shade, massage the cramped muscles to relieve the spasms, and take sips of water. If cramps don't subside, the recommended first aid dose is ½ teaspoon of table salt per half glass of water every fifteen minutes for one hour.

It might seem like a good idea to ride without gear in hot weather, but that just allows your skin to absorb more heat.

Heat Exhaustion

If you don't pay attention to those headaches and cramps and just keep on riding, you may get to heat exhaustion before you get to your destination. You'll just run out of energy as a result of that lower blood pressure and shunting of blood away from the brain and muscles. You may not recognize heat exhaustion because it's normal to feel hot and tired during a long, hot, windy ride. And note that you can lose all your energy without a significant rise in body temperature. Symptoms of heat exhaustion include headaches; dizziness; nausea; momentary fainting; cramps; tiredness; weakness; profuse sweating; and pale, clammy skin. Body temperature will be approximately normal.

If you didn't drink some water for those cramps, that's a high priority now that you're getting exhausted. Find someplace where you can get off the bike and into the shade. First aid books suggest adding a little salt to the water, same dose as for heat cramps. Remove your riding gear and wet down your skin. Pour a glass of water down your neck or onto your head. Wet your shirt. The evaporating water will actually help cool your body down. If you're still trying to tough it out on the bike, pull over at the next fire station and ask for help. Or stop at an intersection where you can read the street signs, get on your cell phone, call 911, and tell them where to find you. Yes, it's an emergency.

If you feel faint, lie down before you fall down, and elevate your feet above your head to increase blood flow to the brain. And if you start to vomit, you're in worse shape than you thought. It may be necessary for you to go to a hospital for an intravenous salt solution. Get out of the sun and stay out of the heat for twenty-four hours. If the symptoms have gotten this far, don't plan to get back on the bike today. Check into a nice air-conditioned motel, and sip ice water every half hour. Avoid sugary or alcoholic beverages. Your body just needs replacement fluids and some time to recuperate.

Heatstroke

I've seen motorcyclists who ignored all the symptoms of heat cramps and then heat exhaustion and eventually just sat down in the sun in a daze. One British couple on a tour to Mojacar had already been several days on the road under a blazing Spanish sun. They hadn't taken any liquid since breakfast tea that morning and were quickly succumbing to heatstroke, with all the classic symptoms. They were incoherent, with red, dry skin hot to the touch and rapid pulse.

Fortunately for these riders, someone else saw the symptoms and organized help in time to get medical aid. They wasted an entire week of their Mojacar vacation in bed, slowly getting their bodies to function again.

If you're heading into a really hot place like Death Valley, you need to get serious about staying hydrated.

Had they not been discovered, their core temperatures would have continued to rise, and their temperature-regulating mechanisms would have begun to shut down. As the sweating stops and the heart beats faster, skin temperature may climb as high as 106 degrees Fahrenheit. Heatstroke victims are first confused, then incoherent, and eventually comatose.

Heatstroke is a medical emergency. Without immediate medical care, the person can die. If you recognize these symptoms in a riding buddy or in yourself, take immediate action. Get the victim into some shade, out of riding gear, and cooled down by any means available. As soon as possible, get the victim to emergency treatment. Don't be bashful about calling 911. This really is life-threatening.

While you are waiting for the medics, you can sponge water or rubbing alcohol on the victim's skin, apply ice wrapped in towels, fan air over them, or whatever you can do to help cool them down. Your target is to get the body temperature below 102 degrees Fahrenheit. Don't give any stimulants, especially not any alcoholic beverages. And forget about riding for a while. It may take four to six days for a heatstroke victim to get over the intestinal upset and start functioning again.

Running Cool

When you're riding in hot, dry climates, the tactics for avoiding heat problems are simple: drink lots of water, insulate your body from the hot air, and use evaporative cooling. Plain old tap water is fine, if you can stand the taste and tolerate the local microorganisms. Bottled water is available almost everywhere in the world in plastic bottles and is usually cleaner. Exercise drinks containing electrolytes are acceptable, unless you have high blood pressure. Carbonated soft drinks are better than nothing, although it would be smarter to get plain water without large doses of salt, high fructose corn syrup, or chemicals. Alcoholic drinks such as beer are unwise because alcohol increases abnormal heartbeats, depresses the pump function of the heart, degrades judgment, and dehydrates the body.

Insulate Your Skin

People from cool climates tend to remove clothing in layers to cool down. As the day warms up, off come the riding pants, then the jacket. Then, if the temperature continues to climb, the rider is really getting hot, so off comes the shirt and the blue jeans get swapped for shorts. But guess what? The rider gets even hotter. Why doesn't baring more skin cool the rider down? It's a matter of physics. You can't give off heat to air that's hotter than you are. If you expose your skin to air that's hotter than you are, the heat flows in one direction—from the air to your body. There are two critical areas of the body where there are large arteries close to the skin: the groin and the neck. The neck area is key on a motorcyclist because it's exposed to the wind blast.

Once air temperature climbs above 99 degrees Fahrenheit, you should keep your insulation on and the vents closed. That's why I wear my leather gloves and insulated riding boots in the summer as well as in the winter. Insulated boots in the summer? Well, my feet are down in the air stream that's first been heated up by the pavement and then heated some more by the engine. Are my feet hot? Sure, but not as hot as if I were wearing thin boots or shoes that exposed my ankles.

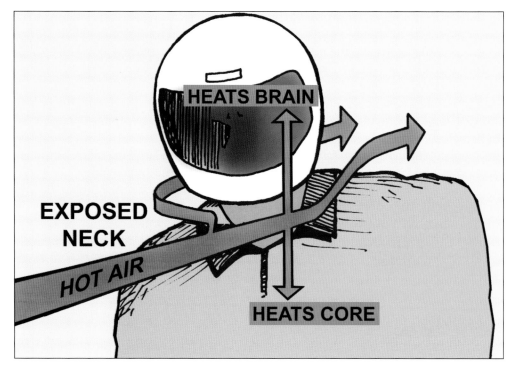

HEATS BRAIN

EXPOSED NECK

HOT AIR

HEATS CORE

When air temperature is above 99 degrees Fahrenheit, exposed skin will absorb heat from the air, and the heated blood will get pumped to the brain and body core. The neck area is critical because there are large arteries on both sides.

Mesh or ventilated riding jackets are a good answer for riding in hot climates, but only in temperatures below 99 degrees Fahrenheit. Once temperature climbs above body temperature, ventilation only allows more hot air to blow through, helping to heat up the skin and transfer more heat back to the core.

Evaporative Cooling

Before leaving the park in Nebraska, I changed my neck protector for an evaporative neck cooler and wet it down. I filled the water bottle and stowed it in the front of the tank bag where I could reach it while riding. Evaporating water absorbs heat from the skin and transfers it to the air. Motorcyclists can augment sweat by wetting down clothing. The most important area is the neck between the ears and the jacket collar because that's where large arteries are most exposed to the airstream. A wet cotton bandanna around your neck will help cool down your core, although you will need to wet it down every few minutes. A neck band that holds a lot of water will provide evaporative cooling for about an hour before it needs to be replenished.

I've tried those tubular neck "snakes" filled with water-absorbing crystals. They work reasonably well for walking, but for me they aren't efficient enough for motorcycling. The crystals hold a lot of water, but it evaporates too slowly. For motorcycling on a seriously hot day, I need a lot more evaporation, and I need it positioned under my ears, not draped loosely around my neck.

Evaporative cooling vests are a functional option and work well with mesh or ventilated jackets. The vest is soaked in water, then worn under the riding jacket. Air blowing through the jacket evaporates the water, and the vest cools down the skin

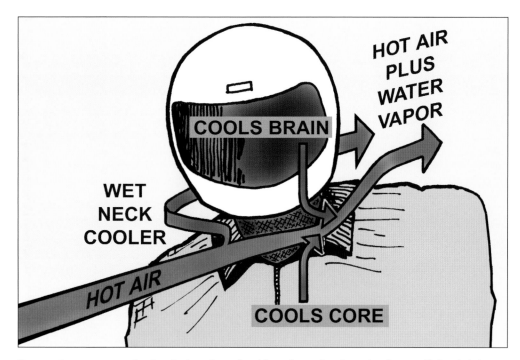

WET NECK COOLER

HOT AIR

COOLS BRAIN

HOT AIR PLUS WATER VAPOR

COOLS CORE

Evaporating water actually absorbs heat from the skin and transfers it to the air, even if the air is hotter than the body. An evaporative cooler over the neck is very efficient because it covers the large arteries and because the neck can be exposed to the wind.

around the core. The two big advantages of a cooling vest over a neck cooler are cooling area and style. A cooling vest worn under a mesh jacket doesn't look dorky, and it has a huge cooling area. Of course, you can wear a cooling vest and a neck cooler at the same time.

The bad news is that evaporative cooling works well only in dry climates. When the humidity is already high, neither perspiration nor the water in your cooling vest can evaporate as well. Slower evaporation means less cooling. Of course, in humid states there is always shade, so the best approach may be to simply take more breaks and consider alternate tactics.

Adjust the Schedule

In Arizona, it's standard practice to nap until midnight and cross the desert between midnight and dawn. In California, you can find cooler air by heading for the mountains or following the coast. Mountains and coastal roads are scarce in states such as Kansas or Iowa, but you can take advantage of the typically cooler morning air. Get up at dawn and get your riding in before the sun starts to warm things up again.

Crossing Nebraska, now in my desert survival mode, I made a point to take more frequent breaks, drink more water, and keep my gear zipped up and my neck cooler saturated. The heat and the wind abated as the sun set, so I decided to keep riding after dark to cover some miles in the cool of the evening.

The next time you're making a long transit on a hot day, remember my little flirtation with heat exhaustion. Trust me here, motorcycling is a lot more fun when your body temperature is steady in the green band and your electrolyte level is up at the full mark.

Gusting cross winds can be frightening for those who don't understand how to quickly lean the bike upwind.

Dang Wind

Cruiser Carla finally saved up enough vacation to take that big cross-country trip to Sturgis, and today she is heading west on Interstate 90 across South Dakota. Last night, there was something on the television about high winds across the plains, but she was too tired from yesterday's ride to get the message. This morning the breeze is kicking up little whirlwinds in the parking lot, but the sun is warming up the air, and it looks like another good day to lean back on the cruiser and motor off toward the horizon.

Carla likes the feel of her cruiser. The low seat allows her to reach the ground with both feet. The forward-mounted foot pegs give her room to stretch her legs. She has added a windshield on the front and has her gear stacked up on the back of the saddle and strapped to the sissy bar. For the first hour, there are a few disconcerting wind gusts, but the sky is blue, the cruiser is thrumming along sweetly, and she continues to enjoy the freedom of the road.

Carla takes a break at Mitchell to see the famous Corn Palace, and when she comes out to get back on the bike, she realizes the blue sky is rapidly disappearing behind dark streaky clouds. Back on the superslab, the wind has shifted to the southwest, and the gusts are getting stronger and more frequent. When gusts suddenly slam into the bike from the left front, Carla can barely hang on. The bike slows as if she had jammed on the brake and points off toward the shoulder. The leather fringe on her jacket whips against her neck. The wind takes her breath away, and grit blows into her eyes behind her sunglasses.

Crossing the bridge at Chamberlain, a malevolent gust suddenly hammers into the bike, slowing it and pushing it toward the railing. Carla's heart jumps into her throat as she struggles to lean the bike upwind. Then, as the gust suddenly passes, she is barely able to keep from shooting over into the oncoming lanes and into a huge truck. For the next 100 miles, she can't shake the image of a bike and rider cartwheeling off the bridge into the Missouri River or slamming head-on into an eighteen-wheeler.

The ride has ceased to be fun, but she sticks to the plan and forges ahead. By the time Carla has battled her way to Wall, her eyes are stinging and watering and she is scared, fatigued, flayed, windburned, dehydrated, and angry. To top off her frustration, the engine sputters onto reserve earlier than expected. And when she parks the bike at the gas station, a gust slams into the bike and pushes it off the sidestand before she can catch it.

Dang wind!

"Dang wind!" Carla screams into the gale. "I hate wind!"

Most of us can empathize with Carla. Motorcycles can be tricky to control in crosswinds, especially in gusting crosswinds. You try to keep the motorcycle balanced, but the gusts suddenly blow it sideways and then just as suddenly let up. It's a constant battle to stay between the lines. You're being assaulted by blowing grit, and your fuel mileage suffers. Is there some method to riding in this windy madness, or do you just have to tough it out?

Sometimes riders contribute to the problem without realizing it. For instance, the fringe on Cruiser Carla's riding jacket is stylish, but it flails around in the wind, adding another distracting annoyance. Her sunglasses are cool looking but don't cover her eyes sufficiently to keep out blowing grit. Carla likes her cruiser because of the image and the low seating position, but the forward-mounted foot pegs make it more difficult to quickly make steering corrections. Stacking her gear on the sissy bar is handy, but that also creates a sail that pushes the bike around. Let's take a moment to consider how different motorcycles react to wind and how the motorcycle/rider ergonomics relate to ease of control.

Sails

A bike with a lot of sail such as a tall windshield or a large fairing is more susceptible to crosswinds. The shape and location of the sails is just as important as the size. Remember, a motorcycle tends to roll around its center of mass. Wind pushing on the area below the CoM has less effect, but wind blowing on the sail above the CoM can have considerable effect. A large frame-mounted fairing acts as a sail, pushing the bike downwind. A passenger seated on the back of the saddle also adds to the sail area. The combination of a frame-mounted fairing; large, boxy tail trunk; and a passenger creates a large sail high up on the bike, making some big touring machines harder to control in gusting crosswinds.

The relative position and shape of the windshield and front fender affect how the bike reacts to crosswinds. More sail ahead of the steering axis, such as a fork-mounted windshield, can actually help roll the bike upwind.

The combination of a frame-mounted fairing; large, boxy tail trunk; and a passenger creates a large sail high up on the bike, making some big touring machines harder to control in gusting crosswinds.

The relative position and shape of the windshield and front fender affect how the bike reacts to crosswinds. Obviously, wind pressure on a frame-mounted fairing or windshield would push the bike downwind. But a fork-mounted fairing, windshield, or fender can have a different result because wind pressure on sails attached to the front fork can apply a steering force to the front wheel. Saddlebags mounted no higher than the machine's CoM will be less likely to push the bike downwind than will bulky sails, such as a sleeping bag strapped up high on a sissy bar or a duffel strapped on a rack over the taillight. Bare bikes can theoretically be as stable as a faired machine, except the wind tugging at the rider's arms will impart some unintentional steering input. For instance, a strong gust from your right can push your elbows toward the left, resulting in countersteering the bike into even more of a left lean.

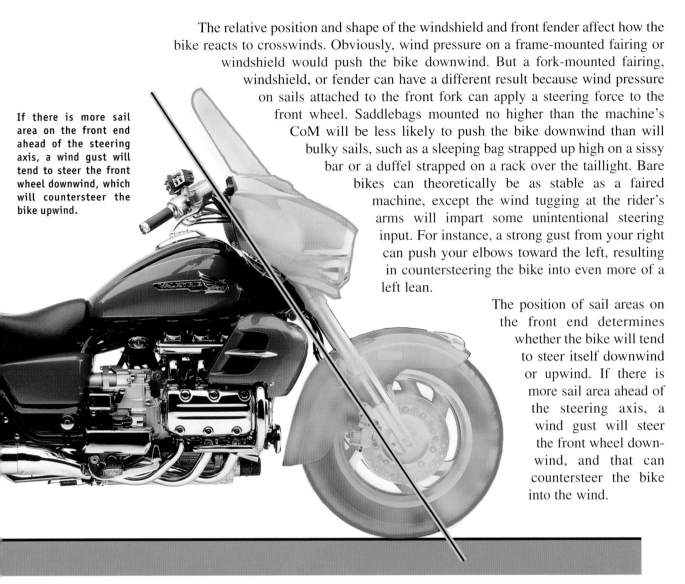

If there is more sail area on the front end ahead of the steering axis, a wind gust will tend to steer the front wheel downwind, which will countersteer the bike upwind.

The position of sail areas on the front end determines whether the bike will tend to steer itself downwind or upwind. If there is more sail area ahead of the steering axis, a wind gust will steer the front wheel downwind, and that can countersteer the bike into the wind.

Ergonomics

The way you sit on the machine and reach for the controls (the ergonomics) also has a dramatic effect on how well you are able to control the machine. For best control in gusting wind, you need to steer the handlebars to quickly adjust lean angle. When you push on the grips, it helps to have your legs in position to counteract the steering effort. The best ergonomics for steering is with your torso leaning slightly forward, arms slightly bent at the elbows, hands grasping the handlebar grips at a natural angle, and body weight supported over the foot pegs. Having the footrests positioned beneath your center of mass allows you to grip the tank with your knees for stability and brace your body against the steering input. What we're describing here is essentially a sport touring posture.

Cruiser-styled machines with forward-mounted foot pegs and high handlebars like the one Carla rides may look stylish, but the ergonomics are far from ideal for windy conditions. Even sportbikes can be difficult to steer if the handlebar position

The foot-forward ergonomics of a cruiser may be comfortable in calm air, but when riding in gusting crosswinds, balance would be easier to control if the seating position allowed the rider to brace his or her legs downward against the foot pegs.

is too far forward or if the bars are too narrow or too low. The upright seating position on a typical touring bike may be comfortable for the long haul, but the sit-up-straight ergonomics can also make it more difficult for the rider to make the quick steering inputs that are needed to counteract a wind gust. It isn't just the style of the bike at issue; it's how the individual rider fits a particular machine.

Consider that the ergonomics determine which muscles are used to lean the bike. Quick, powerful steering input requires quick, powerful muscles, such as those in your arms. To understand this concept, lean your torso forward in your chair with your feet flat on the floor. Stretch both arms straight forward as if you were reaching for some imaginary handlebars mounted too far forward. Reach out far enough that your elbows are locked straight. Now, turn your imaginary handlebars a little to the left and then a little toward the right and think about which muscles are doing the work. With your arms locked straight, you must use your back and stomach muscles, right? And you're probably bracing with your legs, too.

Now, pull your imaginary handlebars toward you just enough that your elbows are bent, and try steering left-right again. With your arms bent, you can steer with your arm and shoulder muscles, which happen to be quicker and more accurate than the larger muscles in your stomach, back, buttocks, or legs. Try steering your imaginary handlebars with your feet stretched forward, and you'll realize that your stomach and back muscles come into play. The bottom line is that ergonomics make a big difference in your ability to control the bike as well as in how you feel at the end of the day.

Whatever your favorite machine, if you find it difficult to control it in windy conditions, take a serious look at both the sails on your bike and the ergonomics. If you have trouble getting the bike leaned upwind or certain muscles always ache halfway through the ride, consider how you might modify the bike to fit you better. And if your current machine can't be adjusted to fit you, the message should be obvious: think about swapping to a different machine.

Control Skill

Even if the machinery, loading, and ergonomics are perfect, your balancing and steering technique has a lot to do with accurate crosswind control. Riders who consciously countersteer have better control and less frustration in windy situations than do riders who merely think *lean* or who try to steer with their knees or feet.

When riding through strong winds, you must lean the bike into the wind, and that may require a quick and forceful push on the grips. For example, with a strong but steady crosswind from your right, pushing on the right grip will lean the bike right (upwind). If the bike drifts too far downwind, you need to lean it even more into the wind. Pushing a little harder on the upwind grip will lean it over more and point back toward your desired line. Of course, when the wind suddenly decreases or changes direction, you will need to quickly countersteer to whatever angle is needed to maintain your line of travel.

When riding through crosswinds, you may get some strange feedback from the front wheel. Front-end geometry wants to roll the bike vertical. You'll need to hold more pressure on the grip than during a curve since the contact patches are way over on one side of the tires, even though the machine is traveling straight ahead. Just concentrate on countersteering to make the motorcycle go in whatever direction you wish, and let the tires swerve around under you. Many of us have ridden for miles through strong steady crosswinds with the bike leaning over at a startling angle, controlling the bike by a firm push on the upwind grip.

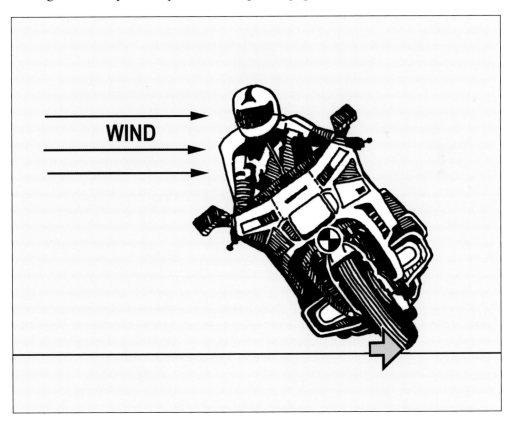

When you're leaned over into the wind, steering geometry tends to roll the bike vertical. You'll have to maintain steady pressure on the upwind grip to keep it leaned.

Gusting Crosswinds

The most difficult situation is one with strong gusting winds. Suddenly, a gust slams into the bike, pushing it off on a tangent toward the shoulder or into the opposing lane. What's needed to counteract gusts is to lean the bike into the wind quickly. And the way to lean a bike quickly is to countersteer forcefully, the same tactic you'd use to initiate a quick turn or to swerve around an obstruction. To lean the bike left, push on the left grip. To lean right, push on the right grip. When you get hit by a stronger crosswind gust, just push a little harder and be prepared to push on the other grip to straighten up again as the gust passes.

Since we can't see the air, it helps to have some understanding of what wind does around other vehicles and structures. Wind tends to reflect off obstructions and swirl into vortexes on the downwind side. That means the air is unstable on the downwind side of hills, billboards, or large trucks. Oncoming trucks push a powerful bow wave of air that curls back on both sides of the cab in still air. In a gusting crosswind, the turbulent bow wave curls back on the downwind side. That's especially dangerous if you are approaching a truck head-on with the wind blowing from your left or are attempting to pass a truck on its downwind side. Be especially wary of large vehicles that will pass upwind of you from the opposite direction.

We might also note that Cruiser Carla's wind troubles grew worse toward afternoon. That's because wind typically gets stronger and more turbulent as the earth warms up. There are many locations in North America where a strong wind is expected every summer afternoon. For example, in the Columbia River Gorge

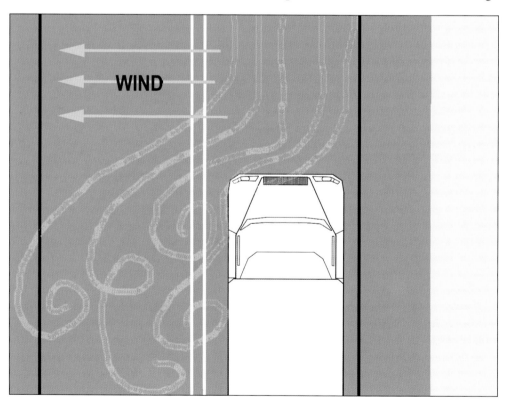

Trucks push a bow wave of air, and when there is a crosswind the wave curls back around the downwind side.

When the wind is from your left, move as far away from oncoming trucks as possible to avoid the wind turbulence curling around the cab, and be prepared to push the grips left to counter the wind blast.

between Oregon and Washington, the cool coastal air rushes inland to replace the hot air rising over the inland areas. For the wind surfers, it's heaven. For motorcyclists, it's somewhere else. The narrow steel-grated Bridge of the Gods crosses the river at right angles to the afternoon wind direction, and it can be a very exciting ride. In such locations, wise riders plan the transit earlier in the morning, before the wind gets serious.

When riding into strong headwinds, be prepared for sudden gusts reflected off steep cliffs. Rounding the cliff, you can encounter a very strong gust at an angle to the prevailing wind.

There are many locations in North America where strong winds are normal every afternoon, including the Columbia River Gorge between Oregon and Washington. The prevailing winds are from the west, in this photo from right to left. The Bridge of the Gods is a narrow two-laner with a grated steel deck over the water.

When you're fighting a strong headwind, be prepared for very strong gusts bouncing off the upwind side of cliffs like this one on your right. In this situation, the prevailing wind is from straight ahead, but the gust will be from your right as you round the cliff.

Body Armor

Obviously, in gusting wind conditions, there is an increased possibility of a crash, so smart riders zip on their best armor. Most important, getting irritated or frustrated can distract you from road hazards. Wear sensible riding gear that covers all skin, and keep everything zipped and buttoned closed. Wear your earplugs because the wind velocity when riding into a headwind generates noise levels way up into the injury range, and the blast may not be deflected by the fairing or windshield. Wind noise results in fatigue and slower reaction time. It's also important to wear eye protection that keeps wind and windblown grit out of your eyes and to use an eye lubricant to keep your eyes from drying out. Your fingers will thank you for wearing durable, full-fingered gloves that protect against wind chapping and sunburn.

Know When to Fold 'Em

You don't have to like wind, but you can gain the confidence that comes from knowing you can control the bike under most wind conditions. I mention most, because sometimes winds are so violent that it is unwise to continue riding. I know of riders who have lost traction in wet, windy conditions and been blown off the road. I can recall dropping down off a pass early one spring to find myself headed straight into a sinister silver-streaked cloud moving across the valley ahead. I was just wondering what I was seeing when a snarling sleet squall hammered the bike so hard the tires were starting to slide into the other lane. I made a quick downwind U-turn, sped back to a road maintenance area I had just passed, laid the bike on its side in the lee of a gravel pile, and hunkered down until the squall moved on. In the so-called tornado alley between Texas and the Great Lakes, motorcyclists must be aware of the extreme hazard of tornadoes. If you observe a funnel start to form, you should immediately seek shelter beneath some heavy structure or make a U-turn and beat a quick retreat.

Homework

The homework exercise for gusting winds is to practice countersteering (push steering) all the time as you ride along. Approaching a curve to the right, consciously push the right grip toward the right. Changing lanes to the left, push on the left grip. If the ergonomics of your machine have you leaning back and pulling on the handlebars as you ride along, try pulling both grips toward the direction you want to go. For a right turn, pull both grips toward the right. For a left turn, pull both grips to the left. If you practice countersteering every time you ride, you'll lean the bike into sudden wind gusts without having to think about it.

Even in the desert, you can run into winter conditions at higher altitudes.

Freezing Your Gas on the Pass

I couldn't believe how cold it was for a desert ride in Southern California. Up on the Angeles Crest highway, only thirty miles uphill from sunny Pasadena, my dual sport sidecar rig was crunching into packed snow and black ice. I'd missed an important turnoff into the desert on the Los Angeles-Barstow-Las Vegas dual sport ride and had continued on the highway far enough that I didn't want to go back and try to find the off-road route. I didn't realize I'd have to follow the crest highway another fifty miles at elevations above 6,000 feet before getting back down to the desert and connecting with the dual sport route again.

The moral of this tale is that even in balmy Southern California, with warm breezes wafting through the palm trees down at sea level, you can find yourself in winter conditions just by gaining a little altitude. Now, whether you are heading out on an April tour from Amarillo, taking a September trip from Seattle, or just itching for a December spin in Duluth, my advice is to be a little smarter than I was up on that Angeles Crest highway. Let's consider some of the implications of cold-weather riding.

Turning Back

There is a lot of wisdom in knowing when to turn around. Ascending the Angeles Crest highway, I was passed at warp speeds by a rider carving corners on a Ducati. But at the first sign of frost in the shadows, the Ducati rider wisely turned around and zoomed back downhill. On the dual sport sidecar rig, I had additional options and continued. But if I had run into sleet up there, I would have turned around also. It's not smart to keep motoring ahead into worsening conditions if you've got a choice.

On the other hand, if you're in the middle of a cross-country trip when you're caught in a storm, the only sensible option may be to continue ahead. Say you're making a transit across Utah and get caught by a cold front blowing down from Montana. The next warm restaurant is forty miles away in Salina, and the last one was sixty miles back in Green River. That front is going to run over you whether you stop, retreat, or continue, so you might as well keep moving toward Salina.

When you're faced with worsening conditions, don't just keep rushing off across the landscape hoping the situation will get better. Pull over, shut down the engine, and spend a few minutes focusing on a plan of action.

Now, one of these days you're going to find yourself in this situation, and I want you to remember this: before you continue rushing off across the landscape into worsening conditions, pull over alongside the road, shut the engine down, and spend a few minutes focusing on the situation. OK, it's cold and the wind is howling. But get out the map. Huddle down in the lee of the bike, warm your fingers on the engine, look at the options, and make a decision. Is it wise to keep going, or should you beat a retreat? If the only option is to keep going, what extra insulation can you add under your riding gear? Remind yourself of the symptoms of hypothermia.

The Human Heating/Cooling System

To understand the tactics for protecting the body against cold, let's remember how the human heating and cooling system functions. The body burns food to generate heat and pumps warmed oxygen-rich blood throughout its system. Blood near the skin surface gives off heat to the air. The lungs absorb oxygen from the air and expel warm water vapor and carbon dioxide. The body automatically adjusts blood pressure, blood flow, and breathing rate to maintain an almost constant temperature of the central core (the heart, lungs, kidneys, and other central organs), regardless of outside air temperature. If the core temperature begins to increase or decrease, the system quickly attempts to correct it. A core temperature that is too cold is called hypothermia. Only a couple of degrees below normal temperature can be life threatening.

Hypothermia

When the body senses a drop in core temperature, the response is to shut down blood flow to the extremities, starting with fingers and toes. If necessary to save the vital core organs, the system will sacrifice fingers and toes to freezing (frostbite). What isn't so obvious is that the head is an extremity, too. Large arteries along both sides of the neck carry warm blood to the head. So when the heating system decreases blood flow to the extremities, there's also less blood (and less oxygen) to the brain. The bottom line is that as you become hypothermic, your woozy brain may not recognize what's happening.

For motorcyclists, the hazard is that a chilled, oxygen-starved brain starts making silly mistakes. At first, maybe it's just stopping the bike without putting a foot down or cruising off the road onto the shoulder, then laughing giddily at the result. It should be obvious that in a hypothermic state, a rider can make serious or even fatal control errors, such as crossing the centerline or going wide into a power pole. If you really begin to chill down, it may seem perfectly sensible to run off into a field, lean up against a tree, and go to sleep.

The head and neck can lose up to 50 percent of body heat. That's why it is so important to insulate your neck from the windblast.

Insulate the Neck

One of the most important defenses against hypothermia is insulation of the head and neck. That's because there are big arteries in the neck. The major blood flow to the head means it can radiate a lot of heat unless it is insulated. Insulating the neck slows down heat loss from those big arteries and provides warmer blood to the brain. Neck insulation is vitally important to a motorcyclist because our heads and necks are hanging out in the wind stream.

The crushable EPS liner in a helmet is similar to a foam ice chest and helps insulate the head. But it's important to close off that gap between collar and helmet. Luckily for me up on the Angeles Crest, I was already wearing one of my favorite neck protectors: a windproof Aerostich Wind Triangle. Other riders prefer a synthetic fleece (Turtle Fur) neck tube, a heavy bandanna, or a balaclava that covers both head and neck. Whatever your choice of neck insulation, don't leave home without it.

Electric Heating

A fellow moto-journalist described his electric jacket liner as a quantum leap in cold-weather riding gear. One reason an electric vest is so useful is that keeping the chest and core organs warm keeps more blood flowing to the extremities. OK, I'll admit it. For years I was reluctant (or perhaps not sufficiently motivated) to buy an electric vest. After that chilly ride up on the Angeles Crest, I finally caved in. These days, on chilly rides I've got an electric cord hanging out of my suit, too.

However, I consider electric heating only a supplement to insulation, not a replacement, especially for trips into more remote areas where there aren't any warm restaurants to duck into. A little electrical failure can leave you freezing. For example, Ironbutt rider and *MCN* contributor Mike Kneebone had a charging failure on the return trip to Fairbanks from Prudhoe Bay (Alaska) in freezing weather. To keep the engine running, he had to unplug all nonessential electrics, including the electric vest. His knees are still knocking.

Crash Padding

While I was up on the Angeles Crest at 7,000 feet, a motorcyclist on an old BMW airhead eased by heading the other way. On the black ice and snow, he was riding very cautiously and managing to keep the bike upright—at least while he was still within view. But on such slippery conditions, there's a thin line between vertical and horizontal, and frozen ground is awfully hard. Considering the risks of a falldown, I'm sure he was glad to be wearing durable riding gear. If you have a choice in your cold-weather crash padding, go for armor that's shock absorbing as well as abrasion resistant.

Rest Breaks

If you know you're going to be on the road all day in miserable weather, plan frequent rest breaks to warm up and refuel your body. The weather doesn't have to be freezing—you can become hypothermic at 50 degrees Fahrenheit. It's not a bad idea to stop once every two hours, or once every hour in really bad conditions. Get into a heated room, have a snack, and drink one or two glasses of water. Remember that the body gives off water vapor through breathing, so you need to replenish your water, even if you've just ridden through a downpour.

Hot soup is good for cold rides because it provides both nourishment and liquid. Coffee or tea are acceptable, but they go through the body faster than plain water does. Definitely avoid alcoholic beverages. When you take a break inside a warm building, remove or unzip enough outer insulation to allow your body to soak up room heat, and move around to get blood circulating to the extremities again. Spend long enough inside to get warmed, refueled, and rehydrated and your body core cranking out heat again. That may take a half hour or longer if you spent too much time in the cold since the last stop. If you're still shivering, that's a sign the core is bordering on the cold side. You need some additional warm-up time before continuing.

Survival Tactics

If you know you're really freezing your gas up on the pass but there are no warm indoor facilities available, don't just keep riding until you pass out. Take steps to conserve heat while you're still shivering and still thinking. I remember a rainy ride years ago when I began to feel sort of disconnected and uncaring. The temperature was in the 40s, but a light rain was helping suck the heat away. I finally recognized the symptoms of hypothermia, made a U-turn, and rode back to the nearest motel where I could get a room, crank up the heat, and huddle in blankets. Two hours later, I was barely getting over fits of uncontrollable shivering. Had I continued much farther, I might have gotten too confused to realize what was happening.

Got some dirty socks in the saddlebag? Wear 'em over your thin gloves. Wrap a spare T-shirt around your neck. Put on your rain gear for a little added insulation. Buy a newspaper and stuff it inside your jacket. Riding the freeway, stop at the rest

You've got to be serious about motorcycling to ride around on ice and snow.

areas and use the MPW (the Motorcyclist Power Warmer—otherwise known as a hand dryer). If you spot a laundromat, take a break while your gear is cooking in a dryer. The point is, don't just keep riding and hope you'll survive—take steps to conserve that important core heat while your brain is still functioning.

Yes, It's an Emergency

Frostbite and hypothermia are nothing to sneeze at. If you or your riding buddies appear to be confused, can't seem to stay awake, or start making silly riding mistakes, those are signs that hypothermia is setting in. Other symptoms include irritability, slurred speech, attention loss, lessening of pain, and stiff muscles. The symptoms are similar to being drunk. Shivering is a good sign—it means your body is still trying to generate more heat. When shivering stops in cold conditions, you're in trouble. You may start to feel very relaxed and peaceful, with a reduction in muscle coordination and judgment.

When you recognize the symptoms of hypothermia in yourself or in others, take action. Get emergency assistance immediately. Hypothermia is a life-threatening emergency, even if the victim hasn't lost consciousness or crashed the bike yet. The top priority is getting the victim warmed up. If you're in an exposed outside location, get the rider off the bike and out of the wind, cover him or her with whatever insulation is available, and get a volunteer to share body heat. As soon as possible, get the victim into a warm room where the body core can gradually return to normal temperature.

Don't be bashful about flagging down a passing vehicle and asking for help. Yes, we know you want to be independent out there, but when you're hypothermic, you can't just tough it out. Got a CB radio? Get on the horn and explain the situation. You may find truckers more sympathetic to your plight than other drivers are.

Be cautious about applying external heat since the victim may not be able to feel burning temperatures. Remove wet clothing. Pat the skin dry; don't rub vigorously. Wrap the victim in blankets that cover feet and head. Provide warm liquids such as soup, broth, or warmed milk to help restore core heat. It may take several hours for the core to regain normal temperature.

Keeping the Shiny Side Up

All right, let's assume you understand all about body protection, and you've got the gear and the tactics to avoid hypothermia. The next question is: how do you keep the shiny side up? On slick surfaces, the tires don't have much traction. You know it's a thin line between a little slip or slide and an instant slam-dunk onto the ice. One of the advantages of a motorcycle is that you can put your tires over the most tractable surface. If the wheel tracks are polished ice, you can usually improve traction by moving over onto the shoulder or riding between the wheel tracks.

If you are determined to ride a two-wheeler on snow and ice, look for the best traction, such as that crunchy snow over at the edge of the road.

Most of the same traction management tactics for dry pavement also apply to slippery roads. Ride as smoothly as possible, avoiding any sudden steering, throttle, or braking changes. Even at slower speeds, follow cornering lines that maximize the turn radius and minimize lean angle. For really slippery roads, slow down to an appropriate speed for the radius of curve and angle of camber, and weight the bike to keep your wheels perpendicular to the surface. Too fast for a flat curve, and centrifugal force pulls the bike toward the outside. Too slow for a banked curve, and gravity pulls the bike toward the inside. Speed is correct when the wheels are perpendicular to the road surface.

You can lessen the risk of falling on slippery surfaces by placing more of your weight on the foot pegs rather than on the saddle. With your weight supported on the foot pegs, you can lean the bike to keep the tires perpendicular to the road surface. That way, even when the bike slides sideways, it's less likely to slam onto its side. You may be tempted to put your feet down to help stabilize the bike, but if your tires don't have enough traction to hold the bike upright, your boot soles probably won't do any better. And if you do fall, it will be less painful if your ankles aren't in the way.

Be aware that bridges freeze sooner—and stay frozen longer—than does adjacent pavement because the cold air can refrigerate the bridge from underneath as well as from the top. Approaching a downhill section, slow to a crawl at the top, stay in a lower gear, and use both brakes lightly to hold back speed. If the tires start to slip, let speed increase. Riding uphill, approach a little faster at the bottom, then ease off the gas and let forward energy carry the machine up.

Remember that bridges freeze sooner and stay frozen longer than does the pavement on either side.

For a slippery downhill section, slow to a crawl, stay in a lower gear, use both brakes lightly, and look for the best traction.

You can also increase traction by letting some air out of the tires, say dropping pressure down to 20 psi. Soft tires are less likely to skid. Just remember to pump them up to normal pressures again after you get off the slick stuff.

The Third Wheel

If you tend to get motorcycle withdrawal symptoms from not riding during the cold winter months and think you can successfully stave off hypothermia and frostbite, maybe it's time to think about a sidecar rig. A sidecar outfit can slip and slide without any major penalties such as falling down. That's the main reason motorcyclists who choose to ride during the winter months add a sidecar outfit to their stable of machines.

But if you're thinking seriously about a sidecar, be aware that a motorcycle-sidecar combination is not just a regular two-wheeled motorcycle with this big thing on one side but an entirely different three-wheeled vehicle with different operating characteristics. Getting a sidecar attached is only half of the deal. Learning to drive a three-wheeler is another level of motorcycling that the casual motorcyclist may not be willing to accomplish. I'll talk about that a little later.

Night Owls

Remember old Paul Revere pounding through the streets in the middle of the night? Wouldn't you think that Paul would have been smarter to do his fast riding in the daylight? Well, he had a schedule problem. The enemy was coming. He *had* to ride at night. At least he was riding a horse. Sometimes we motorcyclists choose to do the same. We need to cover some miles, and there isn't enough daylight. Or maybe we want to cross the Arizona desert at night rather than beneath the scorching sun. Let's consider some tactics for night riding.

Night riding requires some different tactics.

Stay Alert

The very first problem with night riding is that most of us have our bodies programmed for sleep at night. Unless you change the programming, it is extremely difficult to keep your eyelids propped open while staring into the darkness and listening to the hypnotic drone of the engine.

One way to change the body's schedule is to change sleep timing. For example, let's say I want to be at a rally in the next state by Saturday noon and I can't leave until after work on Friday. Rather than hit the road immediately after work when I am already fatigued, I could go home, have dinner, and take a nap for a couple of hours. That not only gives me a fresh start but also avoids the evening traffic rush. Taking a nap before leaving eats up some time, but it may make the difference between being able to keep going at 3 a.m. or being too fatigued to continue.

Perhaps the most important night-riding tactic is to take frequent rest breaks. I make a point of stopping about every 60 miles, or once each hour. When I pull over for a break, I don't just sit on the bike and nod off; I get off and take a jog or do some exercises to get the juices flowing again. As a practical technique, stopping for a coffee break at a restaurant provides a good cue for a subsequent stop at a rest area. If you don't drink coffee, drink a couple glasses of water. Later, your bladder will make you an offer you can't ignore.

Even with some pretrip shuteye and frequent exercise breaks, my body sometimes rebels and refuses to stay awake any longer. I oblige by crashing on a picnic table at some reasonably safe rest area and catching a few z's. I don't take off my riding gear because it provides insulation. Usually, I wake up within a half hour or so and can then continue. However, I choose my spots to crash carefully. If there are suspicious-looking persons hanging around a rest area, I get just enough exercise to refresh myself and then keep moving. If the situation seems reasonably safe, I lock the bike and put the ignition key in an inside pocket to discourage thefts. Some long-distance riders just pull over and take a nap in the saddle, which is known as the Iron Butt Motel.

The Eyes Lose

When riding at night, we need to maximize the view ahead to give us time to react to problems. Human eyes have some interesting characteristics that can get us into trouble, and we're not talking just about winking at the sheriff's daughter. Be aware that every eye has a small blind spot, usually off to one side of center. It's something doctors can measure during a good eye exam. Fortunately, the blind spot of your left eye doesn't overlap the blind spot of your right eye, so both eyes together can cover the whole field of vision. But consider that a bug splat or a scratched face shield in a critical area can totally blot out a portion of the view. That's one good reason to keep your head and eyes moving and your face shield clean.

Vision also tends to fade as we get older, and most of us age another year about every twelve months. One common problem is floaters that drift around on the surface of the cornea and interfere with clear vision. As the years go by, you may become nearsighted or farsighted and need corrective lenses, then discover that your reading bifocals have the wrong focus distance for reading motorcycle instruments. If you have trouble reading the instruments, you might consider some special bifocals just for motorcycling.

Some people gradually develop vision problems such as loss of peripheral vision, cataracts, macular degeneration, or loss of color distinction. Because vision is so important to a motorcyclist, it is smart to have your vision checked every couple of years, preferably by an eye physician (ophthalmologist) who is trained to spot medical problems. There are also sports optometrists who dispense lens prescriptions and can also spot conditions that might require the attention of a specialist. If you know you have more trouble seeing at night, that's a good reason to avoid night riding altogether.

The eye can adjust to bright daylight by closing down the iris. But the vision receptors in the back of the eye also adjust chemically to the average light intensity, and that chemical change takes a while. Our eyes can't instantly adjust as we go from bright light to darkness to bright light again. This is most obvious during a night ride when you walk out of a brightly lit building and stumble blindly over the curb while your eyes are adapting to the dim nighttime level. That's one reason why some veteran truckers wear sunglasses in the restaurant at night and why experienced night riders wait a few moments in the dark before riding away.

Blinding Lights

Consider what happens when someone takes a flash photo of you while you're staring at the camera. The instantaneous flash of bright light overwhelms vision for three or four seconds. The same thing happens when you ride from bright daylight into an unlit tunnel or when another vehicle goes by in the opposite lane.

But what do you do when you're cruising down a narrow road and an oncoming vehicle approaches with its lights blazing at you? As the other lights approach, your eyes begin to adjust to the higher light level, and when the vehicle passes, it takes several seconds to adjust back to low light again. In the meantime, you're almost blind.

The trick is to avoid focusing on bright lights. Instead, as the other vehicle gets close, temporarily shift your focus to the white fog line along the right edge of your lane. The vision receptors in your peripheral vision may be temporarily overwhelmed, but your important central vision is saved for the dark road you need to see after the vehicle passes.

If you haven't tried this before, it may be unnerving to not be focused on that other vehicle hurtling at you, but your peripheral vision is able to track movement and lane position, and your focus on the fog line helps you maintain your lane position. After the car passes, you'll be able to focus on the road again. If you stare at the oncoming lights, you'll be temporarily blinded for several seconds. It is far more important to be able to see that narrow bridge or that deer in the road during the critical seconds after another vehicle goes by.

One other odd characteristic of human eyes is that color relates to distance perception. In other words, you might be able to accurately judge the distance from you to a green light but not to a red light. As it happens, it is more difficult to judge the distance of lights in the red spectrum. Since taillights are red, it pays to occasionally count out your following distance in seconds, rather than assuming your eyes are giving you an accurate distance. At night, avoid following another vehicle closer than four seconds away; locate an object the vehicle is about to pass and count out loud, "one thousand and one, one thousand and two," and so on until you pass the same object. If you pass the same fixed point before you count to four, you're too close.

As the other vehicle gets closer, temporarily shift your focus to the white fog line along the right edge of your lane to avoid being blinded by the bright lights.

FOCUS ON
FOG LINE

Keep on Truckin'

Commercial truckers keep on truckin' day and night. And these nights, truck traffic is more aggressive than ever. It is likely that today's big eighteen-wheelers will run a lot faster at night than you are willing to risk, which means you may be getting passed frequently. It is awfully easy for the trucker to lose track of a tiny two-wheeler in the mirrors, especially if the biker isn't helping. Give the truckers a better chance of not squashing you by staying out of their blind spots.

If you find yourself in the middle of a convoy, try to maintain the same speed as the trucks around you so that a driver doesn't have to pass. When a trucker does pass you, it's difficult to see where you are in relation to the end of the rig. To give you some idea of what a truck driver can see in his mirrors, let's consider two daytime photos. Notice that the lead bike right alongside the cab is barely visible and is partially hidden behind the window frame. The second bike is hidden from view. At night, the driver can see the motorcycle headlight but can't really gauge where the bike is in relation to the end of the trailer. That's why the area alongside a big rig is called the no zone.

Here's a daylight shot of two motorcycles alongside a typical tractor-trailer rig.

From inside the cab, the driver can see part of the lead bike and very little of the second bike, even in daylight.

When a trucker passes you, it is polite to flash your high beam once or twice as a signal that the end of the rig has cleared you. The signal tells the trucker that you're aware of the situation and that it's OK for the trucker to pull back in the right lane. If the trucker appreciates the courtesy, he will flash his running lights as a thank you.

Night riding is one good reason to run with your CB radio on. Jabbering back and forth on the radio is a good way to stay alert. Just as important, the truckers you are talking to are more likely to be aware of you and cut you some slack. You might even learn some important information, such as an accident ahead.

Drunks, Crooks, Creeps, and Weirdos

The most dangerous hours to be on the road are between 11 p.m. and 2 a.m., especially on weekends. Those are the hours when the drinkers are heading home from the taverns. Your risks double during these hours. If you are making a long transit at night, be especially wary of cars and pickups in the outskirts of towns and cities. Drunk drivers tend to be erratic, wandering out of the lane, making sudden steering corrections, or suddenly jamming on the brakes for no apparent reason. Give the drunks lots of room. If you're wired for communication, do the rest of us a favor and report the vehicle before someone gets killed.

Nighttime seems to bring out the creeps and weirdos. Some people are just looking for a confrontation. Psychologists suggest that about one out of ten people are at least borderline unstable. Now and again, you may encounter an aggressive person who picks you as a potential victim. There is no lack of criminal behavior around. We all know to pull the key out of the ignition when going to the restroom and to lock the forks while having coffee. But there are scams to watch for other than getting your bike ripped off. More than one rider has come out of the restroom to find that a leather jacket has disappeared or the GPS is missing.

As a general rule, I don't flash the contents of my wallet near strangers or pay for anything with bills larger than a $20. I once had a $50 bill magically turn into a $20 while I was fumbling with my helmet and gloves in a Nevada gas station. There is little you can do to recover from such scams once you allow them to occur.

While I am still rolling into the parking lot at a rest area, gas station, or restaurant, I scrutinize the people and vehicles already there. If I don't like the smell of the situation, I keep rolling through and look for a different place to take a break. For example, I would avoid a group of tough-looking young men hanging around a car with others inside, especially if all eyes turn to check me out as I ride in. These kids may be friendly, but I don't need to find out. I avoid eye contact and just disappear.

One night at a quiet restaurant, a weirdo several seats away began to make insulting remarks about bikers. I was the only one within earshot wearing riding gear and carrying a helmet. I simply pretended I hadn't heard, avoided eye contact, finished my coffee quietly and confidently, paid my bill with a stone face, and departed. This guy was obviously looking for an argument or a fight, and I wasn't interested.

On the road, I maintain separation from other vehicles. I never allow someone to pace me in an adjacent lane, especially if anyone inside appears to be checking me out. I move out of the way of tailgaters, and I make a point of not cutting closely in front of other vehicles when I pass them. When I become aware of someone invading my space, I immediately take evasive action, changing lanes, dropping back, accelerating, or using a truck as a blocker.

Punching Through the Dark

Obviously, it helps to have some big candlepower punching through the darkness to illuminate the deer, potholes, and tire carcasses you might otherwise not see in time.

If you're going to do any serious night riding, consider upgrading your lights. You might think about replacing your headlight bulb with an 80/100-watt bulb or adding some high-intensity driving lights wired through a relay controlled by the high-beam circuit. Obviously, there are laws about such things. Check on legality before bolting on any extra lights, keep your headlight adjusted, and dim your brights courteously for approaching traffic. You don't want to find out the hard way that the guy you just blinded is driving a patrol car and that your high-intensity discharge night cutters are not legal in the state.

Over the years, I've had more than one occasion when my headlight suddenly failed at night. From personal experience, I can confirm that it's a little scary when your headlight suddenly quits while you're rounding a curve at night. In both cases, there was some hint of a problem earlier, such as the headlight taking a second to come on after the ignition was turned on, or both high and low beams occasionally coming on together. If your bike exhibits electrical problems, it would be smart to fix them before heading out on an all-night transit.

Don't forget about the rear end of your bike. Many motorcycles have only a single bulb for both taillight and stoplight. Either filament can burn out while you are riding along, and you won't know about it. As a test, park your bike on a dark street with the lights off and walk back for a look. Observe what happens when other vehicles pass by. That's what following drivers would see with your taillight burned out. If your bike looks a little gloomy back there, you might think about adding extra tail or clearance lights or at least additional reflectors. Light-emitting diode (LED) rear-light modules are available to replace the light bulb with an array of LEDs that are extremely reliable and draw less power. Do your jacket and helmet have reflective patches on the back? Would it help to wear a reflective vest over your leather jacket at night? At least give other drivers a good opportunity to see you at night.

Body Care

Considering the increased hazards of night riding, it makes sense to wrap yourself in a good crash suit. If tonight is your turn to go sliding down the tarmac on some spilled diesel oil, you'll be a lot happier if you're wearing your best abrasion-resistant duds and skid lid when it happens.

Retro-reflective panels on riding suits help increase your conspicuity at night.

Even during the summer, nighttime temperatures can be surprisingly chilly. Don't forget to wear insulation under your crash padding, slip on your neck warmer or balaclava, and plug in that electric vest. There are enough problems to deal with while riding at night that you don't want to get hypothermic, too.

One final note: it's always smart to avoid alcohol while riding a motorcycle, but it is critical at night. Alcohol not only degrades your judgment, hearing, and muscle control but also upsets vision, including the ability of your eyes to focus and adapt to changing light levels.

Obviously, the risks of riding increase after the sun goes down. If you have any reservations about being a night owl, just say no. Take a day off work and make that rally transit in the daylight, or have an early snooze tonight and get up at dawn to start that desert crossing. If you have a choice, choose daylight. If Paul Revere were around, he'd probably agree. Come to think of it, if Paul had a fast motorcycle instead of a horse, he could probably have warned all the troops about the redcoats coming and been in bed by sunset.

If you're planning a trip to Europe or Southern California, you should be prepared to split lanes between the cars.

White-Line Fever

Riding the white line between traffic lanes is a subject that motorcycle journalists tend to avoid. First, white lining (lane splitting or lane sharing) in North America is tolerated only in and around a few congested cities in California. White lining is commonplace in countries such as England, Italy, and South Africa, but it's a taboo here in most of the US of A. Second, riders who haven't experienced or observed skillful lane splitting seem to have a built-in resistance to the subject.

Keep your speed down when white lining to allow a quick slowdown for drivers who happen to wander into your path.

You may not have thought about white lining and you may not want to. If lane splitting is illegal or socially unacceptable in your part of the world and you don't ever intend to ride into a congested city where lane splitting is a possibility, you may want to skip the rest of this section. The following will probably just increase your blood pressure. But if any of your future travels might take you into cities such as San Francisco, Los Angeles, or San Diego; or if you are planning a foreign trip that will take you to cities such as Rome, London, or Paris; you should be prepared to split lanes.

Lane splitting is a tactic used daily by many motorcycle officers, couriers, and commuters in congested cities around the world where traffic is so clogged that weaving through the stalled cars on a skinny motorcycle is the only way to get across town in a reasonable time frame. As congestion gets worse, you are more likely to see increased lane splitting by local motorcyclists. Motorcycle activists in some states are lobbying to make lane sharing legal. Or, rather, they are lobbying to make lane sharing not illegal.

Dangerous? Illegal?

Is white lining dangerous? Is it illegal? Let's deal with the danger issue first. Of course, lane splitting isn't safe! Squeezing between moving cars and trucks with your legs in a position to get crushed is definitely not without risk. But, before you reject white lining as just a foolhardy stunt pulled off by a few nutty Californians, consider the risks of getting knocked down by inattentive tailgaters while creeping along in stop-and-go freeway traffic.

For example, let's assume you are dribbling along in stop-and-go traffic in line with the cars. After thrumming your fingers on the brake lever for five minutes, traffic finally starts to move out, you roll on the gas, and then the brake lights come on again. Meanwhile, Crusher Carla behind you in her bigwheel Ramcharger with the FOBYFO plates is closing fast on your taillight, and there's no escape. Bam! You're crunched between Carla and the car ahead of you.

In other words, if you are faced with the choice of either creeping along in bumper-to-taillight traffic or white lining, the risks aren't increased by splitting between the cars. It's a lot more difficult for Crusher Carla to rear-end you while you're easing down the white line. I'm not aware of any formal traffic studies that would shed some statistical light on the relative risks of creeping versus lane splitting. A Santa Barbara motorcycle club did an informal poll of some local CHP officers who confirmed that there were a lot more rear-end accidents than lane-splitting accidents involving motorcycles on California freeways. You'll have to draw your own conclusions about the relative risks for you.

I'm not going to go out on a limb and suggest that lane splitting is a risk reduction advantage for everyone. However, I will suggest that proficient urban traffic warriors can split lanes without increasing their risks by following several iron-clad rules. First, lane splitting must be both tolerated by local drivers and not illegal in the eyes of the law. Second, traffic must be moving slowly enough that surrounding drivers can't quickly change lanes. Third, the rider must have sufficient mental skills to predict the movements of all surrounding drivers and must have sufficient control skills to accurately position the bike within inches, including sudden swerves and quick stops.

Is It Tolerated?

In parts of the world where motorcyclists routinely split lanes, it's not only tolerated but also expected. If a motorist expects you to cruise on by between traffic lanes and you don't, that may cause a surprise that leads to a crash, and that expectation includes other motorcyclists as well as car drivers.

On the other hand, if you are in an area where no one splits lanes, then other motorists don't expect it and won't take kindly to you doing it. Legal or not, to manage the risks, you should go along with the riding tactics in the area where you find yourself.

Is It Legal?

You may have heard that white lining is illegal in your state or that it's legal but only if you don't ride faster than 20 mph above surrounding traffic or only if all other vehicles are stopped. Almost everywhere in North America except in California, lane splitting is not considered legal, not expected, and not tolerated by other motorists. Don't assume that lane splitting is legal somewhere just because you see some other motorcyclist doing it. What really counts is how the local police prioritize traffic problems. If you have any question about the legality of sharing lanes, call your state or city police and ask. When we talk about what's legal, we need to remember that many of the traffic laws on the books were created shortly after the Ford Model T came out and are equally outdated. Some states cover the issue by making it illegal for two vehicles to share the same lane. The bottom line is that no states currently define lane splitting, lane sharing, or white lining.

Because California represents a large percentage of the nation's motorcyclists and because Los Angeles and San Francisco are well known for lane splitting, let's see what California laws say about lane splitting. Hey! Surprise! There's nothing in the California vehicle codes about lane splitting on a motorcycle. It's just not in there. The reality is that various existing laws potentially apply to what we (and the police) know as lane splitting. With no specific laws about splitting, the responsibility falls on the individual police officer to find some code that can be used to keep you in line.

One handy law often used by the CHP is the Basic Speed Law: "No person shall drive a vehicle upon a highway at a speed greater than is reasonable or prudent having due regard for weather, visibility, the traffic on, and the surface and width of, the highway, and in no event at a speed which endangers the safety of persons or property." (California code 22350)

That's a pretty handy law. Think about it: since the wording includes "reasonable and prudent," that means Officer Ollie can make a judgment call. Even if you are well within the posted speed limit, Ollie can cite you for riding at a faster speed than surrounding traffic if in his judgment you weren't being prudent. And if you tick someone's mirror while trying to zip between two creeping cars, you could also be cited for "endanger(ing) the safety of persons or property."

A spokesman for the CHP suggested that when lane splitting, you should go no faster than 10 mph over surrounding traffic. However, a general consensus among CHP motor officers hints that 20 mph faster than other traffic is reasonable or prudent.

There are a number of laws on the books that could be used in a lane-sharing situation. The point is that the practice isn't defined by the laws. It's up to the officer

This rider is pushing the limits of "prudent" by zipping between the lanes at a speed much faster than the speed of traffic.

to make a judgment call and pull whatever law out of his hat that happens to fit the circumstances.

To clarify the legal issues and police attitudes surrounding white lining, I stopped off at a district CHP office in the San Francisco Bay area. Two officers gave their unofficial interpretations of the laws, plus personal advice. Officer A, who had no motorcycle experience, suggested that although lane splitting wasn't technically illegal, he felt it was never safe or prudent under any circumstances. At the adjacent desk, Officer B, a motorcycle patrolman, believed that lane splitting was reasonably safe and prudent, providing the motorcyclist used some common sense. He split lanes on his patrol bike all the time.

Think about that. If Officer A caught you lane splitting at just 5 mph faster than traffic, he would probably cite you on two or three counts. But tomorrow you might find yourself following Officer B on his patrol bike down the same white line at 30 mph without a raised eyebrow. The obvious conclusion is that whether you get cited in relation to splitting lanes depends greatly upon the situation, the officer, and how you react to being stopped. Give Officer Ollie some lip and you might morph a conversation into a triple whammy ticket.

When Is Splitting Prudent?

OK, let's get down to the nitty-gritty. Let's say your trip takes you into San Francisco, and you're motoring south on Highway 101 toward the bridge at 7:30 a.m. All the lanes are full of cars and trucks creeping along a few feet at a time.

For most of the ride, there's a high-occupancy vehicle (HOV, or diamond) lane, so that's the place to be. Even if the diamond lane is slowing down, it still makes more sense to stay between the lines as long as traffic is moving. But well before the bridge, the HOV lane ends. You can creep along with the cars wearing out your clutch or slip over between the lines of cars and keep moving. Other motorcyclists are doing it. It's your call.

WHITE LINING

If you do decide to split between traffic lanes, here are some suggestions:

DOs

- Maintain your awareness of the pattern of movements of vehicles ahead, especially those that are constantly changing lanes for no apparent reason.
- Watch the head and eye movements of drivers ahead and to both sides to predict what they may do next.
- Keep your speed down to no more than 10 mph faster than traffic.
- Cover your brakes and apply the front brake lightly when approaching an erratic driver to reduce your braking reaction time.
- Use more caution approaching interchanges or merging lanes.
- Split between the lanes farthest left, not the right side lanes where vehicles are more likely to merge.

Lane splitting is least risky when traffic is so dense and moving so slowly that drivers don't have room or maneuverability to make sudden lane changes.

- Put your tires to either side of shiny lane markings such as those white plastic dots or glued-down plastic strips.
- Monitor your rear-view mirror for other, faster-moving riders or motor officers.
- Watch for extended mirrors on trucks or vehicles towing trailers.
- Politely move back into one lane if the lanes narrow or are blocked by wide vehicles.

DON'Ts

- Don't try to force your way between vehicles if you don't think you can get through without bumping a mirror or scraping a bumper.
- Never position yourself between another vehicle and an off-ramp.
- Don't move outside the lines defining the far left and far right of the roadway, except in emergency situations. Don't even think about splitting over the yellow lines into oncoming traffic (at least not in the United States).

Lane splitting is least risky when traffic is so dense and moving so slowly that drivers don't have room or maneuverability to make sudden lane changes. Let's be clear about this: if traffic is heavy but still jogging along at speeds of 30 to 40 mph, that's not the time to be splitting lanes. Other drivers can (and often do) jump from lane to lane, and you should never assume they see you coming in their mirrors or that they will signal before yanking on the steering wheel.

In the Los Angeles basin, some bikers are zipping along the white lines 30 or 40 mph faster than moving traffic and weaving over to the lanes that provide a clearer shot. Never mind that such antics are an advertisement for arrest. The point is that weaving through moving traffic really increases the risks of getting sideswiped by a driver who suddenly decides the next lane is the place to be and doesn't see you coming up.

Urban Commuter Weapons

If you find yourself wandering north into Los Angeles traffic at 7:30 a.m. on your 1800 UltraTourer (complete with hard bags, engine guards, highway pegs, and double CB antennae), you can forget lane splitting. A motorcycle with full-size hard bags is too wide, and it's too easy to bang into another vehicle. Rather than inch along in commuter traffic risking a rear-ender, why not make a side trip to the coast highway or have a leisurely breakfast at San Juan Capistrano? If you don't need to be in the big city at the same time as everyone else, why expose yourself to the frustrations and dangers of bumper-to-bumper traffic?

For commuting, a 650cc machine is powerful enough to get around and narrow enough to get through traffic. An older model with cosmetic flaws is less likely to become a target for thieves.

On the other hand, if you are making the same commute through traffic every day, why not consider a motorcycle that's a more ideal urban weapon? Today's narrow V-twin machines such as the Suzuki TLS or the Honda VTR Super Hawk might make good commuter bikes with a few changes to the ergonomics. What's more, you don't need 1,000cc's to haul one human body through traffic, and you might not want a shiny temptation parked on the street all day. For commuting, consider one of the dual sport machines such as the Kawasaki KLR 650, the Suzuki SV 650, or the BMW F650. Single-cylinder engines provide a narrow profile, lots of low end grunt, excellent economy, and less plastic to get scuffed or broken. The light weight translates into easy handling. In the interests of antitheft, hang a bundle of stray wires drooping out from under a side cover, apply some duct tape to the saddle—even if it isn't split—and crudely dab some epoxy filler on the lower corner of an engine cover.

The bottom line is that lane splitting by motorcyclists is a fact of life in more and more congested big cities, as too many vehicles try to share too little road space. Don't let anyone pressure you into lane splitting if it isn't legal in your area, if you aren't comfortable with your skill level, or if you aren't willing to accept what you perceive as an increased risk. But where the climate allows, a sharp motorcyclist on a narrow two-wheeler can carve through congested traffic and shave hours off an otherwise frustrating commute without increasing the risks.

CHAPTER 7

Sharing the Ride

BATCHES OF BIKERS

Given my choice of traveling alone or in a group, I'd prefer to travel alone. When I'm cruising toward the horizon all by myself, life is much simpler. I have to make decisions for only one person. I can change plans instantly without having a roadside conference. When I'm ready to go, I just go. If I want to stop, I just stop. If I run out of gas, I—wait a minute! Who's going to help me if I'm all by myself?

What's more, even if I don't have a bike problem, it gets kind of lonely after a while. When I peer over the rim of the Grand Canyon to absorb the awesome view or stop at an overlook with Mount Rainier gleaming in the twilight, I feel like sharing the experience with others. I've had some great canyon rides with small groups of proficient riders. And I can remember a few spectacular rally parades where there were thousands of riders in one never-ending formation. The flip side is that I've also had some group rides that were dangerous, frustrating disasters. Let's consider what's involved in group rides to help you avoid disappointments.

Novices to the Front, Please

When less-experienced riders find themselves in a group ride, the tendency is to wait around, watch what everyone else is doing, and fall in at the back of the pack. That way, the others can't see what the novice is doing wrong. But let's note that the action gets more demanding at the tail end of a group. So novices should be directed to ride immediately behind the leader. That also helps the leader establish a speed that's appropriate for the group since he can see what the least experienced riders are doing.

But We Don't Really Ride Fast

I've been in a number of group rides that were faster than I would have preferred. And I've led a few rides that in retrospect were faster than I should have allowed. There's something about motorcycling that brings out our competitive spirit. *Boy, those other riders are really aggressive. I'd better crank up the wick so they won't think I'm a wuss!* It's easy to get stampeded into riding a lot faster than I feel is safe. And it's just not macho to say anything about the pace or to drop back.

Some groups are more aggressive than others. If you find yourself in a group that makes you nervous, consider dropping out and finding another group that's closer to your expectations.

Some groups are more aggressive than others, whether a matter of speed or poor leadership. If I want to ride aggressively, I'd rather ride by myself and not have to squander my attention on other riders around me. When I realize a group is more hazardous than I'm willing to tolerate, I take action to separate myself from the group. I can either ride by myself to the next group stop or quit the group and go somewhere else. It's polite to announce to the ride leader that I'm dropping out. If there is resistance to my separating from the group, I might have to make a "wrong turn" and get lost.

I've noticed that experienced riders tend to jack up the speed year by year. If nothing goes wrong, it seems reasonable to ride a little faster than you did last year. You've also gained a little additional skill and knowledge, and that should allow you to ride faster without getting in trouble. Many of the big-mileage riders I know ride well over the speed limits. That's your decision, but I've noted over the years that increasing speed year by year eventually results in punching through the envelope. It's not wise to keep jacking up speed until you crash.

Buddy Bashing

Two riders are making a cross-country trip together. They are both veteran motorcyclists and equally skilled. Either one could travel independently, but they enjoy the company of another rider. Betty is in the lead today, with Bob following along. Late in the day, they enter another small town along the secondary highway they are navigating. Betty observes a small dog darting around near the street and instinctively rolls off the throttle. The dog isn't chasing the bikes, it's chasing some small animal, perhaps a squirrel, but Betty is concerned the dog might run out into the street. As she had predicted, the dog does dart out into her path, and she pulls off a perfect quick stop to avoid hitting it.

That should be the end of the problem, except that Bob isn't prepared for a quick stop. Before he can reach for the brake, his bike rams into Betty's. The impact slams Betty's bike forward a few feet where it wobbles into a crash, fracturing her leg and ending her ride.

That should also be the end of the story, except Bob is embarrassed and needs to save face. Bob argues that Betty should not have made a quick stop just for a small dog. Bob believes that if he had been in the lead he would have kept going and swerved around the dog—so that's what Betty should have done. In Bob's mind, Betty caused the crash. As we might imagine, Betty blames Bob for running into her.

This crash isn't an isolated incident. Over the past several years, I've heard similar stories of accidents during group rides, and some have resulted in life-threatening injuries and even fatalities. Rather than try to fix the blame, let's see if we can spot some typical group riding errors that lead to accidents.

But My Buddies and I Think Alike

One assumption that sets a group up for an accident is the idea that we're all on the same wavelength. It's a common misperception that after riding with others for X miles or Y years, we've all learned the same skills and habits. That's part of what got Bob in trouble. He assumed that Betty would ride exactly as he would under all circumstances.

The truth is we're all different, with different risk awareness and different risk acceptance. The idea that we're all thinking alike is an illusion. There's nothing wrong with getting to know your riding buddies and their habits. But it's essential for everyone to understand that when we're riding down the road, each person is responsible for controlling his or her machine. It's not so much a group as several different riders who happen to be on the road together. It's healthier to maintain some suspicion that those other riders on the road with you are potentially hazardous.

It's an illusion that all the riders in a group are on the same wavelength. It's essential to understand that everyone is responsible for controlling his or her own machine.

Back in 1980, I participated in a tour from England to southern Spain led by the late Ken Craven. Ken had led a lot of tours through foreign countries and had some sage advice to offer. For one thing, Ken suggested that we voluntarily break up the large group of forty or so riders into small groups of three riders. In Ken's experience, those crashes that had occurred on previous tours had all been with groups of four or more riders. That's not to say that you can't have an accident because you're riding with only one or two buddies; the point is that more riders create more potential problems.

Consider this: three riders in a group can all see each other. With four or five riders, one or more riders can be hidden behind someone else. And that also applies to how other motorists see us. A large group may be seen as a rolling roadblock that's holding up traffic. If the group leader has defined the ride as one large group in formation, you'll need to adapt to large group tactics. But whenever I have a choice, I fall in with one or two other riders and separate from the main group.

When the group is composed of riders of relatively equal skill and experience, it's customary for everyone to take a turn at leading the ride. No matter who the leader is, it's a good idea to have a rider's meeting before departure to explain what's going to happen. If there are navigation concerns, printed route sheets can be handed out. When I'm leading a group, I may suggest that if anyone doesn't want to ride with the group, they may depart first and meet us at the next scheduled stop. That way, if they have a problem, we won't leave them behind.

As the crash between Betty and Bob reminds us, it's not so much the skill level or experience of the riders that allows accidents to happen but rather confusing reactions to road hazards that occur without warning. We need to be in control of our bikes, but more important, we need to be in control of the situation.

Hey, We Can Make Another 100 Miles Today!

Another big factor that sets groups up for crashes is fatigue. Riding all day takes a lot of effort and concentration. After six or eight hours duking it out with traffic, your skills will likely have degraded, and your reaction times will be longer.

A group of three seasoned riders leaves the Seattle area for the 49er BMW rally in Auburn, California. The weather in Washington has turned cold and wet, which slows them down. To stay on their planned schedule, they press on farther than planned. The next day in Oregon is also rainy, cold, and windy. After only another 250 miserable miles, they turn in, exhausted. All three riders are getting concerned that they might not make the rally, but they keep that fear to themselves.

On a long-distance ride, it makes sense for every participant to take the lead on a rotating schedule.

On the third day, they awake to blue skies. Suddenly, their attitudes get brighter, and all three realize that an aggressive dash through Northern California will get them there on schedule after all. But two hours later, one of the bikes spins a bearing in the transmission. The other two riders are frustrated by the delay, but they refuse to leave their buddy stranded. Locating a rental truck to transport the ailing bike puts them another four hours behind schedule.

Now the two remaining riders urgently need to make up time, and they press on aggressively. Late that evening, they are just a few miles short of the rally when suddenly, at a confusing intersection, the two riders collide. Both riders are carted off to the hospital, and both bikes are towed away to the impound yard.

As one of the riders relates afterward, "Mistakes were made but the underlying cause was fatigue. We simply pushed too hard and didn't stop often enough. We were thinking about getting to the rally on time, and we were unwilling to say anything to each other about how tired we were."

That business about trying to make the destination on time regardless of setbacks is a dangerous mindset that many of us share. I've known riders to continue over mountain passes at night in blizzards, head off across the desert without sufficient water, keep riding through hurricanes, or keep rolling at speed on plugged tires. It's awfully hard to admit defeat and delay the trip or, worse yet, turn back. And I'm speaking from lots of personal experience here.

Riding a motorcycle over long distances requires careful planning and good preparation. There is a long-distance community of riders who know how to manage the risks. Two excellent books on the subject of long-distance motorcycle travel are *Going the Extra Mile*, by Ron Ayres, and *The Essential Guide to Motorcycle Travel*, by Dale Coyner. Both books are available from Whitehorse Press.

I'm Here, Where Are You?

More than a few crashes have occurred as a result of someone getting separated from the group. That's more of a problem when the riders have no plan other than to follow the leader. Without some sort of backup plan, a separated rider can panic.

Case in point: Two very experienced motorcyclists are returning from a rally, the husband riding his machine, and the wife riding hers. Their riding style is the follow me approach, usually with the husband leading. About two days into their homeward leg, the riders become separated in traffic. The husband, failing to see the other motorcycle in his mirrors, pulls over and waits by the side of the road. After waiting a few minutes, he decides to turn around and retrace his steps to find his partner. But, while attempting to make the U-turn, he is struck broadside by another vehicle and fatally injured.

That terrible incident points out that trying to hold a group together visually can distract a rider from observing traffic or surface hazards. When riding in traffic, we must expect that a group (even a group of two riders) will get separated by other vehicles or traffic signals from time to time. So we should have a plan for what to do when we get separated. The most hazardous tactic is to double back looking for the other riders.

If it's a large group, one basic rule should be that the group will not stop to wait for riders held up by one traffic signal in a string of intersections. If the tail end of the group gets separated by a red light, odds are they will eventually catch up. If not, the leader can pull over on the way out of town to allow the group to reform. The clever ride leader will also issue route sheets showing when and where the group will be.

Clubs who ride in groups often equip their bikes with CB radios to maintain voice contact. Cell phones also provide a quick way for riders to find each other. The plan could be to stop and call the other rider if a certain time period has passed without a visual. For instance, if you haven't seen your riding companion for twenty minutes, stop and call.

If the riders are independently capable, the plan could be for each rider to continue to the specified destination. The meet-up destination can be an hour away, a half day away, or at the end of the day's ride. The establishment can be contacted and a message left for the other rider.

The Ride Captain

I suppose my preference for traveling alone isn't so much that I don't like groups, but that I'm cautious about joining groups that aren't organized well. I remember a group led by a rider who turned a day ride into a nightmare. Daffy Don didn't tell us where we were going or offer any advice about riding style or speed. Daffy didn't do hand signals, check his mirrors, or use a radio. Taking off from a stop sign, he would just peel out in front of a line of cars, leaving the rest of us playing catch up. When Daffy instantly decided to make a fuel stop, he slowed in the left lane of an arterial and dove across two lanes of oncoming traffic into a gas station without signaling. The rest of the group was abandoned on the busy highway in confusion. I had survived two hours of that nightmare and decided I needed to separate myself from the group after the fuel stop. I just delayed until after the group departed and no one noticed. Looking back, I wonder what took me so long.

By comparison, I remember a well-organized group that I joined for a ride through the mountains and canyons north of Los Angeles. Boss Man Bill explained where we were going and maintained a pace in traffic suitable for the least experienced member. Bill also explained that once we turned off onto the narrow, twisty canyon roads, each rider should ride at his or her own pace. The more aggressive riders could zoom on ahead, enjoying the curves. Average riders could motor along enjoying the scenery. And the slower riders could bring up the rear, riding at a comfortable speed. The key to keeping the group a group was that at critical intersections Bill pulled everyone over for a break until the slowest rider caught up. That way, no one felt pressured to ride faster than their skill level just to avoid getting lost.

The difference between the two groups is that Daffy Don had no idea of how to lead a group, while Boss Man Bill had an excellent understanding of group riding dynamics and set some simple rules that allowed everyone to enjoy the ride without creating dangerous or frustrating situations. Most of us have gone for a ride with two or three companions, although we may not have recognized them as group rides at the time. If you haven't had the humbling opportunity to lead a batch of bikers yet, you should, even if it's just one other machine. Whether the group is large or small, the ride will go better if you follow some commonsense rules. Let's review some of the dynamics, consider some techniques for leading a formation ride, and evaluate some alternate ways to move a group of motorcyclists down the road.

Let's say you are asked to lead a club ride with a potential for twenty bikes. Hold it! Don't run away just yet. We'll talk you through it. You'll be the leader, or ride captain, but you should arrange for another experienced rider to be the Tail End Charlie to bring up the end of the group. Now, don't just fire up the engine and zoom into traffic just yet. First, here's a trick question for you:

If you immediately pull out onto the street and accelerate up to 55 mph, how much time will pass before Charlie starts to move, nineteen bikes behind you? Well, if there aren't any other vehicles on the road and riders manage to follow you exactly two seconds apart, Charlie will be sitting in the same spot for thirty-eight seconds. At 55 mph, you'll be 3,078 feet down the road before Charlie even eases out the clutch. What's more, if you maintain 55 mph, each following rider will have to go faster than 55 to catch up with you. If Charlie throttles up to 110 mph, he can catch up to the group in maybe thirty seconds. If Charlie is willing to risk only 80 mph, it will take him about a minute and a half to catch up, assuming you hold 55 mph. So you shouldn't be surprised if he's hotter than a rear Heritage header long before the lunch stop.

Think of a group of motorcycles as like a train with the cars hitched together by twenty-foot bungee cords. That's why the sharp ride leader pulls out slowly and creeps along at 30 mph or so until Charlie finally gets rolling. You can either watch in your mirrors or listen for Charlie on the CB if you are wired for radio. Once the entire group is rolling, you can pick up the pace to cruising speed. To avoid holding up other motorists, it's wise to maintain at least the speed limit or the average speed of traffic if the road is busy. You don't want to encourage other motorists to attempt passing the group two or three bikes at a time.

When approaching a slower speed zone, the clever ride captain decelerates the group well before the speed sign, so that as the first bikes arrive in the slower zone, Charlie has also slowed and isn't doing a stoppie to avoid jamming his front tire up someone's muffler.

When approaching a slower speed zone, the clever ride captain decelerates the whole group well before reaching the sign.

The Formation

You have probably seen motor officers (and also big bad bikers) riding side by side in two columns. The side-by-side formation may look really impressive, but it severely limits maneuvering room. Even motor cops have had accidents where one bike has bumped into the one alongside. A staggered formation allows more maneuvering room. In a staggered formation, you ride in the opposite wheel track from the rider ahead of you. That is, if he's in the left wheel track, you take the right wheel track.

The staggered formation moves the same number of bikes in the same road space as a side-by-side formation does, but it allows machines in either column to temporarily move sideways to avoid a hazard such as a car door, pothole, or edge trap. The staggered formation also provides a slightly better

The staggered formation gives everyone more maneuvering room.

view of other riders. If you follow one second behind the rider in the other wheel track, that puts you two seconds behind the rider directly ahead of you. Two seconds is the minimum distance to provide a space cushion while keeping the group as compact as possible. If everyone pays attention, it is easy to establish and maintain a staggered two-second formation. It's the captain's choice to ride in the left or right wheel track.

The bad news is that we must be prepared for a Daffy Don to join the group. When you are signaling "start your engines," Daffy may still be nattering with that chickie-babe on the pink Sportster, with his helmet and gloves still parked inside the coffee shop, his keys in an inside pocket, and an empty gas tank. During the ride, you can expect Daffy to constantly be drifting over into the wrong track with following riders all doing the lane samba trying to reestablish the staggered formation. If we know Daffy, he will drop back an extra eight or ten seconds, just enough to allow a following car to pass and cause the last three riders to miss the green light.

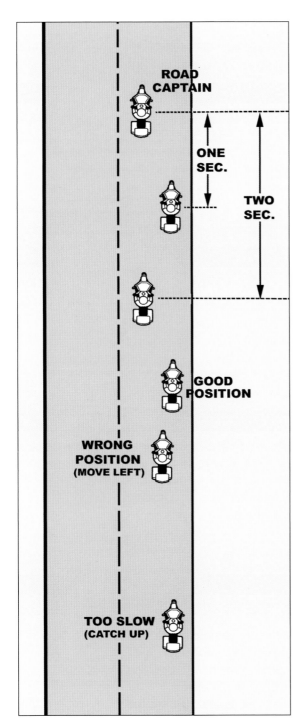

ROAD CAPTAIN

ONE SEC.

TWO SEC.

GOOD POSITION

WRONG POSITION (MOVE LEFT)

TOO SLOW (CATCH UP)

And of course, Daffy will expect you to find a gas station in a few minutes because he fills up only after his bike has gone on reserve, and that won't occur for at least another five miles. Don't think you can ignore him—he'll roar up through the formation to tell you he needs gas.

When It's Time to Go, GO!

My suggestion for ride captains blessed with a Daffy is to expect everyone to conform to the group and to make that clear at the riders' meeting before the ride. Explain your expectations for the ride, along with any rules you think would help. For instance, you might suggest that if any rider in the group can't maintain the specified following distance, it is acceptable for following riders to pass. Explain where the group will be stopping and where the ride is expected to end. Make it clear that when the group stops for fuel, everyone is expected to top up their tanks and drain their bladders.

When it's time to go, go! When I was directing tours, I would post some odd start time, such as 8:17 a.m., and then leave exactly at 8:17 a.m. to make it clear that I wasn't kidding. Leave Daffy running around in circles back in the parking lot if he's not ready. And keep the rest of the group moving when Daffy runs out of fuel during the ride. Maybe poor Charlie will take pity and handle the problem. Don't let the Daffy Dons of the world ruin the ride for everyone else.

Getting Through the Green Light

When you're leading a group through a controlled intersection in traffic, it is unlikely you'll get everyone through before the light turns red. There is a temptation for following riders to speed up and run the yellow to stay with the group, and riders at the tail end may panic and run the red, too. Explain at the start that riders are expected to obey all traffic signals and that you will slow down as necessary to let everyone catch up after a series of intersections.

In practical terms, with a series of signal lights, the leader will get stopped as often as the tail end riders, and everyone will pass through all the intersections at about the same rate. I've been in big groups where some riders are assigned as escorts to pull over and block intersections so everyone can run the red light, but I don't recommend that tactic unless the escorts are on-duty cops. The real legal eagles tend to look askance at motorcyclists taking the law into their own hands.

All you usually have to do is keep speed in check as you leave town to give everyone a chance to catch up before you roll the group up to cruising speed. Once in a while, you may have to creep along in the slow lane or even pull the group off the road to wait for riders caught at a long light. With a group of only five or six riders, it is easy to find a place to stop and also to get rolling again, but with groups of thirty or more, it is best to keep going at a slower speed and let the stragglers catch up.

Don't even think about stopping a group on the shoulder of a busy highway just because one rider has a problem. I've seen some extremely dangerous stunts, such as a whole gaggle of bikes coming to a screeching halt in the middle of a busy freeway, just because one rider dropped a glove.

Communication

Even if you're just going for a ride with three or four friends, it's a good idea to have a riders' meeting just before taking off to explain where you're going, what sort of formation you'll use, the meaning of various hand signals, the CB channel you'll be using, and what to do in case of a breakdown. That also establishes in everyone's mind who the leader is. If you've made up route sheets, this is the time to hand them out. As the ride leader, you might also suggest that you be informed if anyone needs to split from the group so you won't have to run the whole route backward looking for a supposedly lost rider who just split without letting anyone know.

Clubs who ride together on a regular schedule often find it useful to have CB radios. The captain can explain what's coming up next, and Charlie can report what's happening back at the tail end. For example, Charlie can whine that he's had to stop with Daffy, whose dry battery has finally expired, and would the next participant with a radio kindly drop back and assume the Charlie job?

Hand and light signals are quick ways to communicate with or without radios. I once happened to pull into line behind a group of Gold Wing riders during our state's Governor's Run and was privileged to observe their proficient group skills. The ride leader maintained a slow enough speed to allow the others to quickly catch up as they pulled onto the road. Once rolling, the captain accelerated the whole group together. All riders maintained exact position and following distance in a nice staggered formation. At the sight of a pothole, the leader flashed his brake light twice, and all the others passed the warning signal back. Where the road narrowed, the leader held up one finger and everyone merged smoothly into single file. Through a twisty section, the riders cornered briskly at the same pace. Where the road widened again, the leader held up two fingers and the group immediately changed back to a staggered formation. To change lanes on an urban arterial street, the leader positioned the group next to a space in traffic and signaled. Charlie immediately signaled and the whole group moved over as one. Their ride was truly a performance.

Different groups have different ways of signaling a surface hazard. I think the best way to signal is to tap the brake two or three times, rather than attempting to point to the hazard with a hand or foot. Alert following riders that there is a hazard and let them find it.

Getting Stopped

OK, you got the group rolling, you've managed to herd everyone through eighteen signal lights and twelve intersections without losing Daffy or causing an accident,

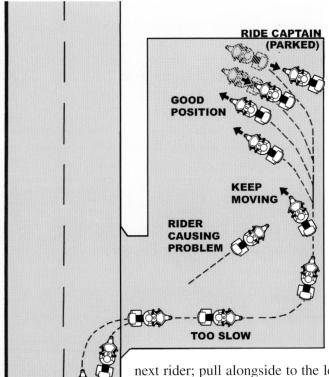

RIDE CAPTAIN
(PARKED)

GOOD
POSITION

KEEP
MOVING

RIDER
CAUSING
PROBLEM

TOO SLOW

RIDERS
EXPOSED
TO TRAFFIC

and it has been a pleasant ride. Now, how do you get a long string of motorcycles stopped and parked for lunch without creating a traffic hazard? The most important consideration is having a parking area that's big enough for the whole group to ride into. You don't want to get half the group off the road and leave the other half stranded out there like sitting ducks. The best scenario is when the group has space to motor into a parking lot and park side by side to conserve space. Riders should pull up to the left of each rider ahead so that everyone can immediately back into the parking space without waiting. With a little experience, the whole group can get parked quickly, which helps move everyone off the road efficiently. When your group pulls into a parking lot, don't try to be creative. Follow the parking drill with everyone else. Don't ride up behind the next rider; pull alongside to the left and immediately roll your machine back into the parking space. Creative parking decisions tend to slow down the process and leave tail-end riders still trying to get off the street.

The larger the group, the more important it is to have specific stops arranged. When I led groups of 80 to 100 riders, I would ride the entire route prior to the tour, both to identify specific problem areas such as construction zones and to find suitable parking areas. If stopping for lunch with more than a dozen riders, I would also either make arrangements for a meal or call ahead to give the restaurant an opportunity to have enough help on hand. If you are making arrangements for a really big group, you'll need help to direct traffic.

A large group like this requires a good plan to get everyone down the road safely.

Back in the Pack

Group rides are a lot more enjoyable when the leader is more like Boss Man Bill and less like Daffy Don. If you've never ridden in a group, make a point of staying close to the ride captain rather than at the back of the pack. It's a lot easier to maintain speed and position if you are no more than two or three bikes from the front. Fill your tank and empty your bladder well before the scheduled departure time. When the leader puts on his helmet and gloves, get your gear on, get your key in the ignition, and get ready to roll.

Once underway, maintain the requested interval and lane position. Try to avoid drifting back and creating a big hole in the formation. If someone ahead suddenly wakes up to being in the wrong track and moves over, every following rider should immediately reestablish the proper staggered formation. Watch the leader for hand signals. When riders ahead give warning signals, pass the signal back down the line. If another rider has a problem and pulls over, stay with the group and keep rolling unless the leader also pulls over or asks that you stop to help. It's Charlie's job to deal with the problem.

Alternate Ways to Move a Group

When we think *group ride*, we usually imagine a long string of bikes in formation, but there are other ways to move a group down the road. One technique I have used is printing up route sheets, which detail the route and schedule. It's relatively easy to make up route sheets by snipping pieces out of an official state tourist map and adding schedule information alongside. Poker runs and mystery tours are different forms of a group ride, where all riders do their own navigating and ride at their own pace.

One word of caution about creative rides with complex navigational instructions: try to avoid complex written instructions that require a rider to read small print while riding. That would increase the risks for everyone, and slow or inexperienced riders would be very likely to get lost or run out of time. One good tactic is to provide an escape envelope with instructions for a direct route to the destination in the event of weather problems or traffic delays.

Try It, You Might Like It

If you've been avoiding group rides, consider joining up once in a while as part of your skill improvement program. Maybe you'll even discover some fellow enthusiasts you enjoy riding with. If none of the others measures up to your standards of group leadership, maybe you'll just have to be the ride captain and show them how it's done. But remember: riding in a group once in a while doesn't mean you can't go droning off toward the horizon by yourself when you feel like it.

The Second Rider

I've ridden motorcycles in some scary situations. Once, crossing Nebraska, I faced two converging tornadoes. In Colorado, during a torrential downpour, I sprinted into a restaurant a few seconds ahead of a lightning bolt. In a canyon in the French Alps, I barely managed to swerve out of the way of a Mini driver in a four-wheel drift around a blind turn. I narrowly avoided a moose collision in British Columbia and a troop of baboons in South Africa. Been there, done that, got the Scary Ride T-shirt.

If you enjoy company on the ride, you need to keep your passenger comfortable and informed.

But the scariest rides of my life were those rare occasions when I had to thumb a ride on the back of someone else's bike. *Hey! There aren't any handlebars back here—what am I supposed to hang on to? Where's the brake lever? I can't see where the bike is headed! I don't know which way we're going to lean. Uh-oh, I think I'm slipping off the back! Slow down!*

Most motorcyclists I know ride solo most of the time. Sure, there are couples who ride two-up on every trip, but many riders seldom carry a passenger. So when you do ask someone to share the ride, you may forget to explain what they need to know or not remember that the additional load will require different riding tactics. Let's review some of the basic concerns for carrying passengers.

The Safety Briefing: Informing the Passenger

When you board an airplane, you assume the pilot knows what to do, but the passengers may need some coaching about whether the flight includes breakfast and whether it will arrive in time for the connecting flight. First-time passengers may need some coaching about things like emergency exits, toilets, and seat belts. When you have a passenger lined up to ride on the back of your saddle, it's part of your job to provide the necessary riding gear, explain how to climb aboard, discuss what to do when the bike leans, and suggest how to communicate at speed. After a few rides, passengers will know what's expected.

For a novice passenger, you should explain the need for riding gear that is warm and durable, including a heavy jacket that won't flap around, leather boots to prevent burns on hot exhaust pipes, gloves to protect the hands, a helmet to protect the brain, and a face shield or goggles to protect the eyes. You don't need to bring up the possibility of rain if the weather that day looks sunny. You should discourage any potentially harmful clothing, such as a long, floppy scarf, which could wrap around a helmet in a crosswind; a long drover coat, which could snag its tails in the rear wheel; boots with dangly things, which could catch on a foot peg; or spiked heels, which could melt down on your mufflers.

For first-timers, it's also helpful to explain that you will saddle up first and get the bike balanced, and then the passenger can stand up on the left passenger peg and swing onto the saddle. Mention that motorcycles lean into corners, that leaning over is normal, and that the passenger should lean the same as the rider. There are a number of other little points you could cover, such as the passenger keeping feet on the pegs when stopping and that you will do the traffic signals, thank you. New passengers want to do the right thing and will probably appreciate some coaching.

Expect Handling Changes

What's most important for the rider is that a second person on the bike not only increases the total weight but also relocates the center of mass and adds sail to the rear of the bike. Those changes affect your control of the machine. Acceleration, braking, and cornering tactics all change, not just because of the additional mass and where the weight is loaded on the bike but also because the second rider's weight can shift around when you're not expecting it.

Quick Stops

For example, consider what happens during hard braking. There is more total mass to stop, so you can expect a somewhat longer stopping distance. With more weight on the rear wheel, more rear braking can be used in a quick stop or on slick pavement. On a machine with integrated brakes, you won't notice much difference except that it takes harder braking and more distance to stop quickly. More weight means increased traction, so you might think the limiting factor would be brake efficiency. But what you will discover when you try a quick stop is that the passenger slams forward during hard braking, limiting how much brake effort you're willing to apply.

It's your job as the rider to ensure that your passenger is prepared for the ride.

Once, when riding with my wife on the back, I observed what appeared to be a brown log in the left ditch. But as we got closer, the log suddenly raised up its antlers, leaped up onto the pavement, and clattered into a U-turn. I immediately

When you brake aggressively carrying a passenger, the passenger's mass slams into your back. You may have to ease off the brake just to keep from being pushed up onto the tank.

squeezed on the brakes, but my wife wasn't prepared for a quick stop and slammed into my back, pushing me forward onto the tank. Even though she is a relative lightweight, I had to modulate the brakes well short of maximum just to keep from being pushed into the handlebars. We managed to miss the deer by inches, but the lesson to me was clearly that I must always allow more stopping distance when carrying a passenger. Remember that the passenger can't see ahead as well as you can, doesn't know when you are going to suddenly squeeze the lever, and during a stop doesn't have much to brace against except you.

If you regularly carry a passenger, you might consider practicing quick stops with the passenger aboard. Some training sites allow passengers to be carried during the practice exercises. The typical drill is for the rider to take the course with no passenger and then repeat the same exercises with a passenger the next day. Passengers may find it helpful to listen to the classroom presentations, too. It helps them understand why you're doing what you're doing and why you must concentrate so much on traffic and surface hazards.

Acceleration

When accelerating, you have more control over the situation because you can roll on the gas smoothly to help the passenger stay put. Heavyweight touring machines with top boxes and passenger backrests provide a relatively secure perch for the second rider, but many machines don't offer much in the way of passenger handholds. Those silly straps that manufacturers used to stretch across the middle of the saddle were supposed to be grab handles for passengers, but no one ever explained how a human being might have braced against acceleration or deceleration with their hands between their knees. Some machines provide solid grab handles around the rear of the saddle, but it is still difficult to hold on if the bike is accelerating quickly.

Just remember that your passenger may not have much to hold on to except you. You can suggest that the passenger grasp you lightly around your waist. If your passenger gives you a little squeeze while riding along into a beautiful sunset, the message is probably, "Gee, Honey, I'm glad you brought me along." But if your passenger suddenly strangles you in a bear hug as you roll on the gas, it's probably a sign you are getting a little too aggressive with the throttle. If you want to enjoy the company of a second rider, you've got to make the rider comfortable, which really means riding more conservatively than if you were all by yourself.

Cornering

When you are carrying a passenger with little or no motorcycle experience, you shouldn't be surprised when the passenger panics as you lean the bike over into the first sharp turn. Of course, it will be your turn to panic if the passenger manages to lean toward the outside while you're trying to get the bike leaned over toward the inside. The wise rider takes corners sedately for the first hour or so to allow the novice passenger some time to adapt to this leaning business and to allow you to adapt to cornering with the additional mass.

If your bike already has limited leanover clearance, don't be surprised when the bike starts making sparks while cornering with a passenger. That's because the additional weight of the second rider compresses the rear suspension more, reducing leanover clearance. You can reduce the touchdown problem by following a larger-radius cornering line, by reducing entry speed more than for solo riding, and by rolling on the throttle more as the bike is leaned over. But if your machine makes sparks too easily, that's a message to get the bike jacked up off the pavement a little more.

First of all, check your tire pressures. When carrying extra weight, your tires need extra pressure. Typically, the tire chart for your bike will suggest 3 psi to 6 psi more pressure in the rear tire. If you've already been lazy about checking your rear tire pressure, you could easily be 10 psi under passenger specs.

While you're checking the bike, take a close look at the rear suspension. The springs on your shocks may have been on the weak side right off the showroom floor, and most springs sag a bit as the mileage builds up. If you have an agile and cooperative passenger, you can check the shock preload by measuring the travel with a tape measure. With the bike unladen, measure the spring length. Then measure again with both rider and passenger weight on the machine. Ideally, the springs should compress only about halfway to the limit with the full load supported on the wheels.

If the shocks are close to bottoming out just sitting there, jack the spring preload to maximum and check again. If that doesn't get the preload back into an acceptable range, it's time for stronger shock springs. Shock suppliers can usually provide similar-looking but stronger springs or dual-rate springs. There are also specialty shocks with multiple springs for a wider range of preload adjustment and spring spacers for front forks. The suspension specialists are always willing to offer advice. Talk to your parts person, or call the aftermarket suspension people directly. Be prepared with the model number and year of your bike and the weight you intend to carry, including rider, passenger, and typical baggage. Don't settle for off-the-shelf suspension just because it's described as heavy duty.

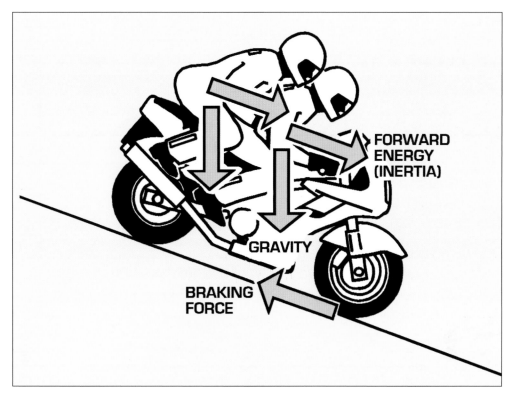

When braking downhill, the brakes have to overcome both forward energy and the down slope pull of gravity.

Hills

Hills can provide some surprises, too. Consider where a passenger's weight is positioned on the bike. Typically, the second rider is sitting over the rear axle. On level pavement, that means the rider's weight isn't applying any load on the front wheel. But when the front end is pointed downhill, more of the passenger's weight is transferred to the front wheel.

When you are braking on a downhill section, the weight shift forward will increase front-wheel traction. Obviously, the brakes have to overcome the forward energy of both riders and machine. What's less obvious is that when the bike is pointed downhill, the riders' weights are being pulled downhill by both forward energy and gravity. And kinetic energy increases dramatically with increased speed.

If you're approaching a steep downhill turn, you don't want to delay braking until the last second and then find you can't get the bike slowed to an acceptable entry speed for the corner. More than a few riders of heavy touring machines have made sightseeing excursions into the weeds when they discovered they couldn't get the overloaded bike down to speed on the available pavement.

When pointed uphill, it's a different ball game. Remember, if the passenger is perched over the rear axle on the level, then on an uphill slant the passenger's weight may actually be centered behind the rear axle, and the rider's weight will also be carried more on the rear wheel. That's why a bike, especially a short wheelbase sportbike with a passenger aboard, wants to do a wheelie when you're trying to get started uphill.

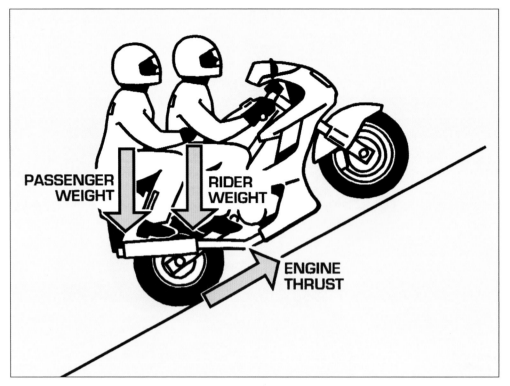

With a passenger aboard, the weight is biased toward the rear, and when starting uphill a bike with a short wheelbase may tend to do a wheelie. You'll need to be very smooth with the clutch to keep the front wheel on the surface.

The wheelie problem can be even worse when there is a heavy load carried behind the passenger. If you find yourself in a situation in which the front wheel starts to float as you ease out the clutch, try to get some weight shifted forward. You can try standing on the pegs and leaning up over the tank, but that's not easy when balancing the bike with a passenger. If you encounter this situation more than occasionally, you should take steps to unload the rear of the bike, one way or the other.

For instance, consider what you're carrying in the top box or saddlebags. Perhaps heavier objects could be moved to the front of the saddlebags or to a tank bag. Maybe you don't really need to carry that set of ½-inch drive sockets strapped over the taillight. Or maybe it's time for a bike with a longer wheelbase.

Even if the bike doesn't show any air under the front wheel when the bike is climbing uphill, be aware that the weight shift rearward unloads the front tire, and that decreases traction. In an uphill turn, the front wheel has more of a tendency to drift wide.

When you're carrying a passenger, the front tire will have reduced traction in uphill turns. Carry a little more speed entering an uphill corner so you don't have to roll on as much throttle while turning.

You can help maintain front tire traction in uphill corners by entering at a slightly higher speed than in a comparable level corner so that the machine's forward energy continues to pull it uphill. Remember, rolling on the gas tends to lift the front end, so you don't want to roll on just where you're also leaned over. If the machine's inertia can carry it uphill, you won't have to roll on the gas in midturn. That's a good tactic when riding by yourself, but when carrying a passenger it is much more important.

Whether you're intending to carry an occasional passenger or your significant other wants to go along on every ride, the experience is bound to be more fun if everyone understands what's needed and there aren't any hazardous surprises. If your life has been getting a little boring recently, I highly recommend a ride on the back of someone else's saddle to gain a little experience and a lot of feeling for what it's like to be the second rider. After that, you'll probably appreciate a conservative rider who takes off gradually, stops smoothly, and corners uphill or down without any unplanned sightseeing excursions off the road.

Carrying Children

If you're suddenly faced with the dilemma of choosing between children and a motorcycle, the obvious win-win situation is to take the kid along on the ride. The problem with that is that children younger than perhaps nine- or ten-years old tend to be not equipped physically or mentally to stay put on the back of a motorcycle at speed. The potential problem for the adult rider is that even a minor injury to a child from motorcycling will probably spell the end of the ride for another ten or fifteen years. Statistically speaking, very few children under age twelve are injured in motorcycle accidents, but if you're the unfortunate parent or grandparent holding on to the handlebars when the kid gets hurt, you're going to receive more trouble than you bargained for.

A variety of imaginative approaches have been invented for carrying children on the back of a motorcycle, but none of them are foolproof. The most obvious hazard is that the child can fall off. So there are belts with passenger handles for the child to hold on to and belts that strap the child to the rider. Providing a belt with handles for the child assumes the child can stay awake and hang on tightly enough to stay

If you are faced with the dilemma of making a choice between children and motorcycling, the win-win situation is to add a sidecar.

put. If the approach is to belt the child securely to the rider, the child gets dragged along with the rider if the bike goes down. Either way, there is the potential for serious injury.

The safer approach to carrying children is to go for a sidecar outfit. Not only is it unlikely a child will fall out of a sidecar after they fall asleep, but in the event of an accident the child has some protection by the sidecar body and chassis. Most important, a three-wheeler is much less likely to take a spill if the tires lose traction on a surface hazard, so there is much less risk of anyone taking a tumble. If you aren't quite willing to risk carrying a child on your two-wheeler but you're willing to learn how to drive a three-wheeled motorcycle, maybe it's time to look into a sidecar.

Be aware that driving a three-wheeler is an entirely different experience, but fun in its own way. There are no statistics available from the insurance industry, the federal government, or the motorcycle industry in the United States that give us any conclusions about the lowered risk of sidecars, but veteran sidecarists believe that outfits are inherently less risky than two-wheelers. Be aware that there are sidecar-trike training courses where you can learn the appropriate driving skills.

Let's Get Loaded

A few decades ago while on a gypsy tour of Northern California, our group was temporarily delayed by a road construction project. Since the road would be closed for an hour or so, most of us took advantage of the break to do laundry and bike maintenance. I was standing around kicking tires with Hawgbone Hal. Hawgbone was snorting about the extra "junk" his "old lady" felt were necessities on a motorcycle tour:

hair dryer, travel iron, portable radio, high-heeled shoes. I understood his concerns. The amount of weight a motorcycle can carry is limited. My wife and I had wondered whether we should bring our heavy-weight rain gear in addition to the load of camping gear and clothing. We were already pushing the weight limits on our Moto Guzzi Ambassador. Hawgbone had a homemade top box the size of a steamer trunk on the back of his Harley Davidson.

While we were waiting for our significant others to finish the laundry, Hawgbone decided it would be a good time to adjust his drive chain. From the bottom of his monster top box, he started extricating tools, included a full set of ½-inch drive sockets, an impact driver, large-size locking pliers, a monster adjustable

If you enjoy long-distance travel or regularly carry a passenger, you should be concerned about the GVWR.

wrench, a selection of drift pins, and a hydraulic jack. My jaw dropped open. Peering over his shoulder, I could see he still had a three-jaw bearing puller, a serious ball-peen hammer, and a full set of combination wrenches in there.

Here I'd been concerned about an extra 5 pounds of rain gear—and this XXL-size rider had brought along an extra fifty or sixty pounds of serious tools! I don't know what the suggested weight limits were for his H-D, but Hawgbone was so far over any reasonable limits he gave new meaning to the term *gross.*

If you ride a sport- or sport-touring bike, you'll have to work hard to exceed the gross vehicle weight restriction (GVWR) for your machine because sportbikes don't provide a big enough platform to attach much luggage, and a heavy passenger probably won't become a regular on a tiny pillion pad. You, your tank bag, and your throw-over saddlebags will probably be within the limits, even if you are six foot six inches and 240 pounds. But, if you often carry a second rider plus a pile of camping gear, you can be close to the limits. And, if you or your passenger are packaged in the XL or XXL sizes, you may be well over the GVWR for your bike, even with empty saddlebags.

Gross Vehicle Weight Restriction

Motorcycle manufacturers determine the maximum weight they'd like to see you carry on a specific machine. Gross weight is the total load of motorcycle, passengers, fuel, and gear that you would register riding across a truck scale. The permissible gross weight, or GVWR, is determined by such things as frame and wheel strength, steering geometry, suspension damping capacity, braking systems, and tire load ranges.

Carrying Capacity

The GVWRs are a quick way to compare different motorcycles, but GVWRs aren't the bottom line. You need to subtract the wet weight of the motorcycle from the GVWR to get the maximum load that you, your passenger, and your gear can share. The wet weight includes battery, fuel, oil, and fluids but not passengers or baggage. For example, the GVWR of the 1996 Harley-Davidson FXDS Convertible is listed as 1086 pounds. Subtract the wet weight of 675 pounds, and that leaves you a carrying capacity (CC) of 411 pounds. That 411 pounds is the maximum load for you, your passenger, and your gear, including the hair dryer, tent, hydraulic jack, and whatever else you intend to carry on board.

You may think that 411 pounds sounds like a lot of carrying capacity, but it gets used up very quickly when you add a second rider. Without getting too precise, let's say my weight is . . . ah . . . around 200 pounds wearing leathers and helmet, and my wife is maybe 135 pounds. So we add up to 335 pounds. Subtract that from the CC for the bike, and we can strap on an additional 76 pounds. If we stuff 20 pounds of clothing into each saddlebag, we can pile on another 36 pounds of camping gear, tools, and so on, before we exceed the limits set by Harley-Davidson:

FXDS Convertible, GVWR	1,086 lb
Minus wet weight	675 lb
Maximum carrying capacity	411 lb
Big Dave	200 lb
Little Diana	135 lb
Clothing	40 lb
Other gear	36 lb

For comparison, let's check the carrying capacity for a few other bikes:

Machine	GVWR (lb)	CC (lb)
2006 BMW K1200GT	992	324
2007 H-D FLHRS Road King	1,259	515
2007 Honda VTX1800T	1,219	362
2008 Kawasaki KLR 650	788	360
2007 Suzuki GSX-R750	840	403
2007 Triumph Tiger 1050	941	434
2006 Yamaha FJR1300AE	1,109	427

Just looking at motorcycles parked next to the curb, you'd think the giant-killer Honda VTX would be the champion weightlifter, eh? Does it surprise you that the Suzuki GSX-R750 has 40 pounds more carrying capacity than the VTX? Or that the FJR1300 can carry 100 pounds more than a BMW K1200GT?

I'm not trying to step on anyone's toes here, merely pointing out the significance of comparing the GVWR and carrying capacity numbers when you go shopping for a bike, especially if you intend to do a lot of long-distance touring, two-up or with heavy camping loads.

How Much Can I Overload?

Obviously, as Hawgbone Hal demonstrates, you can overload some machines and still keep them more or less under control. But you'll have to accept some responsibility for exceeding the limits. First of all, overloading will affect reliability. Hawgbone has to adjust his drive chain more frequently because that chain wasn't designed to handle the full-throttle power required to push an overloaded machine up steep hills and through gnarly detours. His wheel bearings, fork sliders, shock absorbers, and brakes are all stressed more than the designers intended. Second, overloading affects handling. Hawgbone barely managed to keep his groaning machine from wallowing into a mud bath as we struggled through the detour. And after we got through the dirt, the bottomed-out machine would make sparks if leaned over even modestly in the corners.

So—big deal, you may be thinking. *I can live with a little less cornering speed and a few more jolts.* The ride might turn into a big deal if the corner ahead happens to be one of those decreasing-radius killer corners where reduced ground clearance makes the difference between staying on the pavement and bouncing off a stone retaining wall.

What's more, suspension helps maintain traction. Obviously, the springs will sag more under a heavy load, eating up ground clearance in the corners and bottoming once in a while on sharp bumps. Shock-spring suspension systems are designed to maximize traction with the shock absorber piston in the middle of the suspension range. What I mean by maximize is that the tires can keep a constant grip on a bumpy road. If the tires can't get down into holes or up over bumps quickly enough, they can't maintain constant traction. For instance, if the shock piston is already up at the end of the cylinder when the wheel hits a bump, it can't absorb the jolt. The wheel can only try to lift that end of the bike. The resulting shock can bounce the tires right off the pavement, reducing traction to zero for a moment. So I'm not talking just bouncing kidneys here. I'm talking bikes levering themselves off the pavement, tires losing traction, and maybe even axles or shock rods bending or the frame cracking. I could go on, but you probably get the idea that GVWR and CC are important numbers that you ignore at your own peril.

Staying Within the Limits

There are several techniques for staying within the weight limits. First, pay enough attention to the carrying capacity when buying a motorcycle to be confident it will handle the loads you expect it to carry. If you weigh less than 250 pounds and primarily ride alone with maybe just a tank bag of extra gear, you won't have to worry about the limits. But if you and your passenger add up to some impressive weight

Some riders have developed imaginative ways to carry more gear, but loads like this affect both reliability and handling.

and your style of motorcycling leans toward long-distance touring, you ought to be as concerned about the GVWR as you are about the horsepower and torque charts. *Motorcycle Consumer News* includes GVWR and carrying capacities in motorcycle reviews to help readers make informed decisions. You'll also find the GVWR on the machine, usually on a decal under the seat.

Prioritize, Downsize

When I'm getting ready for a long trip, it is easy to take too much. Wise trip advice: take twice the money and half the gear. One tactic for piling less gear on the bike is to prioritize. Make a list. Or even better, put everything you think you must have in one pile on the floor. Put the items you think you might need in a second pile. Put the nice-to-have-along items in a third pile. Of course, if you will be carrying a passenger, each rider will have separate piles of gear.

Now, take a good look at those gear piles, starting with the must-have pile. What can you reduce in size and weight? Bikers and hikers are faced with the same problem: weight. If you're not a hiker, you might consider spending some time in an outdoor store looking at compact, lightweight solutions to tents, sleeping bags, and cooking utensils. If you'll have a second rider aboard, compare the items and see if you can eliminate duplicates.

For example, maybe toothpaste is a must-have item, but you may not need to carry two economy-size tubes. And do you really need two full camera outfits with 600mm telephoto lenses, or can you get along with one little shirt-pocket range-finder camera? Does a weekend trip require the six-person stand-up-to-put-your-pants-on tent, or can you make do with a cramped little two-person tent? If you can reduce the size and weight of the items in the must-have piles, you may have room for a few more might-need and nice-to-have-along items.

Tom Mehren has a clever little book, *Packing Light, Packing Right,* that helps you choose the most compact gear for traveling on a motorcycle. It's available online at http://www.soundrider.com.

When you have pared down the gear, weigh the load on the bathroom scale. Don't forget to include the extra tools, spare parts, motor oil, and tie-down straps. You should have some idea of the carrying capacity of your motorcycle. If you are stretching the limits, you can forget the nice-to-have-along things and start paring down the might-need piles. Of course, the next question is, how are you going to pack it all on the bike?

Packing the Bike

When you begin stacking everything on the bike, where you pack it is important. Loading extra weight far from the motorcycle center of gravity will contribute to sluggish handling. You could tie a big suitcase on the back hanging out over the tail-light, but saddlebags are a better location for heavy objects because they are closer to the bike's CoG. A tank bag is an excellent place to carry weight, but be smart about what you put in it because you may have to get up close and personal with whatever is in the bag should you become involved in a crash.

Big touring machines often have a capacious box over the rear end called a touring case, top box, or scoot boot. You may also have big racks attached to the top of the saddlebag and top box lids to which you can tie even more gear. Hold on, though. If you check the suggested weight limits for bags, boxes, and racks, you may find the limits surprisingly low. One familiar chrome rack for Honda Gold Wing top boxes lists a three-pound limit. What the manufacturers are trying to tell you is to keep the weight down, even if the volume is large. Load heavier objects in the saddlebags, lighter things in the top box, and only the lightest gear strapped on the bag racks.

Tie One On

If you're a novice motorcycle traveler, consider how you're going to package the load to carry it on the bike. You don't want to have your underwear falling off on the freeway or getting soaked in a rain shower. If you don't want to install hard bags, take a good look at the various fabric bags on the market. Whatever system you choose, be sure it can be secured in place and won't get tangled in the running gear or sag down onto the mufflers.

If you're traveling without a passenger, the rear half of the saddle is a good location for larger, heavier gear because the bike is designed to carry passenger-size loads there. When I'm riding by myself, I often strap a heavy fabric bag over the back of the saddle. Other travelers prefer an upright pack that secures over a vertical rack, but of course that creates a sail that contributes to instability in crosswinds.

The standard device for holding loose items on a motorcycle is the elastic bungee cord. I've learned to dislike bungees because of their bad habits and limitations. For example, a long bungee stretches as the bike goes over a whoop-de-do, allowing something on the bottom of the pile a chance to slip out. Worse yet, when the hook on a loose bungee strap gets snagged by a wheel spoke, it suddenly whangs back in your direction.

These ROK straps are a great way to strap on a bag. Here, a rain cover keeps the bag dry.

Flat straps are good at holding loads in place, but you need to have the correct length and suitable places to attach them. One smart design for straps is two pieces that join in the middle with a buckle. The straps can be quickly unbuckled to gain access to the bag. The best attachment for straps is a closed loop at the end. You pull the loop around a rack or frame tube and pull the rest of the strap through the loop to secure it. There's nothing to scratch your paint, and it can't detach itself when you're not looking. The loose ends of the straps can be tucked underneath the tight part to keep them from flapping around.

Luggage

If your motorcycle didn't come with factory luggage, you may want to add some bags. The most obvious choice is throw-over fabric bags. But hard bags (usually cast plastic) have several advantages over fabric. Hard bags can be rigidly mounted to the machine so they don't sag into the mufflers or flap in the wind. They are reasonably water resistant and are usually equipped with locks to help keep your stuff, your stuff. The disadvantages of hard bags are the extra width on the motorcycle and the difficulty of removing luggage if the hard bags are permanently installed.

Europeans have focused more on removable (quick-detach) luggage systems to provide the security of hard bags with the ease of being able to grab everything off the bike and hustle it up to a hotel room. Quick-detach bags also make maintenance much easier. Quick-detach luggage systems usually depend on a clever bag carrier that attaches to different motorcycles with different brackets. If you don't like what your dealer has available, check out the European luggage.

Adventure travelers typically look for bags that are even more durable than what motorcycle manufacturers offer. Aftermarket aluminum panniers are available in various sizes and configurations and can be fitted to many different machines with

The aftermarket Happy Trails aluminum panniers on this BMW GS are powder-coated black inside and out to prevent the oxide from rubbing off on gear. Each bag is secured with two large screw knobs inside, making the bags easily removable. The lids have special gaskets to make them dustproof and waterproof.

appropriate mounting racks. Aftermarket suppliers include Jesse Luggage Systems, Happy Trails, and Touratech. Plastic hard bags are available from GIVI, and there are reinforced Pelican cases with mounting systems from Caribou.

Wind Turbulence

As you add gear to your bare bike, be aware that it all affects wind turbulence. The shade-tree rule for untested luggage is to avoid speeds above 85 mph, whether it's hard luggage, throw-over fabric bags, or strapped-on duffels. Generally, the closer you can tuck everything in toward the bike, the less wind turbulence you'll encounter. That 85 mph maximum speed is a precaution against turbulence that could cause the bike to wobble. But when carrying passengers or adding accessories, consider that anything on the bike carried above the center of gravity will act as a sail in crosswinds. That's something to remember when you are thinking about stacking a tall pack behind the sissy bar or strapping bulky sleeping bags on the top box rack.

Sidecars and Trikes

When you hear the word *motorcycle*, do you picture in your mind a cruiser, a sport-bike, a heavyweight tourer, a dual sport, or a dirt bike? Whatever the style of motor-cycle that comes to your mind, it's probably a two-wheeler. Sure, you may have seen a sidecar outfit in the movies, but it may not have registered that sidecar outfits and trikes are motorcycles, too.

Mainstream motorcyclists may look down on three-wheelers with both curiosity and disgust, cracking jokes about training wheels and old guys and questioning out loud why anyone in their right mind would screw up a perfectly good motorcycle by attaching a third wheel. Of course, automobilists wonder out loud why anyone in their right mind would ride a two-wheeler, so maybe it's just a matter of prejudice. To be sure, three-wheeled motorcycles have some negative points. Dragging an extra wheel around eats up horsepower; makes the motorcycle handle all funny, and adds extra stresses to the frame, suspension, and wheels. To add insult to injury, a sidecar or trike conversion will probably void your new bike warranty. Considering all that bad news, why do so many motorcyclists take the big plunge? Let's talk about that.

One practical reason for a sidecar is to carry children in reasonable comfort and safety. When you're young and free, kids are someone else's problem. But when kids arrive in your family, there is an immediate crisis of the bike versus the children. A caring parent realizes there is really no safe way to carry small children on the seat of a two-wheeler. So what are the options? Some parents ignore the risks, pack the kid on the back of the saddle, and hope for the best. Others sell the bike or let it gather dust until the kids grow up. Some parents leave the kids with a sitter and accept the guilt of traveling without them. Adding a sidecar allows the whole family to travel together, without taking any unnecessary risks, accumulating any guilt, or giving up the motorcycle.

Converting a motorcycle to a three-wheeler allows people with missing or incapacitated legs to participate fully in motorcycling. A sidecar or trike holds the bike up at slow speeds or when stopped, so it's not necessary to have fully functional legs. The motorcycle can be fitted with special controls such as an electric shifter or a relocated clutch lever.

In the United States, a sidecar outfit is considered a motorcycle.

Passengers who are not comfortable riding on the back of a motorcycle saddle may find that riding in a sidecar is a practical option. And a sidecar is really the only safe way to carry children on a motorcycle.

One recent trend in motorcycling is dual-sport sidecars, such as this KLR/Dauntless Enduro, that are not only fun to drive but also very capable on dirt, loose gravel, or even snow.

For people with physical limitations, a three-wheeler conversion allows a way to keep on motorcycling. After losing his left leg below the knee, Mike Paull continues to lead GlobeRiders adventure tours from the seat of his three-wheeler.

Another practical reason for a three-wheeler is extending the riding season into winter. The threat of dropping your speedy two-wheeler on a patch of black ice is a very real concern. In northern climates, motorcyclists tend to put the bike away for the winter because it's just too scary trying to keep a two-wheeler upright on a slippery road. The addition of a third wheel provides a way to keep on motorcycling even when the roads are slippery wet or icy slick. Even in good weather, a motorcyclist may be so concerned about dropping the bike that it stays in the garage more and more. When the day comes that you are reluctant to take the bike out because you're concerned about dropping it, that's a sign that it's time to stop chortling at three-wheelers and start looking at them.

Although there are certainly practical reasons for three-wheelers, the simple truth is that a lot of motorcyclists get into sidecars or trikes just for the entertainment value. Just about everyone is friendly toward a sidecar. It's fun to motor through a neighborhood on your outfit and have people smile and wave—the same people who normally sneer at motorcycles.

Yeah, But It Doesn't Lean Around Corners

Riders who have limited themselves to two-wheeled motorcycles up to now may think that not leaning around corners would take all the fun out of riding. Over the years, various sidecar outfits have been built with connections that allow the motorcycle to lean, even with a sidecar attached. You might wonder why leaners aren't more popular. The short answer is that driving a rigid outfit is just as much fun as riding a two-wheeler, but in a different way. A leaner has the same liability as a two-wheeler: it falls into a heap if traction is lost. It's a real kick in the pants to hang off and slide an outfit around a sharp turn or drift down a gravel road without the fear of taking a tumble.

Most important, some of us enjoy challenges. Once we've learned how to ride two-wheelers, we're ready to try something more challenging. Sure, a sports car would be fun, but it's pretty ho-hum compared to a sidecar rig. A trike or an outfit is still a motorcycle. You're still out in the breeze, hanging on to handlebar grips, and rolling on the throttle. Yes, it's a big challenge to figure out how to handle these strange, three-wheeled vehicles that are like no others, but some of us are willing to learn. One point to remember about three-wheelers is that you don't have to give up your two-wheeler just because you learn how to handle a hack, too. A sidecar gives you a good reason to have more than one type of motorcycle. Why not set up one bike as a sidecar rig and have a two-wheeler for those occasions when you want to enjoy leaning into curves?

Driving a three-wheeler doesn't mean you have to become a fuddy-duddy. Sidecar outfits are just as much fun as two-wheelers, but in a different way.

There are all sorts of three-wheelers available, from antique sidecar rigs all the way to low-slung trikes that corner like sports cars. Some European sidecar rigs corner with the best of today's two-wheelers without the risks of taking a tumble. The most tip-resistant layout for a three-wheeler is with a single drive wheel in the rear and two steerable front wheels. There are also some four-wheeled motorcycle-like vehicles being built, commonly called street quads. State laws generally differentiate between a motorcycle and an automobile based on the number of wheels. Motorcyclists will have to decide whether we want four-wheeled street quads defined as motorcycles, which would require a change in the laws.

Motorcycle-based four wheelers, or quads, are being built in Europe. Motorcyclists in North America will have to decide whether or not street quads should be licensed as motorcycles.

Trikes

Motorcycle-based trikes are similar to sidecar outfits in many ways and handle much like sidecar rigs of comparable size. The most popular type of trike today is built by replacing the single rear wheel of a big bike such as the Honda Gold Wing with a two-wheel rear axle and differential. A trike corners as well as or better than the typical sidecar rig with surprisingly good tipover resistance; but it tends to bounce more over pavement ripples because of the greater unsprung weight of the single rear axle. A sidecar outfit demands somewhat higher skill to drive because it isn't symmetrical, but the independent suspension provides a smoother ride. A trike provides symmetrical handling, which can be a plus for a driver who is overweight or someone with lower body paralysis, but a passenger must ride motorcycle-style behind the driver. A sidecar outfit provides better passenger accommodations, and the possibilities for custom sidecar bodies are endless. The choices in motorcycle-based trikes are more limited. The cost to convert a bike to either a trike or a sidecar rig is approximately the same for a package of equivalent quality and features.

There are also three-wheelers with the two-front, one-rear configuration, such as the Liberty Ace, being produced by Liberty Motors in Seattle. The Ace is a contemporary iteration of the old British Morgan, but the Ace uses a Harley-Davidson V-twin engine. The Ace handles more like a sports car than a motorcycle-based trike.

Motorcycle-based trikes such as this Gold Wing conversion are surprisingly tip resistant and require less skill to drive than a sidecar rig does.

Most of today's motorcycle-based trikes replace the single rear wheel with a modified automobile axle and differential. Typically, a large trunk is built into the space between the two wheels.

The Can Am Spyder is a new three-wheeled motorcycle with the two-front, one-rear wheel layout.

The Liberty Ace is a contemporary three-wheeler reminiscent of the old British Morgan, with the two-front, one-rear wheel configuration. The Ace is powered by a Harley-Davidson V-twin engine and has an automobile transmission with a reverse gear.

Three-wheeled motorcycles have been around since the beginning of motorcycling. But very few motorcycle-based trikes were produced prior to about 1990. During the 1970s and 1980s, a number of auto-based trikes were built by attaching a motorcycle front end to the rear engine and transaxle of a Volkswagen "beetle" or Chevrolet Corvair. Then in the 1990s, the motorcycle-based trike was created by swapping the single rear-drive wheel of a Honda Gold Wing with a modified automobile rear axle and differential. That left most of the motorcycle stock, simply adding an automotive rear axle and differential and some integrated bodywork. The two rear wheels with automobile tires are driven by the motorcycle's shaft, just as they are in a rear-drive automobile. There are arguments over who designed the first motorcycle-based trike, but today there are several manufacturers who convert two-wheeled motorcycles to trikes. Normally, the bike owner will deliver the two-wheeler to an authorized conversion facility, the entire conversion to a trike will be completed, and the owner will take delivery and drive it home.

Building an Outfit

Building a sidecar rig is more like a treasure hunt because there are so many options. You can't just run down to your local Honda or Kawasaki dealer and pick out a sidecar rig you like. The sidecarist must be ingenious, curious, and persistent to solve all the riddles and find all the pieces. There are a few sidecar manufacturers and installers in the United States who can make the conversion for you if you have the right bike. There are also sidecar installation specialists who will attach the sidecar of your choice to the motorcycle you have selected for sidecar duty. They either know where to find the needed bits and pieces or can custom-fabricate whatever special clamps or adapters are required.

If you're thinking about attaching a sidecar to your current motorcycle, be aware that the sidecar should be matched to the motorcycle in size and weight. Perhaps you found a good deal on a lightweight sidecar at a swap meet, but if your bike is a heavy-duty cruiser, putting them together would produce a poor-handling rig. In very general terms, the empty sidecar should weigh approximately 30 percent of the bare motorcycle.

Attaching a sidecar isn't as simple as dropping a trailer onto a ball hitch. The connections between the motorcycle and sidecar must be strong enough to handle

Some sidecar manufacturers build sidecars to fit specific brands and models of motorcycles. The result, as with this Liberty sidecar on a Harley-Davidson, is a well-matched combination with a foolproof connector system and excellent handling.

the stresses of cornering and braking. The standard approach to sidecar attachment is four mounting points, two along the lower frame rail of the bike and two at the top. To facilitate alignment, the frame ends usually have threaded adjusters or sliding tubes that clamp in position.

Some sidecar manufacturers focus on specific brands or models of motorcycles so they can build a foolproof connector system. For example, Liberty Motors focuses on specific models of Harley-Davidson. The result is an installation with factory fit and finish.

Learning to Drive

The most important lesson about sidecars and trikes is that a three-wheeler has very different handling dynamics from a bike's. Sure, it's almost the same motorcycle with the same license plate. But having a tricycle footprint changes the way it steers and corners. And that can be a real mental shock for the experienced motorcyclist who hops on a three-wheeler for the first time. Trikes are a little easier to handle because they are symmetrical.

There are a number of special skills involved in piloting a sidecar outfit, and it may take a few errors before the correct skills settle in between your ears. If you haven't driven a rig before, it makes a lot of sense to practice some specific exercises away from traffic and fire hydrants before you take an outfit out on public roads. Once the novice sidecarist acquires the new skills, an outfit magically gets a lot easier to control.

Before you take a sidecar out to the street for the first time, you should spend a few hours practicing exercises in a wide open parking lot free of obstructions. Better yet, take the Sidecar/Trike Education Program and get two full days of training under the watchful eye of a certified instructor.

Remember that two-wheelers must lean to turn, and leans are initiated by countersteering. To turn left, you steer right. A sidecar rig doesn't have to lean first before turning. So to turn a rig to the left, you just point the front wheel toward the left. For motorcyclists with years of practice steering two-wheelers, steering a sidecar combination tends to confuse the brain until it switches off the two-wheeler balancing habits. That mental confusion is the major reason why a veteran motorcyclist may initially dislike the feel of a three-wheeler and why it's a good idea to learn how to control the rig before hitting the street. And, in case you're wondering, it is relatively easy to switch back and forth between a two-wheeler and a three-wheeler, just as you can switch between a car and a bike.

What About Rider Training Courses?

Until recently, state rider training sites have focused on a basic learn to ride course that was designed by the Motorcycle Safety Foundation. What is seldom noted is that MSF courses are for two-wheeled motorcycles only. The Sidecar Safety Program (SSP) developed a sidecar driving course to fill the gap. The SSP course was subsequently adopted by the Evergreen Safety Council in Seattle, which assumed responsibility for three-wheeler training nationwide, parallel to two-wheeler training. The three-wheeler course is called the Sidecar/Trike Education Program (S/TEP). Some states are just starting to think about three-wheeler training. Both Virginia and Washington include sidecar/trike courses in their motorcycle safety programs. One big advantage of taking the S/TEP is that you can get some hands-on experience with a sidecar or trike before you spend a lot of money.

Driving a Sidecar Outfit Textbook

The Sidecar Safety Program has a textbook available, *Driving A Sidecar Outfit,* which includes both theory and practice exercises. It is a complete do-it-yourself text, very similar in content to the S/TEP course. If you're curious about driving a rig, *Driving A Sidecar Outfit* explains the skills in detail. It's available from Printwerk Graphics and Design, 800-736-1117. Although specific to sidecars, much of the book is applicable to driving a trike.

Not the Bottom Line

I wouldn't want you to believe that the above is all you need to know about sidecars or trikes. The need-to-know list is about twice as long as for other motorcycles, and I've barely scratched the surface. Now, if all this stuff about building a strange-handling vehicle, sliding the tires, and riding around in the wintertime leaves you colder than a frozen mackerel, you probably aren't ready to move beyond two wheels yet.

But if something I've said has triggered your imagination, let it simmer for a while. However, I advise you to use caution when looking at three-wheeled motorcycles or talking with sidecar or trike enthusiasts. The third wheel virus is contagious, and there is no known cure.

THE END OF THE TRIP

Similar to a motorcycle journey, this book heads off across an intellectual landscape, allowing the curious traveler to file away new memories, and hopefully triggering some fresh ideas. We started this *Proficient Motorcycling* trip by facing the risks of motorcycling openly and honestly, and we've wandered through a whole range of topics that have offered the possibility of becoming a smarter, more skillful motorcyclist. It's up to you to put the information to use, ignore it, or update it with what you discover from your own motorcycling experiences.

As promised, I've focused mostly on riding public roads where controlling the situation is just as important as controlling the motorcycle. If you're interested in becoming more skillful at controlling the bike, I would encourage you to take one or more of the track schools that focus on cornering in a low-risk environment. I've provided some references in the Resources section.

This may be the end of the book, but it's only the start of the journey toward becoming a proficient motorcyclist. One final suggestion to make that journey more fulfilling: share your knowledge with other, less experienced riders. You may discover what I've learned, that discussing motorcycle dynamics around the campfire, scribbling diagrams on a coffee shop napkin, or writing articles to help others learn is an important part of the process. You'll always get back more than you give.

Now, the intellectual trip is finished, and the back cover of the book is not far away. Or perhaps we've just come full circle, back to the place where we started and ready to head out in a different direction. Thanks for the ride.

—David L. Hough

Resources

Organizations

Head Protection Research Laboratory
6409 Alondra Boulevard
Paramount, CA 90723-3759
(562) 529-3295
Fax: (562) 529-3297
http://www.hprl.org

Motorcycle Safety Foundation
2 Jenner Street, Suite 150
Irvine, CA 92618-3806
(949) 727-3227
http://www.msf-usa.org

Sidecar Safety Program
SSP President
15900 Clear Creek Rd. NW
Poulsbo, WA 98370

Sidecar/Trike Education Program
Evergreen Safety Council
401 Pontius Avenue N
Seattle, WA 98109
(206) 382-4090
(800) 521-0778
http://www.esc.org

Magazines and Books

HACK'd magazine
P.O. Box 58
Buckhannon, WV 26201
(304) 472-5507
http://www.hackd.com

Motorcycle Consumer News
P.O. Box 6050
Mission Viejo, CA 92690-6050
(949) 855-8822
http://www.mcnews.com
Subscriptions: (888) 333-0354
http://www.custmag.com/mcn

Coyner, Dale. *The Essential Guide to Motorcycle Travel.* North Conway, NH: Whitehorse Press, 2007

Foale, Tony. *Motorcycle Handling and Chassis Design: The Art and Science*, 2003

Ienatsch, Nick. *Sport Riding Techniques.* Phoenix, AZ: David Bull Publishing, 2003.

Motorcycle Safety Foundation Staff. *Motorcycling Excellence, Second Edition: The Motorcycle Safety Foundation's Guide to Motorcycling Excellence: Skills, Knowledge, and Strategies for Riding Right.* North Conway, NH: Whitehorse Press, 1995.

Parks, Lee. *Total Control: High Performance Street Riding Techniques.* St. Paul, MN: Motorbooks International, 2003

Sidecar Safety Program. *Driving a Sidecar Outfit, Second Edition.* Port Angeles, WA 2007: Printwerk Graphics and Design, 1501 Joliet Street, Dyer, IN 46311

Training Schools

Advanced Street Skills
Puget Sound Safety
(888) 539-7545
www.smartcornering.com

Atlanta Motorcycle Schools
(770) 573-9902
www.jkminc.com

**Freddie Spencer's
High Performance
Riding School**
(888) 672-7219
www.fastfreddie.com

**Keith Code's California
Superbike School**

(323) 224-2734
www.superbikeschool.com

**The Kevin Schwantz Suzuki
School**
(800) 849-7223
www.schwantzschool.com

**Lee Parks Total Control
Advanced Riding Clinic**
(800) 943-5638
Email: leemparks@yahoo.com

Motorcycle Riding Concepts
(703) 491-9102
www.mrcsaddleup@comcast
.net

Penguin Road Racing School
(978) 297-1800
www.penguinracing.com

**Reg Pridmore's CLASS
Motorcycle School**
(805) 933-9936
www.classrides.com

Stayin' Safe Motorcycle Training
(202) 857-8384
www.stayinsafe.com

**Streetmasters Motorcycle
Workshops**
(805) 464-0544
www.streetmasters.info

Reports and Statistics

**The Head Protection Research
Laboratory (HPRL)** offers a
variety of publications specific to
motorcycling, including a high-
quality version of the Motorcycle
Accident Cause Factors and
Identification of Counter-
measures, Vol. I, US DOT
PB81-206450
6409 Alondra Boulevard
Paramount, CA 90723
(562) 529-3295
http://www.hprl.org

**The Motorcycle Accident Cause
Factors and Identification of
Counter-measures, Volume I:**
Technical Report, January 1981
(aka the Hurt Report) is available
to the U.S. public through the
National Technical Information
Service (NTIS). The NTIS refer-
ence number is PB 81-206450.

5285 Port Royal Road,
Springfield, VA 22161
www.ntis.gov

**National Highway
Transportation
Safety Administration
(NHTSA)**
NHTSA is part of the U.S.
Department of Transportation and
includes the National Center for
Statistics and Analysis (NCSA)
and the Office of Defects
Investigation (ODI).
1200 New Jersey Avenue, SE
West Building
Washington, DC 20590
(888) 327-4236
Internet www.nhtsa.dot.gov

**NHTSA National Center for
Statistics and Analysis**
NPO-100, Room 6125

400 Seventh Street, SW
Washington, DC 20590
(800) 934-8517
Email: NCSAweb@dot.gov

**NHTSA Office of Defects
Investigation**
(888) 327-4236
www-odi.nhtsa.dot.gov

**The U.S. DOT Bureau of
Transportation Statistics (BTS)**
collects highway accident
and fatality data. Since 2005,
BTS is a part of the U.S.
Research and Innovative
Technology Administration
(RITA).
1200 New Jersey Avenue SE
Washington, DC 20590
(800) 853-1351
www.bts-gov
Email: answers@bts.gov

Businesses

Caribou Case Systems
(303) 786-8947
www.adventure-motor
cycle.com

Dauntless Motors
(360) 825-4610
www.dauntlessmotors.com

GG Quad North America
(214) 559-4597
KeithSmithPE@att.net

GIVI Motorcycle Accessories
(877) 679-4484
www.giviusa.com

Hannigan Motorsports
(270) 753-4256
www.hannigansidecar.com

Happy Trails Motorcycle Products
(800) 444-8770
www.happy-trail.com

Jesse Luggage Systems
(623) 878-7113
www.jesseluggage.com

Lehman Trikes
(888) 394-3357
www.lehmantrikes.com

Liberty Motors
(206) 568-6030
www.libertysidecars.com

Micatech Aluminum Motorcycle Luggage
RoGo Corp
(888) 464-6494
www.Barettandgould.com

Moto-Sport Panniers
(303) 456-4684
www.motosportpanniers.com

List of Abbreviations

ABS: antilock braking system

BTS: Bureau of Transportation Statistics

BAC: blood alcohol concentration

cc: cubic centimeters

CC: carrying capacity

CODES: Crash Outcome Data Evaluation System

CoG: center of gravity

CoM: center of mass

CP: contact patch

DOT: Department of Transportation

FARS: Fatal Accident Reporting System

GVWR: Gross Vehicle Weight Rating

HOV: high occupancy vehicle lane

HPRL: Head Protection Research Laboratory

LTVs: light trucks and vans; light truck vehicles

MCN: *Motorcycle Consumer News*

MSF: Motorcycle Safety Foundation

NCSA: National Center for Statistics and Analysis

NHTSA: National Highway Traffic Safety Administration

NTIS: National Technical Information Service

SSP: Sidecar Safety Program

SUV: sport utility vehicle

Glossary

This book contains various terms, phrases, and slang words whose meanings may be obvious to some motorcyclists but not to others. Some of these terms are defined in the following glossary to help all readers understand their meanings.

apex: the point on a curve where the rider passes closest to the side of the pavement

balaclava: a knit cap for the head and neck

big dog rider: an experienced and aggressive motorcyclist known for feats of daring and skill, such as riding at high speeds on public roads without apparent fear of accident or arrest

binders: brakes

blind corner: a turn in the road that is partially hidden by visual obstructions such as trees or an embankment, making it so that a rider cannot see the road's path (such as surface hazards, other cars) around the rest of the turn

blind turn: *see* blind corner

blood alcohol concentration: the percentage of alcohol in a person's blood, measured as grams per deciliter

body English: a method used by motorcycle riders to help control lean angle or direction independent of the handlebars by moving body position on the motorcycle

bow wave: a wave of water pushed ahead of a tire, similar to the wave pushed ahead of a boat moving through water

camber: sideways angle or slant of the pavement

canyon bites: serious accidents that occur while riding fast on twisty roads that are often found in canyons of mountainous areas

centerstand: a ladderlike stand that pivots down from the center of a motorcycle frame to support the motorcycle vertically with the rear wheel off the ground

chicken strips: the unworn areas of a tire near the sides of the tread that indicate a rider has not cornered aggressively

contact patch: the spot at which the tire of a bike is in contact with the road's surface

countersteer: to turn the handlebars so the front tire contact patch shifts in the opposite direction from that in which the rider wishes the motorcycle to lean

countersteering: a method of controlling and balancing a bike in which the handlebars are momentarily turned in the opposite direction from where the rider intends to go

crash padding: a motorcyclist's protective clothing, especially abrasion-resistant and impact-absorbing riding gear and a helmet

dicing: (1) taking the risk of racing one or more riders, usually on public roads; (2) riding a motorcycle in dense traffic

dive: to quickly change direction such as suddenly leaning the bike into a tight turn

edge traps: the raised edges of bumps or cracks in a paved surface that can catch a motorcycle's tire and cause the bike to lose balance

endo: pitching the rear of the bike over its front, end over end

fairing: an aerodynamic shell covering the front of some motorcycles to reduce wind drag, provide wind protection for the rider, and enclose the machinery with a stylish skin

fairing pocket: a small compartment in the fairing, usually found in the sides of the fairing, alongside the fuel tank

flickable: unstable; a motorcycle that requires very little effort to roll between an upright position and a lean

fog line: pavement edge

foot skids: a rider's boots that are extended to the ground while the bike is in motion

formation ride: a motorcycle road event in which participants maintain their relative position in a group while riding down the road

full chat: riding at top speed for the rider's skill level and road conditions

gypsy tour: a motorcycle road event, usually several days in duration, in which the participants travel through the countryside and stop at a different destination each night

hacker: a sidecar driver or sidecar enthusiast

hanging it out: riding aggressively, increasing the possibility of injury; continuing to ride when weather and traffic conditions are not safe; riding faster than safe for one's skill level or without proper safety gear, with the potential for losing control of the bike and slamming exposed body parts onto the pavement

highside flip: when a sliding rear tire suddenly regains traction while the motorcycle is leaned over, causing the motorcycle to violently snap from the leaning side to the other side (the high side)

low side: the left side in a left turn or the right side in a right turn

lowside crash: when the motorcycle loses traction and falls onto the ground on its low side

motorcycle: a two- or three-wheeled motor vehicle designed to transport one or two people, including motorscooters, minibikes, mopeds, sidecars, and trikes

motorscooter: a motorcycle with small diameter wheels, equipped with a bench seat and floorboard that allow the rider to sit upright without having to straddle the engine

mystery tour: a motorcycle social and travel event in which participants stop at checkpoints to unravel a clue and solve the mystery of where the tour goes

off the gas: rolling the throttle closed to cause the engine to become a brake

on the gas: rolling on more throttle to cause the engine to develop more power

overcook: any control input that's too aggressive for the situation, such as applying the brake so strongly that the tire loses traction

pillion pad: a small seat attached to the rear fender of a motorcycle to provide seating for a passenger

poker run: a motorcycle event in which participants stop at marked checkpoints to draw playing cards that by the end of the run determine a poker hand

push steering: countersteering

rake: the inclination of the steering head leaning back from vertical

rolling on the throttle: increasing engine power by rolling the valve that controls the amount of vaporized fuel charge delivered to the cylinders

roost: accelerating with so much power that the rear tire throws dirt behind it, preferably into the face of a following rider; generally, showing up or embarrassing another rider

round section tire: a tire that when inflated on the rim forms a round cross section with the width equal to the height

scooter: a tongue-in-cheek reference to a large motorcycle, generally used only among knowledgeable riders

Shoei: a brand of helmet

sidecar: a supplemental chassis attached to one side of a two-wheeled motorcycle, supported by a single wheel, making the combination a three-wheeler

sidestand: an arm attached to a motorcycle that swings out from the left side to support the bike at rest; kickstand

skid lid: a safety helmet

slick plastic arrows: directional traffic control arrows made of smooth white plastic that are glued to the surface of the road

smoking the tires: causing the tires to skid so much that they create smoke, either through engine power or through braking

speed wobble: a sudden instability of a motorcycle being ridden at a speed in which the front end of the bike darts from side to side uncontrollably

stoppers: brakes

stoppie: when braking on the front wheel causes the rear wheel of the bike to rise off the pavement

superslab: a generic term for any multilane, high speed, limited access highway, including a freeway, tollway, motorway, parkway, or superhighway

tank slapper: a speed wobble so severe that the handlebars bang alternately against the sides of the fuel tank

tire profile: the cross-sectional shape of a tire

target fixation: when a rider's eyes focus on a point in the distance or a feature on the road, causing him or her to steer the bike toward the point of focus

tarmac: British term for what Americans call asphalt

time hack: an informal measurement of time, such as counting out passing seconds to determine following distance to sight distance

tire cross section: the shape (profile) of the cross section of an inflated tire mounted on the wheel rim; what you would see if you could slice through the tire from side to side without letting the air escape

tire profile: the lateral curvature of the tread of an inflated tire, usually expressed as a comparison of height to width

trail: the distance from the steering axis to the center of the contact patch; usually measured along the ground

trailing brake: applying the brake as a motorcycle leans over into a corner

trailing throttle: closing the throttle as the bike decelerates to apply engine braking

tucking: a front wheel suddenly turning itself too sharply toward a turn with the bike leaned over

warp speed: any speed that is obviously in excess of the posted limit; "warp 10" would hint at 100 mph, without admitting the actual speed.

wheelie: when a driver rolls on the throttle quickly enough to lift the front wheel of a bike off the pavement

white lining: driving on the broken white line that separates traffic lanes to slip between cars; also known as lane splitting or lane sharing

x-trap: a place in the road where railroad tracks or cable car tracks cross, forming the shape of the letter X and creating a slit in which the narrow tire of a motorcycle can get caught or wedged

Index

A

abrasion-resistant gear, 37–38
ABS brakes, 74, 123, 148, 174
accelerating as evasive action, 146
acceleration with a passenger, 255–56
accidents. *See* crashes
age of rider, 23
aggressive drivers, 138–44, 231
aggressive vehicles, 121–23, 230–31
alcohol and riding, 22–23, 132, 233
alleys, 32, 83, 115, 118–19, 121
aluminum panniers, 265–66
animals in the road
    anticipating presence of, 180–81
    deer, 33, 77–79, 175–80
    dogs, 183–89
    quick stops, 33–34, 77–78
    swerving to avoid (not), 147
antilock brake systems (ABS), 74, 123, 148, 174
apexing, 98–101
automobiles. *See* vehicles

B

balance
    about, 45–47
    contact patch, 47, 49, 50–51
    front-end and, 47–53, 58, 152
    mass shift, 49, 53, 63, 170–71, 254
    rake/trail, 47–49
    self-balancing, 52–53
    steering head rise and fall, 49, 50
    tire profile and, 51
bicycles, 126–27
blinding lights, 228–29
blind situations
    about, 32–33, 83
    curves and turns, 30, 34, 35, 90, 97, 100–101
    intersections, 83, 128
    risk acceptance and, 14
blind spots in eyes, 227
blind spots of other vehicles, 133, 230

body armor, 37–38, 130, 218, 222, 232
body English, 58–59, 60
booby traps. *See* hazardous situations
books, 29, 173, 245, 264, 279
boot covers, 197
brake systems, 73–74, 200
braking
    about, 68, 148
    directional control during, 71–72
    on dirt, 174
    downhill, 257
    hard braking, 68, 75, 79, 148, 254–55
    highside flips from, 71, 77, 145, 200
    laying it down vs., 67, 78–79, 148–49
    on rain-slick pavement, 199–200
    skids, 77, 172–73
    See also front-wheel braking; quick stops; traction
braking forces, defining, 69
breaks (rest)
    at beginning of a rain storm, 154, 197
    in cold weather, 222–23
    for flash floods, 202
    in hot weather, 202, 203–4, 209
    at night, 227
    for overcoming anger, 137
    for rest, 227
brick surfaces, 128–29, 154, 156
bridges in winter, 225
bumps and dips, 51, 95, 128–29, 160–61, 262
bungee cords, 264

C

cable car tracks, 164–65, 198
cambered roads and curves, 159, 198
canyon racing, 13–14
carrying capacity, 261–62
CB radios, 223, 231, 246, 247, 250
center of gravity (CoG), 58, 264
center of mass (CoM), 49, 63, 170–71, 254

centrifugal force, 56
children, carrying, 259–260, 267, 268
city traffic
    about, 113–18
    being respectful, 142–44
    intersections, 118–24
    splitting lanes, 233–39
    suburban driving issues, 124–30
clothing. *See* riding attire
cold weather, 219–26
commuter bikes, 239
coning, 61–62
conspicuity devices, 41–43
construction plates, 165–66
contact patch (CP)
    about, 47, 49, 50–52, 61–62
    steering in dirt and, 172–73
    tire pressure and, 152, 169–70, 226
contact ring, 52, 62, 93–95
control of bike, 78–79, 94–96, 103–4, 111, 169–75, 215–16
cornering
    about, 87–89
    carrying a passenger and, 256
    coning, 61–62
    corner entry speed, 96, 106
    fast flicks, 62–63
    making sparks, 102
    pacing/tempo, 102–9, 105–6
    process for, 54–58, 62–63, 89–92, 91, 101–2
    riding practice, 110–11
    throttle and, 82, 89–92, 95–96, 102, 106–7, 110
    traction and, 159
    See also balance; countersteering
cornering lines, 97–102, 106–9, 256
countersteering
    about, 45, 54–58, 152, 161
    adjustments in U-turns, 64
    direct steering vs., 59–60
    edge traps and, 162–63
    out-tracking while, 60–61
    as push steering, 60
    riding practice, 34, 55, 110, 219, 276
    in wind, 60, 213, 215, 216

courses, 21–22, 29, 260, 275, 276, 280
crashes
about, 15–16, 125, 175–77, 181
accidents vs., 19
attitude of rider and, 20, 21, 179
avoiding, 114
during group rides, 242–43, 245
highside flips, 71, 77, 145, 200
in intersections, 118
responsibility for, 19–20, 40–43,
80–81, 139–41, 242–43
riding in canyons, 13
right pace vs., 102–3
single vs. multivehicle, 19, 25–26
time of day and, 126
See also fatalities; risk
crash jumping, 148, 149
Craven, Ken, 243–44
creeps, avoiding, 231
crooks, avoiding, 231
crosswinds, 46, 210–13, 215, 216–17,
266
cruisers, 46, 50, 65, 102, 210–14
cruising speed. *See* speed
curbs and edges, 129, 160–67
curves, on-ramps, and merging lanes,
135–36

D

deer, 33, 77–79, 175–81
deer whistles, 182–83
dehydration in hot weather, 202–7
delayed apex lines, 100
direct steering, 59–60, 64
dirt riding, 159, 168–75
disabled riders, 267, 269
dog owners, 184, 188–89
dog repellent, 188
dogs, 183–89
driveways, 32, 83, 115, 118–19, 121
drunken drivers, 231
dynamics, 10–11, 67–77, 83, 89–90. *See
also* balance; braking; cornering

E

edges and curbs, 129, 160–67
electric heating, 221–22
elk, interacting with, 180
emergency reactions follow habits,
33–34, 81, 117–18, 123, 148.
See also evasive actions; quick
stops; riding practice
emergency stops. See quick stops
ergonomics, 64–65, 67, 213–14
evaporative cooling, 191–92, 196–97,
204–5, 208–9

evasive actions
accelerating, 146
ignoring need for, 19, 20
left turn–related collision avoidance,
19, 74–75, 117, 118–21
planning ahead for, 127–28, 144–45
swerving, 147–48
unsuccessful, 148–49
See also animals in the road; quick
stops
exercises. *See* information sources; riding practice; training
eye examinations, 228
eye protection, 218. *See also* view

F

fabric riding suits, 37
farm animals, 181–82
fast flicks, 62–63
fatalities
in intersections, 118
statistics, 15, 17–25, 121, 127
talking about, 14
time of day and, 126
See also risk
feedback variances, 58–60, 172, 215
flash floods, 201–2
flickable steering, 47–48, 53, 58
foot pegs
crash jumping from, 148–49
for dirt riding, 170–72
on slippery surfaces, 160, 199, 224
steering and, 65, 211
formation, riding in, 248–49
front-end balance, 47–53, 58, 152
front-wheel braking
about, 69–71
braking tempo, 105–6
on dirt, 174
habit development for, 71, 81–82,
89–90, 106, 117–18
riding practice, 124
See also quick stops

G

GPS receivers, 132
gravel in the road, 153, 157, 159. *See
also* dirt riding
gravity and centrifugal force, 56
gravity and forward energy, 69
Grodsky, Larry, 176
gross vehicle weight restriction
(GVWR), 260–63
group riding, 188, 241–52
gyroscopic precession, 56, 58
gyroscopic stability, 53

H

habits. *See* front-wheel braking; riding
practice
hard bags, 265–66
hard braking, 68, 75, 79, 148, 254–55.
See also quick stops
hazardous situations
anticipating and preparing for,
79–80, 82–83, 163, 166–67
bumps and dips, 51, 95, 128–29,
160–61, 262
curbs and edges, 129, 160–67
dirt riding, 168–75
flash floods, 201–2
lightening, 201
oil slicks, 71–72, 78–79, 151, 159,
193–93, 198
railroad crossings, 147, 154, 155,
164–65, 198–99
on superslab, 135–38
twelve-second rule, 114–16
See also animals in the road; city
traffic; surface hazards; weather
headlights for night riding, 231–32
heart rate in heat, 204
heat cramps, 204
heat exhaustion, 202–3, 205–6
heatstroke, 206–7
helmets, 38–40
highside flips, 71, 77, 145, 200
highway riding, 52–53, 125, 130–38
hills with a passenger, 257–59
hot weather, 202–9
Hurt Report, 18–22, 25–26, 85, 118,
125, 166, 280
hydroplaning, 194
hypothermia, 191–92, 221, 222, 223–24

I

inattentional blindness, 41–43
inertia, 68, 173–74
inertial stability, 52–53
information sources
books, 29, 173, 245, 264, 279
businesses, 281
courses, 275, 276, 279, 280
magazines, 7–8, 8, 25–26, 28, 279
reports and statistics, 280
integrated brake systems, 73–74
international travel, 113, 233
intersections
approach tactics, 123, 128
blind situations, 83, 128
clues of impending hazards, 121
as danger zones, 116–17, 118–20
Hurt Report on, 118

quick stops and, 123–24
in urban areas, 125

L

lane positioning, 133
lane splitting, 233–39
laying it down vs. braking, 67,
    78–79, 148, 149
leaning. *See* cornering
leanover clearance, 91–93, 102,
    256
leather, 37, 197. *See also* riding
    attire
leaves, fallen, 128–29, 193
LED rear-light modules, 232
left turn–related collision avoid-
    ance, 19, 74–75, 117,
    118–21
licensing, 20, 25
lightening, 201
lines, cornering, 97–102, 106–9,
    256
linked brake systems (LBS), 74
loading up the bike, 260–66
loud pipes, 144
LTVs, 121–23. *See also* vehicles
luggage, 265–66

M

magazines, 7–8, 8, 25–26, 28,
    279
maintenance, superslab and, 138
maintenance throttle, 92
mass shift, 49, 53, 63, 170–71,
    254
mechanical problems, 110, 138
merging lanes and on-ramps,
    135–36
mirror adjustment, 28
moose, interacting with, 180
Motorcycle Consumer News
    (magazine), 8, 28, 279
Motorcycle Safety Foundation
    (MSF), 14, 22, 29,
    162–63
motorcycles
    choosing, 104–5
    feedback variances, 58–59
    quads, 270–71
    sidecars, 226, 259–60,
        266–70, 274–76
    size of bike and risk, 23–25
    trikes, 271–74
    water intake, 194
mud, 157–58
mufflers/loud pipes, 144

N

National Center for Statistics
    and Analysis (NCSA),
    19–20, 24
National Highway Traffic
    Safety Administration
    (NHTSA), 15, 20, 23,
    121–22, 177
neck insulation, 197, 221, 233
neighborhoods, riding in, 124–30
night riding, 181, 226–33

O

off-pavement riding, 168–75,
    aka DIRT
oil slicks, 71–72, 78–79, 151,
    159, 192–93, 198
on-ramps and merging lanes,
    135–36
organizations, list of, 279
out-tracking, 60–61
overloading, 262

P

pacing by other vehicles, 142,
    231
pacing/tempo, 102–9, 131–32
packing the bike, 264–66
panic stops, 77–78, 80. *See also*
    quick stops
passengers, 252–60
Paull, Mike, 269
pedestrians, 126–27
push steering, 60

Q

quads, 270–71
quick-detach luggage systems,
    265–66
quick stops
    about, 33–34, 74–75, 77–78
    carrying a passenger,
        254–55
    intersections and, 123–24
    panic stop vs., 77–78, 80, 85
    riding practice, 33–34,
        75–76, 84–85
    stopping distance to speed
        ratios, 72–73, 123–24,
        254
    veterans' tactics, 81–85
    See also braking; front-
        wheel braking

R

rabies, 189

racing, 59–60, 62–63, 98
railroad crossings, 147, 154,
    155, 164–65, 198–99
rain, 154–56, 191–202
rain gear, 194–97
rake/trail, 47–49
reading material. *See* informa-
    tion sources
rear-ended crashes, 137
rear suspension, 256
reflective vests, 232
research. *See* information sources
ride captain, 246–47
riding attire
    about, 11, 143, 253–54
    body armor, 37–38, 130,
        218, 222, 232
    conspicuity devices, 41–43
    helmets, 38–40
    in hot weather, 203, 207–9
    leather, 37, 197
    neck insulation, 197, 221,
        233
    for night riding, 232
    rain gear, 194–97
riding experience, 9, 21, 28
riding practice
    cornering, 110–11
    countersteering, 34, 55, 110,
        219, 276
    on dirt, 174–75
    for edge traps, 167
    hard braking, 68, 148
    quick stops, 33–34, 75–76,
        84–85
    for sidecar handling, 275–76
    skid recovery, 77, 172–73
    on slick surfaces, 160
    swerving, 148
    for windy conditions, 214,
        219
    See also training
riding skills
    about, 21–22, 28–29, 34
    carrying a passenger, 252–60
    ergonomics, 64–65, 67,
        213–14
    maximizing your view,
        35–36
    reducing risk with, 9
    sight distance, 29–30, 83
risk
    age of rider and, 23
    attitude of other drivers and,
        142, 143–44
    attitude of rider and, 16–17,
        143, 179

cornering and, 97
drinking riders and, 22–23
early in a rainstorm, 192–93,
197
of passing, 30–32
riding experience and, 9, 21
size of bike and, 23–25
talking about, 9, 14
training and, 22–23
See also crashes; fatalities
risk acceptance level, 14–15
risk management quiz, 27
road rage, 139–42
Road Rider (magazine), 7–8,
25–26
road signs
about, 79–80, 166–67
speed limits, 96
unreliability of, 166–67, 168
warnings, 178, 179, 180,
182, 202
route sheets, 246, 250, 252

S

sails and wind resistance, 211–13
sand, 129, 169
second rider, 252–60
self-balancing, 52–53
sidecars, 226, 259–60, 266–70,
274–76
sideswipe zone, 32–33, 34
sight distance, 29–30, 83. *See
also* view
signs. *See* road signs
skateboarders, 126–27
skids, 77, 172–73
slick edges, 164–65
slippery surfaces
about, 154–58
brick or wood, 128–29, 154,
156
snow and ice, 224–26
standing in the pegs, 160,
199, 224
third wheel and, 269
traction on, 71–72, 192–93
white arrows and lines, 154,
155, 198
See also rain
slow, look, lean, and roll technique, 89–92, 101–2
slowing down, 67–77, 83, 89–90
speed
carrying a passenger and,
255–56
control vs., 111
for corner entry, 96, 106

deceleration rate ratios,
72–73, 123–24, 254
in dirt, 173
racing, 59–60, 62–63, 98
throttle and, 105–6
splitting lanes, 233–39
sport bikes, 104–5, 174–75,
239, 260–61
sport sidecars, 268
spring preload, 256
stability, 47
staggered formation, 248–49
steering geometry, 47–53, 58,
152. *See also* balance;
countersteering
steering head rise and fall, 49, 50
steering input from rider. *See*
countersteering
stop-and-go traffic, 235
stopping distance, 72–73,
123–24, 254. *See also*
braking; quick stops
straps for securing loads, 265
streetcar tracks, 164–65, 198
suburban driving, 124–30. *See
also* city traffic
superslab, 52–53, 125, 130–38
surface hazards
about, 151–53
Hurt Report on, 166
loose debris, 157–58
traction on, 71–72, 152, 153,
158–60, 192–93
See also slippery surfaces
suspension, checking your, 102,
256
SUVs, 121–23. *See also* vehicles
sweating, 204
swerving as evasive action,
147–48

T

tail or clearance lights, 232
tempo. *See* pacing/tempo
terminology, 282–83
thinking skills, 103–4, 131–32,
133–34, 221, 235, 244–45
throttle
cornering and, 82, 89–92,
95–96, 102, 106–7, 110
quick stops and, 34, 76
riding uphill with a passenger, 257–59
speed and, 105–6
steering with, 94–95, 148
suspension and, 95
throttle control, 94–96, 106

thunderstorms, 201–2
tiered licensing, 25
time measurements of distance,
30, 82, 114, 120, 199
tires
contact patch, 47, 49, 50–51,
61–62
hydroplaning and, 194
knobbies, 159, 160, 174–75
tire profile, 51
traction of sliding vs. rolling,
71–72
tire pressure, 152, 169–70, 226,
256
traction
on dirt, 169, 173–74
going uphill with a passenger, 258–59
maximizing, 158–60
in rain, 192–94
road surface and, 71–72, 152,
153, 158–60, 192–93
of sliding vs. rolling tires,
71–72
in snow/ice conditions,
224–26
swerving vs., 147–48
throttle's affect on, 92–93
tire pressure and, 152,
169–70, 226, 256
traffic control devices, 30–32,
154, 155, 166–67, 198,
249–50. *See also* road
signs
traffic gaggles, 133
traffic ripples, 134
trail, 47–49
training, 21–22, 29, 260, 275,
276, 280. *See also* information sources
trikes, 271–74
turning, 53, 63–64, 66, 152. *See
also* cornering
twelve-second rule, 114–16
two-second trajectory bubble,
134–35

U

unbalancing, 53, 152
urban riding. *See* city traffic
U-turns, 63–64, 66

V

vasodilation, 204
vehicles (other)
aggressive vehicles, 121–23

blind spots of, 133, 230
drivers, 32–33, 34, 40–43,
    138–44
parked, lining the streets, 126
turning bikes vs., 54
See also evasive actions
view
    cornering lines and, 97–102
    eyes level with horizon, 96,
        107, 110
    focusing on what's impor-
        tant, 115–16
    large vehicles limiting,
        119–20
    looking where you're going,
        46, 64, 90, 98, 124
    maximizing, 35–36, 90
    at night, 227–28
    passing slow-moving vehi-
        cles, 32
    sight distance, 29–30, 83
visualizing apex lines, 100–102
V traps, 165

W

warm-up time in cold weather,
    222
warning signs. *See road* signs
water intake, 194
water-resistant suits, 195–96

weather
    hot, 202–9
    rain, 154–56, 191–202
    stopping due to, 218, 220
    thunderstorms, 201–2
    winter conditions, 219–26
    See also wind
weight restrictions, 260–63
weight transfers and traction,
    92–93
weirdoes, avoiding, 142, 231
wheelies, 257–58
white curbs, 164
white lining, 233–39
wind
    about, 210–11
    control skill in, 215–16
    crosswinds, 46, 210–13,
        215, 216–17, 266
    ergonomics in, 213–14
    gusting crosswinds, 216–17
    loading up the bike and, 266
    sails, 211–13, 264, 266
    stopping due to, 218
winter conditions, 219–26
wood surfaces, 128–29, 154,
    156

X

X traps, 165